Men, Sex and Relationships

Achilles Heel, the influential magazine of sexual politics first published in 1978, explored questions of masculinity from a standpoint which was sympathetic to the feminist critique of male power. This selection covers crucial issues in men's emotional and sexual lives and relationships, in particular the repressed aspects of their emotional involvement with others.

Wide-ranging and stimulating, these essays focus upon issues of childhood, sexualities and sexual identities, violence in its different dimensions, men's health, relationships and therapy. The writers are searching for an emotional language which could illuminate the contradictions of both love and power, fear and intimacy, autonomy and dependence, so that men can learn to communicate more openly and honestly within relationships. The book includes an introductory essay by the editor which links the processes of personal change very directly to the larger structures of power and subordination within society.

These writings cover issues that are central to contemporary culture and politics and present a stimulating agenda of subjects for future discussion and research. The collection will be of special appeal to students of gender, sexuality and sexual politics.

Victor Jeleniewski Seidler was part of the collective that founded *Achilles Heel.* He is the author of a number of books on sexual politics, including *Recreating Sexual Politics* and *Rediscovering Masculinity,* and the editor of *The Achilles Heel Reader* (all published by Routledge). He is Senior Lecturer in Social Theory and Philosophy at Goldsmith's College, University of London.

Male orders
Edited by Victor J. Seidler
Goldsmiths' College, University of London

MALE ORDERS attempts to understand male forms of identity, practice and association in the modern world. The series explores how dominant forms of masculinity have helped shape prevailing forms of knowledge, culture and experience. Acknowledging the challenges of feminism and gay liberation, the series attempts a broad and critical exploration of men's lives as well as engaging constructively with malestream definitions of modernity and postmodernity.

Also in this series

Recreating Sexual Politics
Men, Feminism and Politics
Victor J. Seidler

The Achilles Heel Reader
Men, Sexual Politics and Socialism
Edited by Victor J. Seidler

Men, Sex and Relationships

Writings from *Achilles Heel*

Edited by Victor J. Seidler

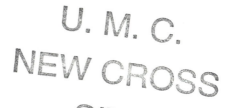

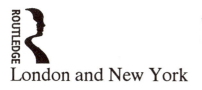

ROUTLEDGE
London and New York

First published in 1992
by Routledge
11 New Fetter Lane, London EC4P 4EE

Simultaneously published in the USA and Canada
by Routledge
a division of Routledge, Chapman and Hall Inc.
29 West 35th Street, New York, NY 10001

© 1992, selection and editorial matter, Victor J. Seidler

Typeset by NWL Editorial Services, Langport, Somerset

Printed and bound in Great Britain
by Biddles Ltd, Guildford and King's Lynn

British Library Cataloguing in Publication Data
A catalogue record for this book is available from the British
Library.

Library of Congress Cataloging in Publication Data
Men, sex, and relationships: writings from Achilles Heel.
    p.   cm. – (Male orders) (Ser. stmt. from CIP data sheet)
  "Edited with an introduction [by] Victor J. Seidler" – P.
  Includes bibliographical references and index.
  1. Men – Sexual behavior.   2. Masculinity (Psychology)
  I. Seidler, Victor J., 1945–.   II. Achilles Heel.   III. Series.
  IV. Series: Ser. stmt. from CIP data sheet.
  HQ28.M46   1992
  306.7′081–dc20   91–43735
                                                        CIP

ISBN 0–415–07468–1
      0–415–07469–X (pbk)

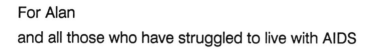

For Alan
and all those who have struggled to live with AIDS

Contents

Preface and acknowledgements

As men explored their responses to the challenges of feminism in the 1970s they got together in the context of consciousness-raising groups. These were often difficult and frustrating experiences for men because we had so little experience of trusting each other and sharing our experience. But sometimes these groups worked and they provided rich and rewarding times. *Achilles Heel*, the magazine of men's sexual politics, grew out of one such group and its attempts to make what had been a private experience much more publicly available. It struck a note for many men throughout the country and provided a forum for the exploration of our inherited forms of masculinity and our attempts to change.

Achilles Heel was sympathetic to feminism and gay liberation, feeling that it was important for heterosexual men to find a way of relating to these movements. We felt that this could best be done by both helping these movements wherever we could, say with the provision of crèches for conferences, while also taking on a particular responsibility for the exploration of our different masculinities. Initially there was considerable suspicion about men getting together in a context of consciousness-raising groups, let alone in a broader anti-sexist movement. Many feared that this was men regrouping and reorganizing their power in the face of the challenges of feminism and gay liberation. It was felt that men involved in anti-sexist activities were somehow presenting themselves as being different, or somehow more 'worked out' than other men. In reality this allowed many men to separate themselves out from these movements for change and it has only been more recently that there has been a much broader involvement of men in questioning traditional forms of masculinity. These issues have become much more central in our intellectual culture.

How were men supposed to change? How could we expect men to give up the power that they largely benefited from? *Achilles Heel* set itself against the tendency of some men to feel that they had to reject their masculinity because it was essentially tied up within a relationship of power. For these men there was *no* way in which their masculinity could be redeemed. Unfortunately these forms of self-rejection were quite undermining for men who learned to despise their anger, power and determination as being somehow inherently threatening to women. Men learned to deny these aspects of themselves and so to shape themselves according to supposedly non-threatening images.

Within *Achilles Heel* we felt this to be a destructive path which sustained a tradition of self-hatred that had often been part of our masculinity. Our appreciation of therapy meant that we recognized that these negative feelings did not go away, but that they lived on underneath the surface of our experience. Often they could make men sullen and withdrawn with an underlying tension which could be experienced as a threat. While we appreciated the good intentions which led men into this direction, we felt that it was to be questioned. Similarly, we were suspicious of men who identified themselves as feminist men because we thought that there were no ways in which men could be feminists. We felt it was more important for men to explore our inherited forms of masculinity so that we could begin to discover and develop new ways of relating both to ourselves, to other men and to our sexual partners.

A number of the men who came together within the *Achilles Heel* collective has been part of the Red Therapy experience which had sought to redefine alternative forms of therapy, such as gestalt and bioenergetics in ways that recognized the realities of class, race and gender. The personal relationships within the group were central and the close relationships emerging from the experience of working together in a therapy group informed our sensitivity. This was very much a collective project in which we were as concerned with learning from each other about how to think about these experiences of men that had for so long gone unspoken.

Achilles Heel is, and always has been a collective in which we valued what we had to say to each other. We had to go through a lot together to bring out each issue. In the early days the collective consisted of, among others, Paul Atkinson, Mel Cairns, Tony Eardley, Steve Gould, John Hoyland, Martin Humphries, Andy Metcalf, Paul Morrison, Andy Moye, Chris Nickolay, John Rowen,

Vic Seidler, James Swinson, Tom Weld and Ian Wolstenholme. There were lots of other men and women who supported and encouraged what we were doing. Dave Bartlett, John Rowen and Harry White were among those who carried the torch through hard times to build the new collective as it exists now.

We were also wary of models of change which saw men's lives in terms of a restrictive men's role. This was often a weakness of visions of men's liberation, which suggested that once these restrictions were lifted, men could somehow be themselves. We felt it was important to recognize the power which men had in relationship to women and in the context of the larger society. But this did not mean that men did not often have a very ambiguous relationship with these traditional forms of masculinity. Men could feel oppressed by these images as they felt they had to live up to certain expectations of themselves. Though we recognized it was crucially important for us to take responsibility for changing ourselves, we fully recognized that the subordination of women, gay men and lesbians meant that we were in no sense in a parallel situation.

Even though heterosexuality functioned as an oppressive norm within a patriarchal society, we did not feel that heterosexuality in itself could be renounced. In this sense our sexuality could not be presented merely as a political choice, but we had to learn to accept and in some sense to celebrate our own sexualities. We had to face how little we understood about ourselves sexually and how estranged we often were from our bodies that we had learned to use in instrumental ways. As men, we had to face our own fear of intimacy and learn to question the ways in which a whole range of needs were somehow compressed into our sexual desire. We had to begin to talk to each other about these issues and to share our experience of sexuality. Some of this discussion is reflected in these writings which originally appeared in *Achilles Heel.*

As we explored the contradictions of our experience as men, we had to face the ways that our sexuality had often been separated from our relationships. We often felt more in control of our sexuality if it could be separated off from our vulnerability. As men we often react defensively, even violently, when we feel threatened around these issues of sexuality, so it became important to explore the relationship between sexuality and violence. This could only be done if we looked at other sources of male violence and the ways in which this had become institutionalized in society. As men we often react violently as a way of defending ourselves and this is so habitual that we rarely recognize how these patterns have been established in our childhood and sustained in institutional life. Different aspects of male violence are also shared within these writings.

Within *Achilles Heel* we were constantly concerned with the ways in which men from different class, race and ethnic backgrounds can change. This involved learning a different relation- ship with our bodies, so beginning to think in different terms about our health as men. We were open to investigating the emotional sources of our illness and beginning to see how the stress and pres- sure which had become such an endemic feature of men's lives, often expressed itself in illness. We were also interested in exploring the connections between consciousness-raising and therapy and sharing what different men had learned from their experience of different forms of therapy. It seemed significant to investigate how psycho- analysis and different alternative therapies embodied particular conceptions of men and masculinity.

As we were exploring different sources for an emotional language which could illuminate the contradictions of both love and power, fear and intimacy, autonomy and dependence, we recognized that the personal could not be separated from the political. But gradually we also recognized that our visions of politics had to be transformed, since they implicitly relied upon particular visions of masculinity. We in no sense wanted to reduce the political to the personal but recognized that we had to take greater responsibility for changing ourselves as part of a process of questioning the larger structures of power and subordination within society.

Much of this writing is exploratory and it reflects a period in which there were more hopes about the possibilities of change. We can still learn from this experience even if many have grown suspicious about the promises of change. We had opportunities to discover ourselves which have in some part been foreclosed in a period when AIDS has become so significant. Since much of this writing was completed before AIDS shadowed our experience, Martin Humphries has written a piece which addresses these issues. From the beginning we were always wary about any sharp divisions between heterosexual and gay men and felt it was important to develop bridges and means of communication. We were open to exploring our own sexualities and felt it was crucial not to foreclose possibilities. If we think differently about some of these issues today, it becomes crucially important to learn from the ways in which gay men have learned to live with the experience of AIDS. This is an issue which vitally affects all of us. The issues that we raise still remain central to contemporary culture and politics. We sought to raise questions rather than to give answers. Some of these questions take on a different form in the 1990s as a new generation finds its own ways of meeting the challenges of feminism and gay liberation. But men are still struggling to change and to find new ways of having more equal relationships. As a dialogue opens up between different generations, so men can share their experience of their different masculinities. As men become more reflective about the processes of personal change, so they become more aware of what is involved in larger political changes. As we develop new ways of relating to ourselves, we can learn to communicate more openly and honestly within our relationships.

Many people have helped in getting this collection together. At a crucial stage I received particular help from Steve Gould, Martin Humphries, Rob Senior and Tom Weld. I would also like to give special thanks to James Swinson for all the work that he has put into the graphics. At Routledge, Chris Rojek has been constantly encouraging and I appreciated the time and attention that Kerstin Walker put into the manuscript. The fact that these issues have stayed alive for me for so long is in no small part due to the support and encouragement of the Men for Men group at Spectrum, London. It has helped to validate my sense of how men can learn both to give and receive from each other. As I contacted men who had initially written for *Achilles Heel*, I was struck by how significant this period remains in their lives. For those I was unable to contact, I can only hope that they will be happy with the form that their work has taken.

Part of the royalties from both collections drawn from *Achilles Heel* will be given to appropriate groups and charities working with men. *Achilles Heel* still exists and is now published by Changing Men Publishing Collective, P.O. Box 142, Sheffield S1 3HG.

Vic Seidler
October 1991

Chapter 1

Men, sex and relationships

THE PUBLIC AND THE PRIVATE

Men have grown up to identify with the public world of work. We have learned to be independent and self-sufficient. We have learned to go it alone and to do without the help of others. We have learned to identify with our work, even when it is not a matter of finding personal fulfilment but simply earning a wage. Class, racial and ethnic differences are obviously significant in men's relationships to work, but male identity is in general an identity which is wrought within the public realm.

Often there is little that prepares us for relationships, for in learning to be self-sufficient we learn to do without others. Often our very sense of male identity is sustained through our capacity for *not* needing the help of others. We learn to take pride in our self-sufficiency and we experience it as a sign of weakness to need the help of others. If we call upon friends, it is often to help us with a particular task. As men we often have little experience of our emotional needs or a language within which to express them. Growing up within a competitive male culture means that to have needs is a sign of weakness and a compromise of our male identity.

As boys, growing up into different class, racial and ethnic masculinities, we learn constantly to diminish what has happened to us, and even when we are hurt we tend to say, 'it was nothing'. We learn in diverse ways to minimize hurt and pain and to take pride in this as a sign of our strength. It is as if something really terrible has to happen, for instance, like crushing a leg, before we can feel entitled to reach out towards others without somehow compromising ourselves. Often as children we have learnt not to expect much from others. We have embodied a fear that others will take advantage or somehow ridicule us for reaching out: 'What's wrong with you then?

Can't you handle it?' So often, even at the moment that we are reaching out, we learn especially in the middle class to use irony as some kind of defence, and at any moment we are prepared to withdraw. Frequently, we feel easier helping others rather than reaching out ourselves.

Since within modern Western culture masculinity has largely been identified with reason, we learn to reject the emotional and feeling aspects of our lives as 'personal' or 'subjective'. They cease to exist as sources of knowledge and they cease to exist as part of our identities as men. It becomes difficult to recognize that when we *lose touch* with our emotional selves, we lose touch with an important aspect of our masculinity. This makes it very difficult for us to *accept* our vulnerability as an integral part of our male identity. Often we feel threatened, even scared, of our vulnerability, and in order to control it, we often move into activities. This is especially true within the public world of work where often there is little space for our emotional lives. It is still very rare for men to cry at work without feeling that their masculinity has been severely compromised and that others will think less of them. They would have revealed a lack of self-control which would often bring into question their capacities to do their jobs well.

Often men experience a real disparity between who they are in the public world of work and how they can allow themselves to be in private. Again this has to be carefully specified in relation to class, race and ethnicity. Since so little recognition is given to our emotional development within the dominant culture, there is often very little balance between the instrumental and the emotional. It is partly because of this that men with diverse backgrounds often seem to exist as children within our relationships. It can be difficult for us to behave emotionally as adults because it is through the suppression of our emotional lives and the control that we exert over our feelings, that we have learned to affirm our male identities. It is as if to have feelings and emotions is automatically to compromise our masculinity. Since it is emotions like anger that are deemed acceptable for men, we frequently resort to anger as a way of fending off our vulnerability or softer feelings. We often move into anger as a way of sustaining control of ourselves and so ward off threats to our male identity which come with our vulnerability.

It is important to discover a new relationship between the public and the private realms. Men have learnt to exercise a whole range of skills, abilities and qualities within the public realm that need to be fully acknowledged as sources of male identity. At this level masculinity cannot simply be conceived of as impoverished. But it is still important to find space within the public realm for men's emotional lives and relationships to be given fuller recognition.

It is with feminism that the distinction between public and private has been reworked, and this has necessitated rethinking traditional relationships which allowed men to think of the public realm as their own, and to set terms for the participation of women. If women are helping to redefine the terms of relationships within the world of work, so men have to rethink their involvement and participation within the private realm. Often as men we take our relationships for granted and we treat the private realm as a background which supports and sustains our involvement within the public realm, which is what really matters to us. Even as we argue that our participation within work is all being done for the family or for children, we are being challenged to find new terms of involvement. But this does not mean that the private realm becomes the only source of meaning and value. It is as much the public world that needs to be transformed as the private.

Robert Bly's work *Iron John*, has been part of a significant movement, especially in the United States, which has wanted to rework men's relationships to feminism. It argues that men have to discover the sources of their masculinity and that men have somehow lost touch with their masculinity in their response to feminism. This touches an important chord but in part reflects a failure to analyse correctly the diversity in men's early responses to feminism. It illuminates particularly well the rejection of masculinity which went along with a rejection of anger, strength, will, determination and other qualities which were discerned as oppressive to women. Since masculinity was deemed a relationship of power, some men did feel that the only way they could cease to be oppressive to women was somehow to cease being men.

But from the beginning *Achilles Heel* rejected this response, thinking that it was important for men to rediscover and redefine our diverse masculinities. We recognized that this was a task that men had to do for themselves, and this was connected to the importance of consciousness-raising groups for men. But this did involve recognizing the power that men had in relationship to women within the larger society, even if it meant questioning some of the conceptions of men and masculinity that feminism had fostered. It is important to stress this if we are not to fall into reacting negatively to feminism but to explore creative relationships with the different feminisms which have emerged. Unfortunately, Bly remains relatively silent on these crucial questions of how we relate as men to the oppression of women and how we can develop more equal relationships. For him the personal realm is still women's realm and men are to be initiated into their masculinity through escaping into the public world of men.

It is also true that consciousness-raising often proved a limiting and frustrating activity for men because it proved so difficult to escape from the intellectualization of our experience. It proved much harder to share ourselves emotionally with other men, partly because of the depths of competitive structures. This was part of what drew some men towards more expressive forms of therapy which allowed men to explore emotions and feelings which otherwise would have been dismissed as irrational. It is because men traditionally learned not to allow themselves to feel unless they knew that these feelings could be rationally justified, that men often build a very tight cord around themselves.

A similar feeling seems to inform the wild man movement, which encourages men to recover a lost masculinity through rituals and emotional work. This can help recover a form of male bonding and help men to learn to support and nourish each other; but there is also something disturbing in the return of the warrior image of masculinity, especially if it means turning your back on relationships with women and children to take this heroic journey on your own. However specific Bly is in relating the warrior to standing our gender ground as men, his language carries resonances which imply men have little to learn from feminism. This can serve to isolate men further, for it does not encourage us to learn *how* to communicate more openly and honestly and *how* to share our vulnerability within our relationships. It can work as a welcome escape from the routines of family and work and provide men with a space in which they can explore hidden aspects of themselves; but it can also too often keep in place the structures of relating within both the private and the public realms which, whatever Bly's intentions, are somehow sustained as a movement from the mother's house to a father's house, which boys alone have to achieve.

IDENTITY AND DIFFERENCE

Within the human sciences it has become almost common sense to argue that gender differences do not have their basis in nature but are socially and culturally constructed. This helped to foster the idea that gender differences are created though socialisation, the ways in which children are related to from a very early age, and the kind of experiences they are offered. This was crucial in helping women recognize that there were a whole range of activities that they had been prevented from doing. Women did not know who they were or what they could do, since so much of their lives had been restricted to the private realm. So it was important for women to have time and space to explore what it was they wanted to do and the kind of capacities they wanted to develop for themselves. No job or activity should *a priori* be limited. Girls should be encouraged to do woodwork just as boys should be encouraged to do needlework and cooking. This helped people argue that gender differences had no basis in reality but were simply the outcomes of different socializations.

Gender differences seem to have endured in a way that brings into question traditional theories of socialization. In this context psychoanalytic theories increasingly have been used to explain the sources of gender difference. Nancy Chodorow's book, *The Reproduction of Mothering*, has had a particular significance in showing how mothers, being largely responsible for childcare, have helped produce an asymmetrical experience for boys and girls. Boys have had to separate themselves from their feelings of need and vulnerability which they identified with their mothers, and have had to learn to identify with a father who was often not present in their everyday lives. This seemed to explain how masculinity could be quite brittle as it was largely built upon an identification with a distant father. Boys continually had to be ready to defend their masculinity against attack. They were often plagued by feelings that they were not men enough. Chodorow tends to argue that if men were more involved in an everyday way in childcare, then boys would learn to accept their vulnerability as integral to their masculinity. They would have more experience of an *ongoing* relationship with their fathers which an earlier generation missed out on.

Robert Bly has helped to focus upon the injury and disappointment that many men feel for not having had closer contact with their fathers. It is something that few men have learned to acknowledge because they felt that it was somehow unreasonable or unmanly to have expected any more. So it is in terms somewhat reminiscent of Jung that we might think that the search for the lost father is somehow connected to a search for a lost masculinity. We need to be careful how we think about this.

As men we often learn to focus on the future and to distance the past as a form of self-indulgence. We learn to be active, and often to assume that if we feel down or frustrated then we can *do* something to eradicate these unwanted feelings. It can be difficult for us to acknowledge that the problems and difficulties that emerge in our relationships are somehow connected to our early experiences in the family. It has been Freud who initially has been important in reconnecting men to their histories and in helping us to recognize that our emotional lives have a history. Often we learn to put our childhood aside, sometimes because it was too painful, and sometimes because we just do not want to remember the awkwardness of that period. We have left childhood behind in our move towards adulthood.

Within a relationship it can mean not dwelling on things when they are going badly. We learn to 'turn over a new leaf' or 'leave the past behind', for 'there is no point in crying over spilt milk'. We learn to look forward and we learn to disconnect from experiences that have been painful or unhappy. Within a protestant culture we tacitly learn to deal with unhappiness through ignoring it or turning aside from it. We learn that to dwell on our childhood unhappiness is just to stir in the pain to no avail. We assume that we can move forward without looking backwards, and that we can use our will to exert our mind over matter.

So it is strange to think that we might need to reconnect with our childhood experiences to *change* the ways that we relate in the present. We want to feel that we can put these difficult or embarrassing experiences behind us. In any case, as I have said, we learn to minimize these experiences, thinking that they were 'not so bad', as a way of proving our masculinity. Somehow this works to undermine our feeling that we are entitled to feel disappointed or upset that our fathers were not available to us. We know that others have had to cope with much worse, and as men we learn 'to take it'. It can be easier for us not to register these feelings, and so it is that we learn *not* to listen to ourselves. So it is that we often fail to develop means of communicating with ourselves, and so it is difficult to communicate emotionally with others.

In this context, at least, it might help to reassert the particularity of a masculine experience. When we silently ache for contact with our fathers, it is for a particular quality of relationship. It does not mean that our mothers were not there for us, but there was something particular that we missed. But as boys we learn not to feel and so *not* to expect very much, especially from our fathers. It might only be years later that we are aware of the disappointment or allow ourselves to feel this need. This is difficult for men because of the pressure to be self-sufficient and to think that we can get on *without* the support and love of others.

Traditionally, the father was a figure of authority who was obliged to sustain a distance if he were to be effective. This was institutionalized within psychoanalysis, where the father's role was to separate mother from infant at a particular age. The father was to intrude externally into this primary relationship at the appropriate moment to set the child free from a potentially engulfing dependence. But there was little sense of an ongoing relationship of fathering within a psychoanalytic tradition. The father remains separate as a potential figure of identification particularly for sons working through oedipal conflicts. There is limited sense of the importance of everyday contact and relationship.

With feminism, men were challenged to take greater responsibility for childcare, but there was limited acknowledgement of the particularities of fathering. Rather, parenting was conceived of as a series of discrete tasks that could be more or less equally distributed between adults. This made it difficult to recognize that at particular times the relationship between mother and baby might be more significant and that the father's relationship with the infant might come into focus a little later. It became difficult to recognize that both partners could take responsibility for children, whilst also recognizing that there might be certain differences in their relationship.

This seemed as if it could too easily become a form of back-sliding, allowing men to escape from their responsibilities for childcare. It seemed to threaten the insight that it was only through an ongoing everyday relationship with children that men could create and sustain a fathering relationship. Sometimes it was only years later when fathers regretted that they did not have a much closer relationship with their children, that men had to recognize the painful truth that the distances that had been created could not be undone easily. It meant acknowledging that relationships were not simply a matter of present attitude, but involved ongoing everyday participation over time.

In men's groups men often talk with sadness about the difficulties they have in relation to their fathers. They talk of the different ways they had provoked their fathers into some kind of response, even through misbehaving so as to provoke punishment, which was at least a sign of caring. Years later we can seek recognition for our achievements, wishing that our fathers would at last acknowledge what we have done. But often we are disappointed yet again. Once we allow ourselves to feel *entitled* to something more, we can feel angry at how little we received. But there are times when it seems that anger has to give way to acceptance and we learn to accept what we can still have in the relationship with our fathers. We might resolve to relate differently to our own children and find ways of nourishing ourselves, so giving ourselves things that we might have hoped to receive from our fathers.

We might also still carry the scars of, for instance, not being able to do woodwork, which was something that our fathers could do well but which they always put us down for. Whatever we did was not good enough. They made us feel cack-handed and incapable and in this way sustained their power in relationship to us. At the time, it might have been hard to recognize the ways in which, for instance, working-class fathers might have felt threatened by children coming home with maths homework that they could not do themselves. So we might inherit a feeling that maths is difficult or that we are not capable of doing it. Often we unconsciously inherit the anxieties and insecurities of our parents. It is only when we face our childhood experiences in this way that patterns can be broken and we will have more chance of relating differently to our own children as fathers ourselves.

Otherwise we unwittingly discover that we are reproducing patterns and even if we do not want to, we are relating to our own children as we were related to ourselves. But it is partly because as boys we are so used to *disconnecting* from painful or embarrassing experiences that we so often attempt to leave our childhood behind before we have worked on our experiences. Often we prefer to remember things as far better than they were so that we do not have to face our unhappiness or isolation as children. We learn to put the past behind us and prove ourselves through what we can achieve now. In this way we disconnect from these deeper levels of our experience in the false hope that they do not affect our capacities to love and care in the present.

SEXUALITY AND RELATIONSHIPS

As boys we have often been spoilt by our mothers. We are used to having things done for us and often we have learned to do very little for ourselves. Learning to be independent and self-sufficient often involved at another level learning to allow women to support and sustain us emotionally. This meant we were very little prepared for emotional and sexual relationships as boys. Often our mothers would do things for us as a sign of love, so that we learned that 'if you love me you will do things for me'. Even if this is not said, it is often felt. If we have been spoilt as boys this does not help us learn to do things for ourselves. It is partly because work can be so stressful and that we learn to give our best energies to it, that we expect to be looked after within the private realm. Women's refusal to do the emotional work for us has created much tension in the wake of feminism. Since men have never learned to value or identify this emotional work for what it is, it is difficult to deal with its withdrawal by women. Often men withdrew into a sullen silence, feeling unappreciated or feeling that all their efforts at work were not being recognized. It was much harder for men to question *why* it was that all their best energies had to go into their work so that often they arrived home exhausted and empty. It meant there was little energy or joy left for their sexuality, which became a marginal, often peripheral, experience.

As boys we often learned to treat love as a scarce commodity which was not to be wasted. We learned to keep ourselves in reserve and often did not know *how* to share ourselves in relationships; for to share our vulnerability as men is to show a 'weakness' and we assumed that others would have every reason to reject us if they saw us as weak. Because we had learned to see our vulnerability as a weakness, it was hard for us to believe that our partners wanted us to share our emotions and feelings with them as part of creating and sustaining a relationship. We still often feel that we should be 'strong' in our relationships and therefore able to support our partners. But often strength is interpreted as independence, as being able to do without others.

As men learn to be self-sufficient they learn to take pride in not needing the support of others. As we deny our own emotional needs it becomes hard to care for ourselves and so difficult to learn *how* to care for others. So the dialectic of giving and receiving which sustains a relationship is rarely developed. As men we are hardly prepared for relationships and sometimes we feel barely *capable* of having them. It is as if we have learned since childhood to construct our lives so that we do not need others, learning to exist at one remove from our experience. We can find it hard to relate more personally and directly. There is an abiding, if generally unacknowledged, fear of intimacy, which is part of our masculine inheritance.

Often this creates an imbalance in relationships, for if we do not acknowledge that we have any emotional needs ourselves, it becomes much harder for our partners to rely upon us. Often in heterosexual relationships our partners can feel as if their emotional needs are overwhelming in comparison with ours. So it is that relationships get polarized and women can feel that they have to carry all the anger or all the sadness of the relationship. Because as men we have not learned to acknowledge these feelings, our partners are left to have them for us. If men identify with their rationality and take it to be their particular task to sort things out in a relationship, then it can be from a removed and impersonal position. Sometimes our partners will feel estranged by this attitude while not knowing how to confront it. They learn not to share their feelings with us so a *distance* is created within the relationship. Often we do not understand our part in creating this distance as men. We often fail to recognize the consequences of our behaviour.

As men we learn often to 'put up' with very little emotionally and because we need so little ourselves it becomes hard to recognize our partner's needs. We are more comfortable with the idea of a relationship as some kind of *background* against which to live out our 'individual' lives. In the 1970s and 1980s more men and women have learned to create more equal relationships on this basis. Both maintain their own friendships and work. They both contribute more or less equally to the upkeep of the house and home. But often this vision of equality can only be sustained by putting off having children, for it is with pregnancy and birth that forms of dependency emerge which are difficult to negotiate in contractual terms.

With the birth of a new child, men often feel silently aggressive for having been displaced from their position within the relationship. Often people are unprepared for this new situation and the lack of freedom that a baby brings. Men unknowingly can seek revenge through a sullen withdrawal or sometimes through seeking a new relationship. With the birth of a new child women often want more emotional support from men, and men can find it difficult to provide it. It can be easy for men to feel that things should be the same as they were before, and so not to appreciate how radically changed the situation can be. It becomes important to negotiate emotional needs but if there is little experience of this, problems are created within the relationship which might only surface years later.

Within a protestant culture we learn to think about responsibility as a matter of blame, and so if there is a 'problem' it must be someone's fault, and if it is not ours, it must be our partner's. It becomes an issue of assigning blame and shifting the burden of guilt. So often men learn to seek new partners, unwilling to acknowledge that we take our issues with us into a new relationship. It becomes harder to recognize our own involvement in the situation that has been created. To be able to take responsibility for our emotional lives involves a transformed relationship to self.

It is mostly only in our late twenties that we can discern certain patterns emerging in our relationships and are encouraged to recognize our own part within them. Before that it is easy to blame our partners and to think that our lives will be very different with a new partner. We learn to obliterate the past and 'turn over a new leaf' in the hope that things will be very different with a new relationship. We still expect our partners to be responsible for our happiness and traditionally women have taken on this responsibility. But with feminism, women have questioned this task and encouraged men to take greater responsibility for themselves emotionally and so for their own happiness. If both partners are equally responsible for what goes on in a relationship, it is also not simply a question of passing blame between them.

Again, this can involve questioning the idea that because men have power, they are to blame for everything that goes on in a relationship. It is unhelpful for feminism to suggest that women are always 'innocent' because they are the powerless ones in a relationship. It is important to recognize that women are in a position of subordination within a relationship *without* this meaning that they can do no wrong. This so easily fosters a false vision of sexual politics as a form of moralism which creates its own traps as relationships, especially in the 1970s, were often conceived in terms of 'correct' feelings and behaviours. This suppressed feelings that were deemed to be unacceptable or unwelcome and encouraged people to present themselves in terms which were sometimes very much at odds with how they felt inside. This created a gulf between inner experience and outer expression. It became difficult, particularly within heterosexual relationships, for men and women to communicate openly and honestly with each other.

Again, this honesty was something that men had to learn for themselves. It was not something that we could decide as an act of will. We had learned so long to present ourselves in particular ways and to deny our emotions and feelings, that it was hard to discover ways of reconnecting to them. Often it was as men learned to trust and communicate with other men, that they found that their issues were shared by other men. It meant that we felt less like freaks and more able to identify with the issues that other men were struggling with. But it was often still difficult to communicate our feelings within our personal and sexual relationships. It was often hard to feel that others would be there for us, or that our needs would not overwhelm our partners if we were to start to express them. It is partly because we express so little as men that we fear being overwhelmed and overwhelming to others.

In part this registers the distance we have from our emotional lives and the limited relationship we have with ourselves. Sharing ourselves emotionally involves its own risk and takes its own form of courage. Part of the attraction of Robert Bly's *Iron John* seems to be that he promises men in advance that they will not lose their power or become 'wimps' if they take the path of emotional exploration and bonding with other men. It might be that some men need this guarantee *before* they are willing to change. But we have yet to see how this helps men learn to communicate openly and honestly in their relationships with both men and women.

As expressive forms of therapy have also shown, often men can feel more comfortable escaping into the intensity of emotion than in communicating directly our sexual needs and desires. We can often feel that sex, if it is to be good, should be unspoken and a matter of physical passion. It can be more difficult to identify what we need and like, the ways that we like to be touched or held. We can fear that to put these feelings into words is to destroy the intensity of the relationship. But this is not true. It is part of taking greater responsibility for our emotional and sexual experience. It also helps us question the ways in which many of our emotional needs are compressed into making love. Often there is a push towards orgasm when other forms of expression would be more appropriate. It is because we cannot identify and differentiate these different needs that there is often such a push towards orgasm for men.

LOVE AND ANGER

How do we learn to care for ourselves? If we have never learned to nourish ourselves, for we have never learned *how* to identify our needs, how can we care for others? It is partly because caring is supposedly 'natural' that we never learn *how* to care either for ourselves or for others.

Because we learn to treat vulnerability as a threat to our male identity, we often learn to keep people away, especially when we are feeling sad or vulnerable. Sometimes we hit out aggressively at others as a way of protecting ourselves in the face of this threat of vulnerability. It is particularly difficult to reach out to other men, especially if we are feeling low. We assume that we have to *do* something about it ourselves, or else that other men, even friends, will not be there for us when we are down. We might feel able to reach out when we feel up but it seems particularly hard to trust that they will be there for us when we are down. It is easier for us to assume that they will be too busy or that we will get them at a difficult moment. It is easier not to make the call.

As we learn to push for orgasm within sexual relationships, so we learn that it is acceptable to use our anger in our emotional lives when other feelings like unhappiness or sadness seem too threatening. Somehow, to say 'I feel unhappy' seems to reflect failure or seems to be an admission of inadequacy. It feels easier to push these feelings away, as if, if we do not acknowledge them, they will be unable to take hold of us. Again, I'm not trying to generalize from a particular experience, but to open up terms in which diversities of class, race and ethnicity can be shared and explored.

So it is that we learn to eradicate feelings that we do not want or which somehow work to compromise our sense of male identity. It works similarly when we eradicate a memory which is unpleasant. We assume, in Weberian terms, that we can create reality in our own image. This is part of a masculine identification with reason, which is especially strong within middle-class experience. It allows us to order reality according to our own cognitive principles. If something does not 'fit', we refuse to acknowledge its reality. We pretend that it does not exist for us. So it is that we block our negative feelings, allowing them no space or reality within our experience. We can behave similarly in our relationships when we withdraw into a sullen silence or 'send someone to Coventry'. We refuse to acknowledge their existence for us and we eradicate them as part of our lives. It is because we are so used to treating our emotional lives in this way within modernity, that we frequently fail to recognize the cruelty we do to others as well as the injury we do to ourselves.

As men we learn to 'manage' our experience by moulding it according to the dictates of reason. This is a question of mind over matter. It is reflected within our rationalist forms of social theory, which insist that we can order reality according to particular classifications or representations. The inadequacy of these traditions is that they assume experience is there waiting to be governed, but in fact reality often refuses to conform to our representations. It is much messier and if our social theory wants to illuminate social reality as it is, rather than as we would want it to be, then we need to break with these rationalist forms of theory.

As men we learn to identify with self-control and, as I have argued in *Recreating Sexual Politics*, this control involves the domination of our emotional lives. Often we insist on sustaining control by refusing to acknowledge emotions and experiences which do not fit our prevailing reality. So it is that men are often very slow in recognizing a crisis situation as it emerges within their sexual relationship. Men often minimize the problems involved and insist that they are of a temporary character. It is often only when a partner has insisted on leaving that men have recognized the gravity of the situation they face. Frequently it is easier to insist that another man must be involved, so as to be able to blame the partner rather than to take responsibility for what has gone on within the relationship.

It is because as middle-class men we are so used to construing reality as we would want it to be, that we often find it hard to acknowledge and express what we are experiencing in the relationship. As far as we were concerned, we might think everything was going well, so it comes as a shock that things are so wrong. A rejection can be particularly threatening to our sense of male identity. Anger can be a way of reasserting control over a challenging situation. This anger can make it harder for us to acknowledge our part in the relationship. It is often much easier to put the blame on our partners, so not having to face our own involvement.

Since as men we learn to plan our lives as a way of exerting control, so we also learn to control our emotional lives. This makes it difficult for our spontaneous feelings to emerge for they might well threaten the image we are presenting of ourselves. It is often preferable to cut out the possibility of this contradiction, for these feelings might well threaten our image of masculine identity.

But if we block our feelings, we also block our love, for love is related to vulnerability. So it is that we learn to *fear* intimacy, for we often find it hard to share our vulnerability without feeling that we are somehow being compromised as men. It is difficult not to treat vulnerability as a sign of weakness. It is as if we do not want to recognize our feelings of vulnerability ourselves, let alone share them with our partners. Frequently, we have learned that to share our vulnerability is in fact to undermine the relationship because it shows us as weaker than we would want to be. Because of this it is difficult to recognize that in sharing our vulnerability we are learning to express our love.

Often anger is a much more acceptable emotion, so that when we are beginning to feel vulnerable we react with anger as a way of pushing others away and unconsciously concealing our vulnerability. Anger becomes a form of self-protection as a whole range of emotions are transmuted into anger, and we fail to learn how to differentiate our different emotions and feelings. This works differently for women, who often feel sad or upset as a way of protecting themselves from their anger that traditionally threatens their femininity.

But often it does not help for men to label their anger as an 'unacceptable' feeling because it coerces others. Anger has its place in both men's and women's lives and it is important to recognize this place, perceiving at the same time that we often invoke it when it is not appropriate. Frequently, anger is not appropriate when it hides our vulnerability, for it creates a space between ourselves and those we love. As men we often *withhold* our emotions and feelings and we never learn to communicate these to our partners.

Anger can often help to express our sense of outrage at injustice. It also has a significant place within our relationships, but we have to learn how to communicate our anger in non-abusive ways. The point here is that our anger is sometimes not rational and experienced at a level which is not appropriate to the situation. As we learn to identify this within our diverse masculinities, we can give it an expression, knowing that our anger might not be appropriately directed at our partner but calls upon childhood experiences of abuse or violation. Therapy can help us understand the importance of expressing this anger, since it is only through its expression that we can become clear about what might be appropriate within a relationship. Often as men we are fearful of our anger and worried about losing control because we have grown up with such little relationship to our emotional lives and often without an emotional language which could help us identify what is happening to us. Within *Achilles Heel* we were beginning to recognize the importance of humanistic forms of therapy, despite their limitations, as a way of providing a language which could illuminate some of these issues.

Within a liberal moral culture cast within rationalist terms, it is easy to treat all emotions and feelings as if they are irrational. This is particularly significant when within modernity masculinity has been so closely identified with reason. It is as if reason gives us a standard by which to judge our emotions and feelings, and so to decide which are to be acknowledged. As men we learn that emotions have to be 'rational' in order to be legitimate, before we allow ourselves to experience them. We are tempted, especially within the middle class, into a situation of living at one remove from our experience, feeling easier with irony and disdain. This is a form of self-protection and often it is insidious and difficult to break with.

It means in relationships that men often find it difficult to experience directly and so to share their emotions with their partners. We need to explore a *whole range* of emotions and it is wrong to judge them in advance as intrinsically irrational or inadmissible. Rather, it is a matter of whether they are appropriate to the situation. Even if they are 'irrational' in the sense that they are more intense than seems appropriate, it can be interesting to investigate them. Intensity is itself revealing and something we can learn from. At the same time, it is important to discover a safe context in which these feelings can be explored and often this is what therapy can provide.

But it can be difficult for men to acknowledge that we need help in this area as much as in any other. We frequently feel that we should be able to manage things ourselves and that it is a sign of weakness to need others. Often it is unreasonable to expect our relationships to take this strain, and one of the strengths of men's consciousness-raising groups was to provide a context in which men could learn to draw support from other men and so relieve the pressure so often put on women's lives. As we learn to take greater responsibility for our emotional lives as men, so we begin to identify our emotional needs and learn how to identify and express these in our relationships. This helps to break endemic patterns of withholding.

ANGER AND RELATIONSHIPS

To recognize that when we block our anger we also block our love, is to question a rationalist tradition which suggests that if we do not express our anger then it does not need to affect our relationship. It is as if our anger only has effects if it is expressed. This makes it difficult within a rationalist tradition to understand how unexpressed anger can spoil a relationship. As Freud grasped, there are all kinds of unconscious ways in which it can influence our behaviour. We can withhold and become spiteful or simply distant from our partners. The intensity of our feelings might indicate that it has a source in early childhood experience.

It might be that we are reacting to our partners because of the ways that we were treated by our parents; if we have never acknowledged this or worked on our relationships, situations in the present are likely to trigger experiences from the past. Unless we have ways of recognizing this, we often react inappropriately in the present. Our visions of self-control are set in rationalistic terms which means we exercise control as a form of domination of our emotional lives. Of course, we might feel frustrated at not getting the recognition from our parents that we would have wanted and we might continually return in the hope that it will be forthcoming; but if our parents are not going to change, at least *we* can. This involves learning how not to be 'hooked' in the same way.

Foucault's *A History of Sexuality*, vol. 1, challenges the idea of our emotions waiting to be expressed. He questions the hydraulic conception of our emotional lives as part of challenging the usefulness of a conception of repression. But both Freud and Reich, to whom Foucault directs his challenge, offer much more complex visions of repression. We do often carry unexpressed emotions and feelings and often it can be many years later before a person has, for instance, learned to mourn the death of their father. Of course if we do this as an adult it is very different from if we had mourned a father who had died when we were young. I know from my own experience how important it has been as an adult to recognize, possibly for the first time, the death of my father. For a long time I had lived with the idea that somehow he would return and that he was some unfocused presence in my life. At a rational level, of course, I knew he had died but I was not ready to accept this emotionally. Somehow I was living as if he had never really died. I had never fully embodied his death. So it is, for instance, that therapy can help to *ground* our emotional lives.

Similarly, I might never have expressed my anger at my father's death, thinking that it would be irrational to feel such a thing. It can be enormously helpful to be told that it is quite natural to feel anger at the death of a parent, to feel forsaken and abandoned. But often these are emotions that we do not allow ourselves to have because they seem 'irrational' or 'unfair'. But our emotions have their own logic which needs to be acknowledged and respected. It is part of learning to respect our emotional lives as part of learning to respect ourselves.

If we allow ourselves to express our anger, things often begin to change, and it might put us in touch with our vulnerability and so allow us to reach out to others. As we withhold our anger so often, we also withhold our love. We cannot will ourselves to feel differently even if we want to. Often as men we are false to our experience because we *want* to feel much more for our partners than we often do.

Finding ways to work with our anger and resentment, rather than simply judging these feelings as 'irrational', is a way of preventing tension building within ourselves. In any case our anger often gets expressed in all kinds of subtle and underhand ways. Frequently, men withdraw and this can itself be an act of violence. It goes along with a withdrawal of love and affection, even though often we are unaware that this distance has been created. Often we fail to acknowledge the consequences of our emotional withholding as men. Within a rationalist culture we assume that it does not have to affect our contact and communication; for we learn that these particular emotions can be put aside, for they supposedly interfere with our communication which is assumed to take place on a rational level alone. Psychotherapy helps us grasp that these emotions and feelings cannot be put aside without consequences. They have to be acknowledged as part of what is going on in a relationship. Otherwise our communication becomes stilted, unreal and formalized, leaving us as men somehow outside our experience, watching from a distance.

Often there is a *gap* between how we feel inside as men and what we are ready to share with others. We are so used to this dislocation that we do not even identify it as such. It is a form of self-defence that has become so routinized and taken for granted that it is invisible. As I have argued in *Recreating Sexual Politics*, we assume an externalized relationship to our experience as men, so that often we are judging ourselves by external criteria and doing our best to adapt or squeeze ourselves so that we fit the images or models we have of ourselves.

Our inner lives become a resistance that needs to be overcome so that we can present ourselves in the best light possible.

This creates difficulties in our personal and sexual relationships, for we have never learned to share our inner lives with others. It becomes difficult to share our emotions and feelings with our partners as part of our learning to care for them. It is easier for us to *do* things for others than to share ourselves with them. It can be hard to trust that our partners can be there for us emotionally. Since we learn to experience our own emotions as a burden we would rather be without, so it is easy to feel that we are burdening our partners when we share ourselves with them. This is part of the difficulty that we often have in relating to others. As we take ourselves for granted emotionally, so it is easy to take others for granted. As men it can be hard to learn to care for others. Little in our background seems to prepare us for relationships.

SEX AND VIOLENCE

For men, sexuality can be a way of working out all kinds of unacknowledged needs and desires. Often it is easier for us to 'go for sex' than it is to acknowledge that we want to be held and touched. It can be difficult to identify our particular needs without threatening our sense of male identity. Masculinity has for so long been identified with activity that it can be difficult to take a more passive position in our sexual relationships. Often we push ourselves to be active as the way of protecting our masculinity. This seems particularly true for heterosexual men, who learn to think of sexuality in terms of conquest.

We think of 'getting off' with women as a matter of affirming our own self-esteem. It is a way of validating our male identity. Since we learn to 'go for what we want' and to 'go as far as you can get', we expect women to place the boundaries upon our sexual activity. They cease to exist in their own sexual identity. There is little sense of mutuality or trust when it is a matter of seeing women as 'blocking' what we think we are 'owed' as men. Some of these patterns are no doubt changing but they are deep-seated within inherited forms of male sexuality. They serve to block our vulnerability and so to sustain our egos.

It is as if we want to deny the link between sexuality and vulnerability. As men we often want to have sex *without* vulnerability;

for when we are vulnerable we fear that we can be rejected. This is not simply a matter of being rejected as individuals but of our very masculinity being brought into question. So it is that control becomes a crucial issue, because in controlling our partners we minimize the risks of rejection. As part of this we can insist on being active. It is we who do, or who order what is to be done to us. It is as if we have to maintain control of the sexual activity so as to protect ourselves. Frequently, it is through activity that we can curb and control our vulnerability.

Often it is difficult to identify the whole *range* of different needs that are subsumed under sex. It is because 'going for sex' is culturally acceptable that we often push towards genital sex as a way of protecting our vulnerability and sustaining our control. This can help to illuminate the idea that for men sexuality often tends to be relatively isolated from intimacy and relationship. It is as if men control threats to our masculinity through this very separation. For women there often seems to be more connection between intimacy, contact and sexuality. But often men want to keep sex separate because it is a potential area of rejection and it is an area of potential humiliation. It is because of this that men often need to know that they can withdraw at any moment. Frequently, we go on the attack as a way of protecting ourselves, with such notions as 'I wasn't interested anyway' or 'I don't think you're attractive' or 'I didn't really want a relationship'. These are all familiar projections, ways in which we learn to defend ourselves as men.

This connects to the ways that often as men we tend to blame our partners and somehow expect them to take responsibility for our satisfaction. It is harder to take responsibility for our own emotional and sexual lives. As men we often blame others, never ourselves, and it is difficult to recognize our responsibility within the relationship. It can be very hurtful to be told that we are not good lovers, so that often the focus for heterosexual men is upon making our partners happy, making sure that they have an orgasm. The insistent question 'Did you have one?', is a way of men reassuring themselves; but this is still sexuality as performance. If men have become more sensitive to the sexual needs of their partners, being prepared to acknowledge the autonomy and independence of women's sexuality, still it can be difficult to negotiate sexual needs and desires.

But often it is when men cannot communicate their emotional needs that they get violent. For if control is threatened we often hit out. This is especially true for middle-class heterosexual men who feel they are being so 'reasonable' and so feel frustrated when their partners want something different. For if a relationship is ending, and men are feeling powerless to *do* anything to sustain it, then this frustration can easily turn into violence. When communication has begun to break down it can be difficult to recreate it as an act of will. Every encounter seems to degenerate into a row and partners often sense the vulnerable spots and unwittingly go for them.

Often there is an unexpressed anger that men can feel at the growing independence of women, for it challenges a rationalism which has traditionally given men a sense that they are doing what is 'best for all'. But if a women does *not* want to do what is 'rational' but feels the need to go her own way, this can be particularly threatening. Feminism has helped women to challenge this 'rationalism' which has worked to subordinate women as they have so often forsaken their own needs and desires for the greater good. Women have insisted on having their own time and space to explore their own feelings and values. This can be difficult for men to appreciate, partly because as men we rarely learn to give ourselves time and space for this kind of exploration.

If anything, we feel threatened by it, and often attack women with the idea that they are 'irrational' because they do not know or seem to know what they want or need. As men we have learned to treat this as an issue of reason alone, and too often it is identified with notions of individual success and achievement. But this conceals a tension between what we feel and what we are capable of identifying through language. Frequently, there is envy at women who seem able to explore these tensions within their experience, while as men we can feel locked into our unspoken needs and desires.

Men can often feel frustrated, for they cannot recognize themselves in the powerful images that feminism projects of them. Often it construes men as self-determining and clear in their wants and needs. Even if women know that the reality is different in their private relationships, in terms of the public images of masculinity this reality is often not reflected. Men often experience a dislocation between their inner experience and how they project themselves externally. We often learn to deal with this through obliterating our inner selves, learning to treat our emotions and feelings as interferences which if allowed would block the ways we would best present ourselves.

Men's lives are often divided between the public and the private realms. We learn to draw upon the support we can get within the private realm to sustain an image of ourselves in the public. But this is an unbalanced situation and often it is only sustained at the emotional cost of our partners. It is when women refuse to do this emotional servicing that heterosexual men often enter a period of crisis. They have grown so dependent upon this emotional servicing that they are often thrown when it is not forthcoming. Men can withdraw into a sullen and resentful silence or act out in violent and aggressive ways. It is as if we are deprived of what is our due, or at least what we have grown up to take for granted in our relationships with women.

If men are challenged, for instance, for being controlling, we can often act defensively. For there is a deep-seated fear that we will be exposed or found out. The dislocation between 'inner' and 'outer' means that we are *not* what we present ourselves to be, for as men we are constantly living out certain 'images' of ourselves, and there is an abiding tension between the inner feelings we do our best to control and the ways we present ourselves to be. If we are challenged it is difficult not to feel attacked, and often we hit out even if we do not want to, partly because we have few ways of exploring what is being said.

This reflects how little inner relationship to self we have and so how hard it is to sort out the particularities of the challenge. Somehow we feel as if our very existence is being threatened, so that it is so much easier to feel that, given that we are being attacked, we have to defend ourselves. Our very sense of masculine identity seems to be tied up with our personal identities, so that if our masculinity is being challenged we fear disintegration. It can be difficult to hear a challenge that is being made and the goodwill with which it is being offered.

Often as men we learn to attack as a way of defending ourselves. This can be a way of controlling our emotions and feelings and so not feeling threatened by the challenges being made. In the public world we know how to defend ourselves, especially if our masculinity is threatened, but it can be much more difficult within the private realm of relationships. Here we often use violence as a way of curbing a critical voice. It can be painful to be told by our partners that 'you were just not there for me, during the pregnancy and first year of our child'. If we are aware of all the pressures at work and recognize that we have been trying to be supportive in the family, it can be particularly frustrating to hear this. It is partly because we expect ourselves to be able to deal with whatever demands are made, that it is hard not to hear this critically. Sometimes we hear it more critically than it was intended because as men we have a strong critical sense and often one that is related to feeling that we are not 'good enough'. It is partly because we are so hard on ourselves that it can be difficult to listen to what is being said. Often we cut off or separate by putting down our partners as 'nagging again' or 'having a go at me again'.

At times when men get violent, it can be as a way of trying to stop or eradicate this critical voice, which is also the voice within themselves. It is partly because men can find it hard to curb or control their feelings of inadequacy that haunt their masculine identity, that it can be difficult to hear criticisms. This makes it difficult to learn and to change patterns of behaviour. It is also difficult to learn to care within the context of relationships unless we also learn how to listen.

Since anger is often treated as an 'outburst', an external event that takes us over, we try to forget about it or put it aside. If it has led to violence and we later often feel ashamed for our actions, we feel that the incident should be forgotten. As men we can use our power in the relationship to insist that it is eradicated from the history of the relationship. It is as if it has never happened. Since within a rational-ist moral culture emotions are not integral parts of our identities, we can treat the anger or violence as an 'aberration' – an 'episode' that does not reflect upon *who* we are. So it is that the violence can be forgotten about until it erupts again. It is a way of avoiding responsibility for our behaviour as we take refuge in the idea that 'I'm not a violent man but I sometimes do have violent episodes'. This can make it harder for us to take responsibility, acknowledging that it is *we* who are behaving violently, not a 'demon' that has somehow taken possession of us.

There are a number of ways in which our violence can be triggered, of which being sexually rejected is often particularly potent. Since within a protestant culture we inherit an abiding feeling that there is something wrong, defective or inadequate in our natures, we are often left feeling that we are concealing this bitter and unwelcome truth about ourselves. A rejection can connect us to these truths that we have done our best to conceal, and so we can react violently at being 'found out'. It is this feeling of fear of being exposed that men often learn to live with.

Since men supposedly have power within the larger society, it can be difficult to recognize the pressures of masculinity. Often men are continually pushing themselves in order to sustain the image they have of themselves and also keep in check these hidden and unrecognized fears. This is part of the tension between language and male experience. Frequently, we carry these unconscious fears so that if, for instance, someone is attracted to us, it does not count in terms of our self-esteem, but simply proves the little value they have. This is part of a process whereby men, despising themselves, learn to despise their partners too. This is part of a negative cycle that is familiar in long-term relationships. There is a boundary between the relationship and the rest of the world such that couples learn to present themselves in a way that is often quite at odds with the reality of their relationship.

LOVE AND INTIMACY

A protestant culture makes it difficult to understand that, unless we learn to love ourselves, it is hard for us to love others. Inheriting a morality of self-denial and selflessness, it becomes easy to dismiss our emotional lives as a form of self-indulgence. Emotional life is not part of *who* we are and so has no place in our fulfilment or self-realization. Only through the ends which are chosen through reason alone can we find satisfaction. This makes it difficult to discover the place of relationships and friendships within our lives for they are established merely as a background against which we are to pursue our individual ends.

Since we never learn to care for ourselves, it is hardly surprising that, particularly as men, it is difficult for us to care for others. Rather, if we have a low self-esteem and feel bad about ourselves, it is easy to curb or control these feelings by taking them out on our partners, saying, 'what do you know anyway?'. It is easy to contrast our relationships negatively with others, thinking that the grass is greener elsewhere. We imagine that with a different partner our lives would be completely different, failing to appreciate the ways that we take our difficulties with us. Therapy has helped men to recognize that history cannot totally be put aside, but that we have to learn to take responsibility for our emotional lives if they are not to disturb our present relationships.

We have to learn to care for others, which partly means sharing ourselves. This is frightening for men because we can feel that in sharing our vulnerability we threaten to disintegrate. It is as if we only have a centre within the public realm but find it hard to establish our emotional identities within our relationships. We can feel silently ashamed for comparing our partners or for making them feel useless or inadequate. Often this is a way of dealing with our own feelings of inadequacy.

Often there is collusion because there is relatively little sharing outside the relationship, and women often stay because they think then can 'reform' their partners. They know, for instance, that they've had bad childhood experiences and so their behaviour is not 'their fault'. So there is a collusion around issues of responsibility. This vision of rescuing which says that 'he needs me, so I cannot leave him', often creates collusion where the violence is not clearly *named* as unacceptable behaviour so that *if* it happens again it means the end of the relationship. Unless it is clearly stated that violence is not an acceptable way of expressing yourself within the relationship, excuses will constantly be made.

Unless we begin to teach children how to identify their emotional needs and wants in school, so they learn to care for themselves as a basis for learning to care for others, these patterns will be continued. At the moment boys still learn to resort to violence as a way of proving their masculinity. It is still respectable and validated behaviour. Radical feminist work has helped to place issues of male violence at the centre of our understanding of patriarchal society, but often radical feminists have denied the possibilities that men can change even though in other contexts they are largely sceptical of an essentialist mode of analysis.

For men to get their satisfaction out of kicking the shit out of other men is a form of brutalization and needs to be recognized as such. It is long overdue for men to take seriously an investigation of the sources of male violence and their links to issues of sexuality and emotional life. A rationalist tradition that has insisted on too sharp a distinction between reason and nature, and which has conceived of identities as being established within the realm of reason, language and discourse, has made it impossible to deal seriously with questions of emotional life. These get treated as part of a realm of nature that no longer has a place in our understanding of social life. To the extent that this has been a guiding assumption of modernity, it is reflected in our prevailing social and political theories.

Men are no less loving, tender or caring than women. But we have to learn to care as we have to learn how to relate to others. This is not something that comes naturally but is something that needs to be learned, and it is important that our educational theories recognize more systematically the links between our thinking and our emotional lives. Emotional development should be an integral part of our education and schooling. This means acknowledging the ways we are educated into an emotional illiteracy within the dominant culture.

Achilles Heel recognized the importance of sharing our experience as men, even those experiences that we felt ashamed and uneasy about. This meant sharing the difficulties of intimacy and the problems we had in caring and loving. This descriptive task could not be separated from the theoretical work of exploring the contradictions of our inherited masculinities. It meant breaking the silence around men's emotional and intimate lives and being prepared to explore tensions between our everyday lived experience and the ways we would want ourselves to be. This was not to speak for men in general but for ourselves as individuals, recognizing that others would have to join in an exploration of their own masculinities.

As men, we were wary of each other because of our long histories of competition. It was not easy to share ourselves without feeling that we might be put down by others. We had to learn ourselves how to be intimate and caring, for it was only then that we could begin to share what we had hidden and left unexpressed for so long. As men we learnt to support each other and recognize the strength of feeling and commitment that could grow between us. We learned to love as we learned to care. Love was no longer a precious commodity that had to be reserved for our relationships but was something that could be freely shared with other men. As we developed our understanding, so we recognized the complexity of men's experiences and the difficulties of generalizing about them. In sharing some of this work with a broader audience, we recognized that even if things have changed, most radically with the advent of AIDS, it has been important for men, both gay and heterosexual, to learn to care and love each other in these difficult times. In exploring our masculinities we learn as much about what we share as about what separates us. We also learn to support each other in our differences.

Vic Seidler
October 1991

Chapter 2

Experiences of childhood

MR PINE: FROM AN ACCOUNT OF MY CHILDHOOD

Mr Pine was the only teacher at Arkwright Street who made any real attempt to reach into my being and touch my soul. As my self-awareness grew during the year in his class the contact with Mr Pine developed. It developed slowly, in fits and starts, and ended quite abruptly at the close of that year. But in a way my relationship with him was the most formative experience of my primary school years.

He was more or less my age then – late twenties. He was tall and quite thin and erect. His face was narrow and bony with slightly hollow cheeks, but it wasn't pokey. His chin and nose were too smooth and rounded, they offered no sharpness.

He was much younger than the other two men on the staff. Mr Skinner who took Class I was close to retirement. He was a product of the 1930s, lower middle class. His age and severity distanced him from and terrified most of the kids. The Headmaster was middle-aged and stood in the middle between Mr Pine and Mr Skinner.

Mr Pine's room was on the top floor next to the art room, the first schoolroom that I remember. It was painted apple green, and the steam pipes ran round its perimeter. We all sat facing his desk – forty of us. There wasn't much room to play about in there.

I suppose Mr Pine was a good teacher. He was always pretty clear and easy to understand. And he did exciting things like show us how you could soak chalk in a sugar solution so that it wouldn't rub off the blackboard or explaining with an electric kettle how water turned into steam. I'd never seen an electric kettle before.

Everyone could read and write in his class. We were streamed by now. Class 4 was the lower stream to Class 3, as was Class 2 to Class 1. Classes 4 and 2 were taken by women. We practised neat writing, read aloud in class, did sums and simple science, bits of history and geography. As the year advanced we began to do more and more tests, and our written work in class was marked and commented on. I was good at it and began to enjoy going to school for the first time.

I'm not sure how it started but I began to get quite close to Mr Pine. There were two of us that were usually top of the class – me and Mike Rogers, who lived in the street next to mine. We were made monitors, which meant clearing up after classes finished, handing out books and paper and things like that. I was embarrassed to be picked out as in any way special, but liked it at the same time.

I was so shy I hated to stand out really, to be made to be public. I certainly never felt better than anyone else. I was much too aware of how complicated the differences between us all were to reduce things to academic success. My lack of confidence was paramount. Being good at writing and reading didn't count for that much really. There was football and being tough or popular in the playground. Most kids were much more there in the external world than me, much more assertive and invulnerable.

Mr Pine recognized my vulnerability I think. He liked me. A strange energy was building up between us. His attention wasn't just to do with me being bright. He got me to do things in class in front of the other kids.

Once he got me to bring two of my pigeons to school and talk about them. He must have asked me about myself before that to find our that I kept them. Partly, I think, he really tried to get all of us to come out of ourselves and talk about our lives, what home was like and what our lives outside the school were like. That was amazingly unlike the rest of the teachers.

I brought the pigeons in, a hen and a cock, and talked hesitantly about them, with Mr Pine prodding and asking questions all the time. I showed everybody how to hold them with one hand around their wings and feet, and talked about how to look after them and keep the loft, how to train them as homers, how they bred and what the chicks were like, and the kinds of illnesses they had and what to do about them. It was wonderful.

It was the first time I'd been public, a centre of people's attention. As I got into it and the kids in the class began to feed them and ask questions, I began to glow with an amazing inner warmth and wellbeing. I loved everybody in the room, I loved their attention and interest. Somehow the group of people in that room felt like a group for the first time to me. I felt part of a collectivity, a warm and loving, supportive collectivity. My shyness fell and vanished.

Mr Pine's authority slipped into the background. No one was in control, everyone was excited and eager. How totally different from what that school had always been like before. Each of us had sat for endless hours in class rooms, glazed, bored, cut off from the teacher and more importantly from each other. Everybody had a few friends, but friendly warmth seemed never to get into the class room. It was always a separating, isolating experience.

Mr Pine was a middle-class person. Like Mrs Pheasant who took Class 4, his accent and vocabulary, the way he expressed himself and the feelings that his words carried over to me were so unlike my mam and dad, and anyone else that I'd ever met at home. He was liberal, not just middle class.

He cared about life and people. I should think he'd been to university. He certainly had a confidence about him that I'd now associate with educated professional middle class. He had no pretensions like John. He probably assumed his status. He didn't have the bitter, competitive edge that I met later with older, working-class teachers at grammar school, teachers who felt put down by their confident, graduate colleagues.

He approached teaching with dedication, a sense of mission even. He taught with enthusiasm, and watched our reactions. He watched not only for the results we got in tests, but for how we were feeling about things, how we were getting on with each other, who was getting left out and isolated. He noticed our behaviour in class and in the playground and in the dining room.

I was aware that Mr Pine was an intense and caring person. But the way he went about it was so unfamiliar. He maintained the distance of a teacher, of his class and his sex. He cared from a distance. He upheld the school rules firmly. His liberalism was in the way he expected us to behave sensibly and with reason – always with reason. Discipline was a self-imposed regime. Self-discipline for our own good and the good of the school. Most of the time his words were beyond me. It was his intensity, his desire to communicate and effect that penetrated.

He lived in West Bridgford – a middle-class suburb of Nottingham. One Saturday me and Mike Rogers visited him. I'm not sure why he asked us. Mike and I were at the top of the class, 'his most promising' pupils, and he'd spent time with both of us in and out of class. We were his monitors. Perhaps he was aware of the excruciating gap his class background presented to us. I'm sure he was aware of it and didn't know what to do with it. It was 1959.

He was very respectable middle class. I got the feeling that he wanted to show us how he lived. He had no class guilt; on the contrary he probably wanted to show us that a different world existed.

One day during the week Mr Pine's wife visited the class, towards the end of the day. They were going to have a baby. I vaguely realized that this had some significance in relation to Mrs Pine's body. She was young and quite beautiful, shy in front of us all, though I think she taught, too.

It was strange to see them together, and to half understand that they were a family like us in some ways, that Mr Pine had a private life – and a sex life. But still they were so unlike my home. They were so formal, prim and proper.

Shortly after Mrs Pine's visit Mr Pine invited us to visit his home. There was an excuse that escapes me. We were to collect some posters or paper that he thought we might like. He invited us privately at dinner time after the other kids had left the room.

We were used by now to being asked to stay behind. It embarrassed me slightly. I felt I was betraying the other kids and that there was something wrong in getting so close to the teacher. I was beginning to feel quite uncomfortable at times. Anyway we were invited and told how to get there.

I didn't tell my mam that I was going. We usually played out on a Saturday anyway so I could just set off. I wore my usual Saturday clothes – old shirt, jeans with the bottoms tucked into my socks and plimsolls. I didn't say anything because I wasn't sure what to say. I felt the arrangement was a private thing between me and Mr Pine. It felt like some kind of bond or trust.

I was quite passive in the relationship. He took all the initiatives. He approached me, I never approached him. I assumed that he liked me and wanted to get to know me, to be close and reach inside me. I was in no way cultivating the boss. If I'd thought that for a second, or if any of the other kids had ever said anything, I would have been reduced and that would have been the end. In a way that's what happened anyway.

So I didn't tell my mam. It had nothing to do with her. I set off in the morning and called for Mike, who lived in the next street. As Mike left his house I knew there was something wrong. He was dressed in his best clothes and his hair was plastered down. His mother saw him off, tucking his shirt into his trousers. She said 'Are you goin' like that?' I blushed and said I was.

We walked over the bridge into West Bridgford. It was an area I hardly knew. It was the main middle-class suburb, outside the boundary of the city – West Bridgford Urban District Council. Its buses weren't city buses. They had different colours – chocolate and cream. Their timetables were more select than the City's and if you got on on the city side of the bridge to ride into town you had to pay more. Funny how they were cleaner than our buses, more looked after by the passengers, less used and more orderly. When the city took them over a few years later the citizens of West Bridgford were outraged. But they weren't prepared to pay higher rates to keep them running as UDC.

The only reason I'd ever crossed into West Bridgford before was to scrump in the gardens of the élite. We called it 'bread and lard island' because people were supposed to be so keen to provide a display of their status over there that they would buy houses beyond their means and have to live on bread and lard.

Maybe, but there were some poshies in that place too. When we moved to West Bridgford ourselves when I was 16, we were instantly isolated as rogue working-class intruders and my mam and dad have never had anything to do with the neighbours, except to take them to court over ownership of the hedges around the garden.

Mr Pine's house was in Musters Road. We arrived on time. How strange the house was then. It was a semi with an arched porch and an electric bell. No one had bells in Sutton Street; our front door went straight into the living room. And there was a little privet hedge and front garden.

Mrs Pine answered and brought us into the hall and through into the back room that was Mr Pine's study. It wasn't a large house by the standards of the world at large, but it seemed massive to me. And there was Mr Pine without a jacket spending his Saturday morning in his study. Christ, what a weird atmosphere.

It was my first study. The idea of having a whole room devoted to such an esoteric activity was staggering. And there were books everywhere, books and papers and pictures. I slumped into embarrassed passivity. I hadn't know what to expect. I'd been excited and expectant, but this was just surreal. I had no idea of what to say, how to act.

He asked if we wanted something to drink. What? Would you like some orange squash? Orange squash? No one ever offered me such a luxury. In our house you had to beg, steal or borrow to get orange. Mrs Pine brought it on a tray and poured it into glasses standing on saucers. I nearly died. What was I supposed to do with the saucer? What did I do with the glass? How fast was I supposed to drink? Was I supposed to enjoy it? The atmosphere seemed to say this is just for show, not for your enjoyment.

I followed Mike, but he was flummoxed too. We both stood around like lamb and lettuce. Mr Pine said a few things to us and we mumbled answers. Mercifully we didn't stay long. He gave us the posters and we left.

It was very bizarre really. I didn't know Mike very well. He never played out in the streets much with the rest of us, and after Arkwright Street the Rogers left Ashling Street and moved over the river to the new huge council housing estate at Clifton. We were never really friends at all, just connected through doing well at school. So I couldn't talk to him about it on the way home. I didn't know what he was thinking.

I was dazed. I could feel that Mr Pine wanted contact with me and that he was somehow trying to get through to me. But I didn't know why and I couldn't relate to the way he was doing it. I just didn't know how to respond. Everything was filled with significance and wonder. The posters he gave me were symbols of an unknown world, a treasure which held a secret coded meaning that one day I might be able to use.

Mr Pine represented a different world from that of my parents and the street. His was a world of vast horizons, of knowledge and expansions. The visit left me feeling for the first time that there was a world outside Sutton Street, that there was more to life than the daily routine that most people I knew were engaged in. I sensed the control over life that his world represented – knowledge and control. Maybe that was why he'd invited us.

When I got home, I told mam where I'd been. She said I should have told her and she would have got me to put different clothes on. I felt embarrassed again that I'd done the wrong thing. I couldn't talk to her about what had happened and how I was feeling. The experience seemed private. More than that, it was totally other than life at home. The new horizons that were shown me of a middle-class educated world were separate from mam and dad and Sutton Street.

Mr Pine planted seeds that were to grow steadily over the next 10 years. As I passed through grammar school a wedge was slowly being hammered between me and my family. My relationship with Mr Pine marked the beginning of a process of hooking into a culture that wasn't mine by birth. Through educational selection I was about to be lifted out of my class and cultural background, and drawn passively and unconsciously into a world that could never quite be mine but which blew open the stifling lack of self-reflection that trapped me where I was.

After the visit to his house my relationship with Mr Pine reached some kind of climax or catharsis. He began to get me to talk about myself in what felt like incredibly intimate ways. He'd get me on my own, by having me stay behind at play time usually. He sat at his desk and asked me about myself. He asked about my family, what mam and dad were like, how they treated me and how I got on with them. I didn't know how to talk about it. I'd never even tried before. I told him about them arguing and being unhappy, and how I felt unhappy at home a lot of the time. The intimacy was excruciating to me.

One day he asked me about sex, what did I know about sex, and how did I know it. I told him about how the older kids in the street talked about sex. What kind of thing did they say? What did they do? I nearly died. I told him about the entries in the street, how they were used for kissing and touching. What else? Well I'd heard that some of the older boys took their girlfriends' knickers down and they bragged about how they did it, but I didn't know what happened after that.

As we talked I was spellbound. I was glued to the spot, transfixed, dying not to be there, for it to end. It was so embarrassing. I didn't know what to say, I couldn't talk about myself, about masturbating. I felt far too guilty, and anyway I was sure he didn't want to hear that.

Tiny beads of sweat were on his forehead. I had an overwhelming desire to touch him in some way, to stroke his face or wipe the sweat from his brow. I stood motionless, mesmerized by the intensity of the interview. Finally it was over and I shot out into the playground.

I don't know what he wanted from me really, I'm sure he wanted closeness and warmth, even love maybe. But the closer we got the greater was the tension of the contradictions of our relationship. A big part of him was still treating me as a kid and a pupil. I was one of his bright pupils. I could get to grammar school maybe. Academic achievement sat there, somewhere at the centre. He was encouraging a bright pupil.

At one level the class difference between us was a challenge. How close could he get to me? How much personal contact could he achieve with his kids, regardless of class? He was proving that he could get through to me, teach me *and* get through to me.

He wanted to be a success, I knew that for sure. He liked my quietness and my consistent good behaviour and attention in class. Hew liked my introspection, the way I reflected on things. I was a bright boy, and a good boy. Good and bright by his own middle-class standards.

Somewhere though he was patronizing me. He treated me like the equal I wasn't. His vision was probably his ability to produce a good grammar school kid out of the working class. Polishing a rough diamond. He couldn't possibly understand how I lived, what home was like. And I couldn't understand where he was coming from either. We inhabited different worlds.

The structure of the school, the fact that he was my teacher, gave our relationship form and made it possible. The structure defined us to the extent that his job was to teach me, to get me through the eleven-plus. Within that he could get close to me personally up to a point. He was allowed to make some inner contact, to try to get to know me.

But the further that moved from the central definition the harder it became. We couldn't really be friends. The differences were too massive – age, class, power. He couldn't make the leap and nor could I. If we tried the world wouldn't let us anyway. I was only in his class for one year. A year after that I would have left the school. Anyway, the other teachers wouldn't like it too much. I don't know what he wanted really, how far he wanted to go.

That he did want to touch my insides though was clear. As the year went on the intensity grew between us. He got inside me like no one had ever done before. He had a self-awareness that I had not come across before. Maybe it was that he was like me. Our contact was direct, like I recognized him as someone that I knew incredibly well. In some ways he was a liberal, caring father – so unlike my own dad.

But most important was that he touched my soul. That he wanted to touch me inside. He had an unspoken knowledge of my inner life, my private world of reflection, of sorrow and joy. He knew what life was about for me. He somehow expressed and touched the core of existence that I knew was in me but had no words for. And really he touched that core because he recognized its existence. He felt it in himself too. He, too, never voiced it in so many words. The knowledge passed between us and was gone.

It was that mutual recognition that was the life of our relationship. It grew through the year, but it could only grow so far. It was trapped in its context. Like all relationships it was defined by its historical situation. We had no way of just being together, close and in love. He was a teacher and in his late twenties. I was 10 and his pupil. It *was* a love affair really I suppose. But we couldn't acknowledge it.

With the talk about sex things went over the top. I couldn't take the intensity any longer. I couldn't passively be the good, intense, introspective boy that he needed me to be. I began to feel resentful and abused. After all he was still the distant teacher with authority over me. He chose to talk to me when it was convenient for him. The rest of the time he retired into his role of teacher.

I began to withdraw and avoid getting into private situations with him. And one dinner time the crisis arrived. He was on dinner duty with Mrs Pheasant. They were quite similar people; they had the same atmosphere. Maybe I was a bit jealous that they were together.

It was a school rule that you had to clear your dinner plate before you could have your pudding. Some teachers enforced it, others didn't bother. Mr Pine did, Mrs Pheasant didn't. Towards the end of my dinner one of the girls on the table with me poured a pile of salt onto what was left. It was a joke. Her name was Gloria Aitchison. She was in Class 3 with me. Something was going on between us. I hardly recognized it at the time. It came more from her than me.

Anyway I couldn't finish my dinner; it was covered in salt. I took my plate up to Mr Pine to look at. He said I had to finish it. I said it was too salty. It made no difference, I was to finish it.

Suddenly I was furious. Partly I was angry with Gloria, but much more than that I was furious at him. I lost control and screamed at him: 'How can I finish it when that bledy Aitchison's covered it with salt.' Tears of anger began to run down my face. The dinner room was totally silent.

Mr Pine just looked astonished and said 'Paul!' in a pained and remonstrative tone. It was my first open rebellion at Arkwright. His shock registered disillusionment. He'd always thought I was such a quiet, well-behaved and contemplative boy, so open to reason. Unlike the rowdy, scruffy, abrasive working-class kids that were my neighbours in the streets.

He didn't say anything else. I took my dinner plate away and got

my pudding, and ate it in silence. I was seething with righteous indignation. My anger was much greater than the salt. It was at Mr Pine and
his reasonable distant authority. There he sat at the teachers' table
with Mrs Pheasant looking down at me. I was just a child, a little boy
among all the other boys and girls far beneath their haughty presence.

In the end he could only apply the rules abstractly. I was to finish my
dinner like a good little boy. No doubt he had told Mrs Pheasant at some
point what a good little boy I was too. I had to shatter the whole thing.

I never talked to Mr Pine with intimacy again. It was over. In my
anger he was cold and distant. He was shocked, not moved. He didn't
understand what I'd felt for him. He gave me no comfort. I was now
just a little naughty, a little rebellious, and could never quite be
trusted again. At least that's how I felt.

I withdrew and he made no attempt to get close again. At the end
of the year I went up into Class 1 with Mr Skinner and neither saw or
thought much of Mr Pine again. But deep inside I held both my love
and resentment for him.

Paul Atkinson
1981

CODES OF CONDUCT

For a number of years, whenever thoughts of childhood and
adolescence surfaced, an insistent little phrase would rattle round my
head like a dried pea in a can. It went: 'They call it growing up but I
call it schizophrenia', and it caught pretty well the keynote of my
existence during that time of my life.

I remember one Sunday, some time in the mid-1950s, when I had,
as usual, sneaked the weekly muck-rakers up to my room before my
parents woke. On that occasion I came across a long article with the
title 'The Twilight Men', plus a picture of a male (in silhouette and
mac) in the park, at dusk, gazing toward a group of young boys. A face
we could not see, but a mind seething with filthy lusts, we were told.
From that moment, with a shock of recognition, I was able to identify
my own desires, until then simply vague moods and imaginings
washing around inside me. The vocabulary of that article gave me the
means to place myself in the world and the tone of it left me in no
uncertain doubt that I had better keep my mouth closed. For about a
year after, it was the vogue at school for the boys to point fingers at
less-than-manly pupils and unmarried masters and whisper 'he's a

Last day at school . . .

Twilight'. So that's what I was, though I was not about to let them know it, and I entered that period of – schizophrenia. I call it schizophrenia in the loose, popular sense of contrasting patterns of behaviour alternating violently. My alternations were not visibly violent – the patterns were mental rather than manifested. Yet (as I'll explain), the struggle between the two versions of 'me' was bloody and violent. A strictly medical academic (male?) mind would probably chide me for sloppy use of a particular word, and indeed I wish we could invent a word for the particular gay experience I'm talking about. We haven't, so I use their jagged word because it's very sound zooms in on the jagged feelings their world imposed on me.

From then on, of a morning, two people would look in the bathroom mirror, get into the same suit of school clothes. There was the bright grammar-school pupil, marked down for university one day, popular with the girls, and there was the boy who wanted desperately to kiss his best friend or be fucked by the history master. The former, in order to bar the latter from making his presence known, set about to develop a set of procedures; an elaborate, sophisticated code of conduct, the prime rule of which was: Check Everything. Looks and glances had to be carefully monitored – don't allow eyes to linger on a boy too long, don't gaze at the history master, never look at a male any lower than the waist. Stance and posture had to be under a constant review – no hint of droop, limpness, don't let those hips swing! Voice of course was crucial – no giggles, high-pitched tones, etc. Facial muscles had to be in control – if the words 'queer' or 'Twilight' came up, no twitch should betray a lack of composure. Clothes and the manner they were worn should not indicate 'fussiness'. Conversation had to be moulded – make it big, authoritative, swear more than most. This and much more was the order of the day, and not just an on–off job, it was a full-time preoccupation, the motor of life.

Now came the difficult part. Having constructed code number one, there was code number two to deal with. The hidden, invisible person, though so carefully screened from the world, was still there. What's more, in my case (and I know now, in the case of many of my gay friends) there was the feeling that this 'other' was really all right. Don't ask me where that feeling came from, I couldn't for the life of me say, but there it was. Then it was hidden away, with its hideous names, but one day, I knew, this person would want to breathe freely and had to be allowed some space in adolescent life. And so double-double code number two. Example: sitting in the coffee-bar with your 'girlfriend' and your 'best friend', you sit, arms around her, deep in conversation with him (careful not to look too deeply into his eyes – he's sitting next to you anyway, all three on the same seat, you in the middle, so you don't have to look straight at him thank goodness). But he's got his arm over the back of the seat. You're wearing a T-shirt, and for a moment, his hand brushes the back of your neck. By accident of course, and barely touching, but you can feel the flesh. Code one says 'withdraw at once or/and make a pouff joke', but code two says 'It's OK, keep cool, he can't see what you're thinking, enjoy the thrill.' Fear and desire fight, desire wins a few moments for itself and in that half-minute you have achieved something tangible – all the fantasies of love and lust, sex and romance, sensuality and friendship *do* have a relation to actual social, physical life. So code two is about seeking for those times when code one can be relaxed. That's a full-time job as well. The thing to do, I discovered, was to beat them at their own game in subtler ways than acting big and swearing more. It was to gain a purchase in the male world of achievement. With the kudos that came with winning cups for running and swimming (thus side-stepping the problem of hated group sports), putting on the end-of-term plays, getting the best exam results, it was possible to win male admiration and respect. This provided a margin of camaraderie, not dependent upon the sexist pack-hunting of young women, in which code one could soften at the edges: you're in a stronger position to admit, yes, you actually like poetry if you won the half-mile on sports day. I tell you, getting really good at history was just as much about getting to visit the history master at his own home at a weekend as loving the subject. (Alas we only talked.) Such was the success of my tactics, that by the end of the sixth form, I'd integrated various bits of myself so well that the tearaway who was clever and won things, could actually play an effeminate dandy in some stage production and get away with it. Could even begin to write moon-calf poems about other boys (never shown of course, to a soul). Yet it was still the fight inside and the world was still a minefield, and I knew it wasn't honest (not to the 'girlfriend', who was being cheated rotten, or to the 'best friend' – who might have had the same feelings).

Undeniably it was exciting at times, and such habits of behaviour have left their mark on those men who feel that life was more exciting before gay liberation robbed them of the bitter-sweet romance of being 'naughty boys'. Yet it was not good. It is a wrong sort of world where young people have to learn habits of slyness and deceit in order to survive. 'Coming out' is, I think, just a start. Not merely in the process of linking sexuality with the outer world of politics and relationships, but in the constant awareness of the shadowy battle that took place between the two personalities in the same suit. I believe that childhood is, for us all, female and male, gay and heterosexual, of whatever creed and colour a process of subterfuge, where often habits can be learnt that cripple for life; the person with homosexual desires can learn that in a particular, focused way.

Funnily enough, it's at this point that often, good-thinking heterosexual friends stick. Prepared as they are to support and listen, change their behaviour and language *vis-à-vis* lesbians and gays, the homoeroticism of childhood pulls them dead in their tracks. When, being presented with 'the children' I have said something like 'I hope the gay ones don't have to hide it at school as much as I did', the look of panic on the face of the proud parent is a picture indeed. Whose childhood are they denying – their offspring's or their own? What childhood coding system of their own haven't they faced up to? What other selves put down and battled with?

Finally, the phrase came out as a song lyric, it goes like this:

They call it growing up but I call it
schizophrenia
They call it being alive but I call it
schizophrenia

They drive a wedge between
your body and your mind
They've got you caught up
in the original double bind
They say you're acting strange,
you've been acting all your life
In a play you haven't written,
in a script that's based on lies

They say it isn't right for a man
to love a man
And a woman in a woman's arms
is upsetting the natural plan

They so confuse your mind
they make you hate yourself
And when they've filled you full of
madness they say they want to help

They call it growing up but
I call it schizophrenia
They call it being alive but
I call it schizophrenia.

Noel Greig
1983

Note

A revised version of this article appeared in *Heterosexuality* (eds)
Gillian Hanscombe and Martin Humphries, London: Gay Men's
Press, 1986.

Why we stick our cocks in other people

because it feels good
because of the beer
because it was meant that way
because it hangs there
because of the night,
a claw, one small forgotten sigh
the wet ocean slapping around the pier,
lances through the night
I said it was because it feels good
because once it was hidden
because size matters
because of the journey out,
the concrete playground,
because aloneness scrapes infant bones,
because helping with the cooking was never enough,
because of clouds across the moon,
mothers distancing kisses
because she ought to want it
because of car lights on the ceiling
because there is nowhere else
because of the lost world
because it's our gear stick and the motorway calls,
because this way there are no smells
and it was always hard out there
it's just because it feels good that way
because of the steel linings to our veins
peek-a-booh games, sky blue baths,
the origin of life, fat rumps of reason,
because that's what turns us on
because of the need to visit the shrine
because we feel divided, lost,
abandoned
because that is the only door back
and because it does feel good

that's why we stick our cocks in other people.

Andy Metcalf

FROM AN AUTOBIOGRAPHY

In Brian's 'letter to a friend' in the last issue (see p. 80) we published a 'live' account of an extreme but in many ways typical sexual/emotional trap. The following excerpt helps us to see some of the ways we are made to suffer as children and how these experiences come to leave their marks in our lives as we grow older. Like Brian's piece, the writing both expresses the repression of the past and reveals something of the possibilities within the present.

I was the eldest of three boys, born 10 months after my parents were married. Their laws prescribe that babies be conceived through a hole in the sheet; though I don't think they went to that extreme, it couldn't have been far off.

I never saw them touch each other, and apart from when I was a baby, or was crying or was smacked they never touched me.

Perhaps if I had been a girl I would have been given some recognizable physical affection, but I wasn't. I must have produced mixed feelings in them. Without a doubt my parents have, in their terms, lived their lives for their children, with special emphasis on me as an example to others, and that has been a great weight for me to carry, particularly as they bred in us no emotional ability to cope with such burdens, but gave us *things* instead.

I have rarely found people with so limited a social life as my parents. They are both exceptionally nervous of new social contacts, and although polite to guests are often extremely critical when they leave. They hardly ever invite people to visit, nor do they go to the pictures or indeed anywhere except for a run in the car. They gossip and never talk about feelings.

My mother is fearfully oppressed and depressed, and is often ill – stomach and nerves mostly – and is always on tablets. It disgusts me that the doctor once told her that she had three clever sons, and she should know there was only a hairsbreadth between genius and madness.

She works part time, something she of course never did when I was growing up, and enjoys the outside contact, though she is never slow to moan about the standards and attitudes of those with whom she works. She enjoys having a bit of money to spend as she pleases. As a child I was threatened by her with all kinds of retribution 'when dad gets home', but mum appeared to be the punisher and dad the one who brought home the treats. Now mum is the one I feel (relatively) sympathetic to, dad the one I try hard not to despise.

He is arrogant and stubborn and can say cruel things, and I fear to be like him. He jokes and is jolly as often as he can be to cover up his snappy nerves. He would like to be devoutly religious and wanted us to be. His job, which he grimly enjoys, involves literally, prosecuting people who attempt to cheat the system. One of my earliest memories is of sitting with an apple in a van in a field while he was outside working.

Both my parents are intelligent, and could have done well academically if they had had the opportunities they helped give me, but I have never seen either of them read a book (indeed, I don't think there is an adult book in the house). They spend their evenings dozing in front of the TV in an overheated living room.

They have not moved to one of the newer estates where the rest of the Jewry live, but remain in an oldish suburb not far from the city centre. My mother says she likes to think of herself as a big fish in a small pool.

They would be revolted to be called working class. When I go to see them, they are delighted and full of chat, but soon they remember all their expectations of me have come to nought, and I am no longer their little boy, and their bickering and torpor sets in. I hate to destroy their dreams and hurt their feelings, but I do the former continually and am bound to do the latter while retaining contact with them and being at all truthful.

When I was little I was so naughty I was put outside the playpen and all the things I shouldn't touch and the cat inside. My mother still carries with her polyphotos of me – grasping, reaching, sulking, hardly ever smiling at the camera. I don't think many of my instincts were well provided for. But it would be wrong to imply that all my memories are bad; I have great nostalgia for my infancy. I remember bedtime stories, two beautiful packs of shiny playing cards I folded into quarters while sitting on the pot, the old cat's kittens scrambling up the big fire-guard, dancing round the room to the 'Archers' tune with the lights out and sparklers lit on a winter's night (this is the closest I ever remember being to my parents), going to the park on a Sunday to listen to the band and feed the ducks, going down in the morning to see the cockroaches scuttling about and spinning on their backs because of the powder, the air-raid shelter full of dusty jam jars. I remember shopping trips to the clinic, dog-meat shop and fish shop, and the streets on slopes down which I was convinced, for some unknown reason, lay the sea (the river lay in the opposite direction). I was brought up on football, and my first word is alleged to have been 'Goal'.

All this dates from preschool days, before I was aware of politics, economics and religion, nuclear families and expected roles, before I was aware of anything except that my parents used to get annoyed with me and give me nice things.

Primary school

My first brother was born when I was nearly 4. He didn't say much because I used to speak for him – if he wanted a drink and coughed, I'd say, 'He wants a drink'.

I enjoyed his company and we were very close, especially as we weren't allowed to play in the street with other kids (a facet of my childhood I look back on with regret) because, of course, they weren't worthy of our company and were ruffians.

When he was still small, I began school. I don't think I felt pushed out or anything, for I was a precocious child, having had largely undivided attention on the cerebral front and being eager to learn. I enjoyed school and did well and behaved perfectly, behaviour which was reversed at home, according to my parents. There I am on an early school photo, a weedy little specimen clinging onto the end of a row, boys and girls whose faces and clothes wouldn't have appeared out of place 20 years earlier.

Girls. A new idea altogether. I had two girlfriends, but don't know if they cared for me. I didn't get involved in the standard kissing or fooling around because I had never mixed with anybody from whom to get such ideas. I did join in a sortie in and out of the girls' toilets; it wasn't very enlightening but fairly bold, and I was severely reprimanded.

During assembly I was put in the book corner at the back of the hall. I could hear and see the service anyway – I think I knew the mysterious Lord's Prayer better than most of the participants.

When I was about 7 the headmistress told my mother that I had a reading age of 13 or something, and that I was a dear little thing and they were very fond of me. My parents teased me endlessly about this latter compliment. I grew into an impressionable and weak child, visiting friends under prearranged circumstances but not generally mixing with other children. Being sensitive, clever and Jewish acted as a triple barb for those who chose to taunt me.

When I went into the junior school they took us swimming, and we were told we could wear swimming hats. I was just about the only one who had a swimming hat (because, you see, my hair was so thick and it wouldn't dry quickly and I would get a cold).

I was scared stiff of the water, and didn't have the sense to hide the hat in my pocket, and stuck out with it like a sore thumb. I still have not managed to conquer this fear (there is hope, though, as I learnt to ride a bike 2 years ago, never having learnt as a child because, of course, we weren't allowed to have them because they were too dangerous). I know they were only trying to protect me, but the barriers they set up proved pretty hard to penetrate.

From the ages of 7 to 17 I was schooled entirely with boys, and though there was strangely exciting kissing at parties, outside of which I never came into contact with girls, I was deprived of puppy love. My sexual feelings were completely internalized, and fantasies took the place of the physical closeness I missed. Only recently have I begun to come to terms with the contrast between fantasy and the fact of enjoying physical contact with men and women, and it has taken much toil and many tears to make inroads into all the guilt I have felt.

Eleven-plus

My second brother was born when I was 10; I was delighted with him, and still in complete ignorance of the reproductive processes. He had a white furry suit on the day I took and passed an exam and small scholarship which entitled me to go to what had been an exclusive grammar school. This exam was harder than the eleven-plus, and nobody from our school had ever passed it (both my brothers later succeeded). I was praised to high heaven, and believed I was wonderfully clever.

My teacher in that last year at primary school was the first master I had had, and I idolized him. He epitomized all the traditional views of sport and fair play and what was good for boys. I was not strong enough or brave enough to be proficient at sports, though I wished to the heavens I was, and this teacher showed me how to spin-bowl, which I rated as my greatest achievement. The only ways I let him down were by failing to learn to swim, breaking a window when mucking about with a cricket ball in the classroom, being caught with *Superman* comics in my desk and saying the record I'd ordered the previous weekend was not classical but 'The Hat Twist' by Max Bygraves (it never turned up at the shop).

We used to go over to the corner stores for chewing gum and sweet cigarettes and firewood and twopenny lolly-ices (we weren't allowed the penny ones as these allegedly had beetles' blood in them). We enjoyed my grandparents' company; my grandfather took me out on my tricycle on Sundays. My grandmother came on Thursdays and took my brother and I to the toy shop. I once wrote self-righteously in my diary that he got something that actually cost more than my thing did.

On Bonfire Night we could look at a distance at the wild, huge fire round the corner, but could get close only to the little one outside a friend's house. Because we weren't allowed to play ball in the street, my brother and I played a variety of cricket using a hula hoop as bat and a cork as missile with the lamppost beyond which we were forbidden to venture as a target. Just occasionally we were allowed – joy of joys – to go to the park, where we actually communicated with some other children.

Such were the pleasures and advantages, snobberies, disillusionments and disadvantages of one's parents taking pride in their 'middle-classness' and believing that this and their centuries-old religious inheritance made your children superior and not needing of the little pleasures of the childish flesh to which other poor people were so sadly susceptible.

Puberty and grammar school

The old-fashioned and fading grammar school I went to intrigued me and offered plenty to keep me busy. A thousand boys and a 'sister' school (with locked gates inside which we never saw) across the road. I worked very hard, worried intensely about not succeeding but continued to be top for a couple of years. Horror of horrors, when I first failed to be top it made me wince to admit such to my parents.

I feared being caught out of school without the statutory cap on. I feared my cap would be thrown down a lavatory. I feared that another Jewish boy, whose father was a minister, would report me for not wearing the dreaded cap when I ate my sandwiches. I feared a large boy who kept mocking my puny stature and threatening me. We all cowered in awe of the prefects, who even now, looking back on the revered panoramic photograph, look like large, heavy tough guys.

There was not an ounce of compassion or sympathy for failure. All expectation and effort was concentrated on us who had been chosen to do O-levels in 4 years, and none on the other half of the school who were so stupid they had to spend 5 years on this menial task.

At 12 I specialized in science (it was a toss up whether I preferred this or classics, but it was clear to my advisers that science was where the money was and where I would have a satisfactory future). I enjoyed it, but it narrowed my life, for I took no further interest in other subjects, which I considered intellectually inferior, or even in reading non-text books which seemed a waste of time. It took me some time to overcome this prejudice and enjoy reading without feeling I was wasting time – I didn't read a work of fiction again until I was about 20. Against this new academic background I went through my religious confirmation, the barmitzvah and puberty. Girls were a mystery, the only intimations of sexuality came from lavatory walls.

Sexual fantasy

Going back to when I was 5 or 6, my earliest sexual fantasies included the (conventionally) attractive mother of one of my classmates. I imagined myself sitting on the wooden swing – the most coveted piece of PT apparatus – and her coming up to me in a long, blue, shining gown, arms outstretched like a biblical figure, and kissing and stroking me.

Later I fantasized about my women teachers both chastizing me and being kind to me. While at primary school I had seen nudie books which had thrilled and excited me – there was a taboo on them, together with the discussion of biological or emotional connections, at both school and home.

When I was 13 I masturbated, by accident, for the first time, playing with myself and contemplating a picture from the *News of the World*. I did not know what was happening, excited but scared at my apparent lack of control over it, I thought, for no apparent reason, that it would stain the bedcover green. After that I bought myself magazines and suchlike and played with myself, stopping short of ejaculation for several months, but naturally I soon began to climax regularly.

Masturbation and unnecessary sexual intercourse wastes further Israelite generations, according to Talmudic law. It was not discussed, except very obliquely with the lads at school, practised in privacy, always waiting for the bathroom door to rattle. I presumed it was downright dangerous, and when I had a torsion of the testicles at 15, automatically imagined a causal relation. I was told no differently, nor did I enquire for 10 years after. Once my mother found a pin-up in the pocket of my trousers, and laughed if off, deriding my taste and saying it looked like a tarty character off the TV. I was glad to let it rest there, hide my material away more thoroughly, and attempted no explanation other than to hang my head.

My fantasies became more complex. They involved most of the females I knew from everyday life or saw in the media. Age and conventional good looks were largely irrelevant as in my mind I dreamt of women who would be nice to me, who would handle me, make love to me and who would enjoy acting out sadomasochistic scenes. To an extent these fantasies still attract me, but have diminished power and impact as I have found completely different involvement and satisfaction in a good, physical sexual relationship, something which I thought would never happen. I feared that once the initial excitement of a new sexual encounter had died down, for me there was no separation of intercourse from masturbation fantasies, about which I felt so much guilt and have only recently begun to come to terms with.

Ardent anti-sexism

In no way do I wish to degrade women or use them to gratify my masturbatory needs. I try to be ardently anti-sexist in all I do. The more I learn to enjoy lovemaking, the more important is the physicality and the less satisfying the fantasies (that is not to say that mutually stimulating fantasies should not be used or are to be forbidden). Sometimes good lovemaking happens, marvellously, without fantasies, but they do not go away of their own accord, I cannot banish them, but they are slowly being disarmed as I begin to actually like, rather than feel neutral or even arrogantly disdain, other people with whom I have begun to allow myself to get luxuriously close. It is still instinctively harder for me to be attracted to and to get close to most men than it is to many women, but I am aware of this and am positively working to change.

Where do these things come from? Mum and dad would say I had a dirty and disgusting mind. I think they come from a morbid interest in sex bred from lack of information, lack of physical and emotional warmth, from a view of women as second-rate articles, servicing machines and sex objects in the patriarchy, from disliking men as fellow competitors and non-sex objects, and from a view of life which involves giving and getting things, but never giving yourself receiving other people's selves, enjoying worldly comforts and self-gratification and using such as a barrier against the fear of the nakedness and vulnerability involved in emotional closeness.

But I knew none of these things when I was 15.

Dave Feintuck
1981

Letter

Dear *Achilles Heel*,
My initial excitement in discovering part of my 'autobiography' in *AH* was mixed with embarrassment, for having somewhat studiously avoided looking at what I had written for 6 months, seeing my words leaping back, together with your photos and headings, made me face up to what I was feeling last summer, something I find harder than dealing with immediate problems or the distant past. Thanks for the push!

I wouldn't contradict a single one of the facts I wrote then, but I have since been using a most useful tool to help deal with the mountain of emotions and patterns of activity I am subject to – this tool is re-evaluation, or 'co'-counselling. For example, I wrote, 'Mum is the one I feel (relatively) sympathetic to, dad the one I try hard not to despise.' This deals with only one side of the feelings I am now aware of, and which counselling has helped me learn to recognize and 'get into'. I have lots of different feelings about my parents; through counselling I have been able to begin to explore them, and by 'discharging' some of the past hurt – getting over past distress, fear, anger, etc. by crying, trembling, talking, raging, laughing, etc. – I re-evaluate behaviour which has caused me to act in predetermined, patterned ways. At the time of the hurtful incidents of the past, the basis for patterned behaviour was laid down because being hurt then meant I did not, could not, act in a sensible way. I wrote, 'I hate to destroy their dreams and hurt their feelings, but I do the former continually and am bound to do the latter while retaining contact with them and being at all truthful.' I have been able to start to dispel this guilt by dipping into some of the feelings aroused by past hurt, to discover and admit I care very much indeed for my parents, and want to be cared for by them, and being able to say this and show it in an appropriate way, at an appropriate time, is an achievable end if I am prepared to work hard enough at it.

In a co-counselling session the helper, or 'counsellor', provides a secure and reassuring present in which to let the worker, or 'client' give some attention back to the hurtful past and to explore the feelings aroused. With the discharge of emotions comes the re-evaluation of past hurt; memories which have shaped the way I act in similar situations can be disarmed, and I am freer to make sensible, flexible decisions. It might seem contradictory to talk on the one hand about getting into feelings, and on the other about acting rationally, but my recognizing that my getting into feelings where appropriate help frees me to act in the best way I can, on the basis of the facts in hand, has been a significant discovery. Co-counsellors believe they need, and can help each other with, 'therapy'; counselling is always two-way – that is, roles are swapped at half-time, thus helping break the barriers between mental health and illness, between client and professional therapist. I learnt of co-co. [co-counselling] through a friend, and was able in the autumn to join the group he was in, since when we have split to take in new people. Our groups are mixed, and there are also single-sex groups.

I feel I have usefully introduced some of the concepts of re-evaluation counselling into the men's group I am now in to good effect. If I allow myself to get into my feelings in the relaxed atmosphere, I can leave feeling refreshed and positive about future activity. If I repress feelings, I sometimes come away feeling unsettled and dissatisfied; I am sure this sort of negative reaction has prematurely broken up other groups. Since I left full-time paid work in the summer, lots of other exciting things have happened to me – beginning Tai Chi, great dietary changes away from meat-eating, finding and enjoying our communal house, having a lovely holiday in Yorkshire, doing some painting, working with a free school – that have helped reshape my old relationships and open doors to new ones.

People usually do their best, but old patterns dictate that we do not make the most of our intellect in that we cannot accept the facts without their being coloured by our past hurts. If people are deliberately hurtful and persist even when this is pointed out, then I feel I can criticise. Otherwise, I hope I can free myself from enough patterns to be able to accept others as fully as I have begun to accept myself – and that includes accepting the painful necessity of change and growth.

Love,
Dave Feintuck
Brighton, 1982

Chapter 3

Sex and sexism

SEXISM AND MALE SEXUALITY

This article is an edited transcript of a public talk given by Michael Singer at the Berkely Men's Centre in the US. We had a lot of discussion about it in the collective. And it has provoked several good discussions at the East London Men's Centre.

We wanted very much to put it out – to open up a debate on male heterosexuality in the magazine and in general that is very much overdue. It's the only attempt we know of – and some of us like it a lot – to provide a general overview within which such a sharing can take place; to begin to deprivatize the most mythologized area of our lives. At the same time, we recognize a problem of the article, one which Michael is aware of too: that of trying to talk about sexuality out of the context of particular relationships and particular histories and experiences. It's hard not to objectify sexuality even in the very act of focusing on it as a separate area of our lives; sometimes the article does that, and this tendency is reflected in the discussion that follows after it.

There have been times within our particular men's groups when we have managed to talk about sexuality in a way which sprang true from our individual relationships and yet posed general questions and perspectives as well. Such accounts have yet to be written up, as far as we know, and we hope Mike Singer's talk will help encourage this to happen.

Introduction

Let me begin with story. I was raised in a Jewish home. So were all of my closest friends. When Jewish boys are 13 they can be barmitz-vahed, which is a ritual ceremony introducing boys into manhood.

When the boys in my crowd were barmitzvahed, they were taken to a whore house. I was no exception. It was part of the initiation rite.

An older woman came into the well-lit, sleazy hotel room. I immediately had an erection and immense anxiety. She inspected my penis. Then she took my money, opened the door, handed it to someone I could not see. She undressed. She slipped something into her vagina and told me to get into bed and climb on top of her. I did and she put my penis inside her. After what seemed like 10 seconds, she asked if I was finished. I said that I wasn't but as soon as I finished saying that, I came. Then I felt terrible. She got up and left the room. That was it.

The boys, waiting in the car, asked me how it was and I said, 'Great...' If this is what making love is about then I think I'll stick to masturbation. I didn't say that, but I thought it. I was sure the other fellows had had a very different experience but I didn't dare ask and they weren't talking.

That was the beginning of what I assumed was a very conventional sex life. I slept with women regularly in college and after I never thought much about what was happening in bed. I didn't think my sexuality was something to be explored, only experienced. Since nothing very strange or bad seemed to happen in bed I wasn't troubled.

When I was 27 I was living in New York. I turned on the radio one day and listened to a conversation two women and a man were having about the difference between clitoral and vaginal orgasms. I realized I didn't know what they were talking about. I didn't know what a clitoris was.

I remember a woman with whom I had had a long affair; she had never been able to have an orgasm when we made love. I had always just assumed she was uptight because no matter what I tried nothing seemed to change. I didn't know she had a clitoris and she didn't either, or she wasn't saying. We did not stop seeing each other because of the sex; but I wondered what might have happened had we not been in the dark? How many other relationships might have been different? What had the women I had slept with felt? We never really talked about it.

In addition to my personal confusion, I began to understand that the problem was not only mine. I realized through reading and discussions that the society I lived in didn't really offer up the information people needed to begin to enjoy or know our bodies, or our responses to our sexuality. Everything was mystified. The irony was I had gotten a 'good education' and had an active sexual and

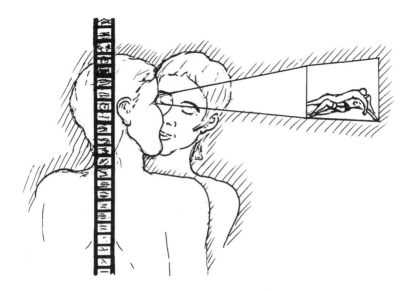

social life. I thought everything was okay in 'that' area. Now it was, like everything else, open to question.

Having been in many men's consciousness-raising groups I know many men have stories to tell which are similar to mine; they are the norm in our culture. After realizing there was something in it for me I began to explore some of the questions raised by these experiences. In no way do I feel expert, 'on top of it' or together. Further, I want to acknowledge that the orientation of this article is heterosexual. I am one and do not pretend to speak about or for any other kind of sexual experience. That is not an apology but a statement of fact. I am indebted to my gay friends whose political courage inspires me. They have been in the forefront of the revolt against sex-role oppression and many have paid dearly for it.

Sexism and the creation of 'men'

What is sexism? The simple definition I accept is that sexism is a prejudice based on gender. Its fundamental message is that men are superior to women. Over time, this idea has been elaborated into an ideology supporting not only the subjugation of women, but the economic and social relations that exist in most countries of the world.

We live in a patriarchal society. All the major institutions in this society are dominated by men. By institutions I mean those major centres of power through which control is exercised over our lives; that includes government, military and police apparatus, corporations, mass media, organized religion and schools. In socialist countries it might mean the central committee of the ruling party and the managerial and bureaucratic élites.

In recent years feminists have made it clear that you cannot separate the personal from the political. The dynamics of personal relationships – the way power gets used, the assumptions about roles, work and sexuality – are a microcosm of the larger social and political relations in our society. Many people, unhappy with their personal lives, are increasingly unhappy with the political situation in which they find themselves and are becoming conscious of the connection between the two.

There is an analogy (which speaks to the similarity of power relations in the public and private sphere) that can be drawn between the situation of bosses or managers and workers on the one hand, and the situation of wives and husbands on the other. No relationship is simply unequal or economic. There are many subtle privileges and benefits that some women and workers experience. But traditionally, women trade sex, their ability to nurture and make a home, for economic security from men. And workers sell their labour to bosses for economic security. In both instances the relationships are hierarchical and male-dominated. It is important that we as men understand this connection because the ways we are trained to be powerful and successful males in the world has an effect on the way we conduct our personal lives.

In this society all influential organizations are hierarchical in form; a form which demands leaders at the top in positions of unequal power. It is primarily white males who are trained to fill those positions. The form and content of learning and the social conditioning (as in sports, for example) men are exposed to is designed to sharpen their abilities to compete for and exercise power. Most real power (political and economic) is concentrated in the hands of a very few people. Consequently, our sex-role training has its own self-generating frustration. The power left for all of us to struggle over is minimal and often illusory. The frustration we feel is often transformed into a vague internal message that we have 'failed'.

For men sex often works out as a trap, because it's the only place where men can really get tenderness and warmth. But they have no skills to evoke these things because there is nothing in the rest of our lives that trains us to do this. So we come into this situation where we want warmth and intimacy and we don't know how to get it. But it's the only place where it exists, so there's this tremendous tension for men getting into bed with women.

In school certain qualities are emphasized. Boys are taught to be rational, to analyse and get on top of things, to be clear and efficient, disciplined and responsible. We are encouraged to accept, re-articulate and strive for socially acceptable goals with an intensity that makes it difficult for us to pay attention or give value to the process we use to achieve them. We are rewarded when our thinking is abstract, linear and consecutive. We are taught how the world 'works' and how to manipulate material, the stuff of the 'real' world. This real world is defined as 'real' and to a great extent built by male minds we are trained to imitate, so the information system is closed, self-perpetuating and male-dominated.

Most importantly, as boys are taught not to pay attention to what we are feeling; competitive work situations demand that we don't feel what we are doing to others. If we start to feel what we are doing, we may experience pain, boredom and confusion about our behaviour or the banality of our work. We might begin to sympathize with those we are supposed to beat.

Some men don't make it. Most working-class men are filtered out very early. When I was in high school I knew some of my classmates were not going on to college and others were. I knew those boys who didn't go on were slated for boring low-paying, dead-end jobs. Those of us who went on to college were being groomed for leadership, to take control from our fathers of these institutions and organizations or do what we were led to believe was socially useful work. The way it runs turns out that the middle-class men compete for limited and often illusory power and the working-class men compete for survival.

In a competitive society success, by definition, must be hard to achieve to be valuable. Sex-role training which is success-orientated presumes there is a scarcity of the kind of rewards men want most. There is one winner at a time, one president at a time, one hundred great rock stars, senators or lawyers. If we want such things we must become tougher, more competitive, less co-operative, more unfeeling; the cost of success is often early death: the physical and emotional mutilation of our heart. In a sexist society the values which impel us towards success and leadership are held in esteem. Those values which allow us our softness, nurturing, openess, willingness to co-operate are hidden from us or ridiculed and seen as weakness.

Sexism and relationships

Woman have complementary training which has often led them to feel powerless and, consequently, worthless and one-down to men. Obviously the situation is changing because of the women's movement. But the majority of women in this country are still operating within sexist assumptions about the limits of their potential.

Women are allowed to be nurturing, close to their feelings, they are encouraged to use their imaginations and be childlike because those modes have not threatened male power.

Sex-role training creates and reinforces power imbalances between men and women. Power comes in many forms in this society and money is one of them. Having a measure of control in your life in the sense that you are earning a living and are financially independent is a kind of power. Often women are unhappy in marriages and don't leave them because they understand they have no training to go out into the world and earn their own way. They have been taught to be dependent on men for money. In this way women are trained into a state of powerlessness and become victimized by it.

Divorce laws speak to this issue. Alimony awards to women often contain a double message. On the one hand, alimony is a recognition that women have actually done work in a marriage for which they have not been paid; on the other hand, alimony is a way of saying to a woman, 'you are a victim, unable to work and support yourself and we shall support your continued powerlessness'. This situation is fluid. Now many courts are not awarding alimony, often women are rejecting such 'help', but others, out of resentment and anger towards their mates try to get everything they can.

Sexism creates guilt in men and women. Usually what we mean when we say we feel guilty is that we are feeling intensely self-critical because we have done something wrong, or failed to do something right. We judge ourselves against some sex-role model which carries

with it a set of responsibilities and expectations we are taught to internalize. Women are expected to be 'good' mothers (a mystified ideal). Men are expected to be 'good' providers. Rarely do we have the power to live up to our expectations of 'good' behaviour. These role models oppress us. We feel bad. We grow to dislike ourselves and become difficult to love.

The pay-off, we are led to believe, for playing out our sex role is that we will make ourselves and our partners happy; as men we will offer our strength, our ability to make money, our aggressiveness. Women will offer nurturing, abilities at home-making and sexuality. Ideally there will be a trade-off; people look for what is missing in themselves in their lover. In the romantic version people complete themselves in the other. The fact is that the exaggeration of certain skills or qualities in men and others in women creates feelings of powerlessness and dependency which often leads to resentment. In trade-off relationships it is assumed that one person will always supply one thing in return for something from the other. For example, men must always work for a living and women must always be available sexually. Most of us are too complicated to fit such rigid styles. So problems develop.

The feelings of worthlessness and self-hatred generated by sex-role oppression are then manipulated in America by advertisers who create mythic men and women who have lived up to this society's expectations of what it means to be a 'good' or successful man or woman with the help of some product. Women get a double dose because almost all the images of what is important in this world are male.

Those images are there in home life, school and the media, all institutions dominated by men. The media, which penetrates our consciousness without our approval or control is owned and operated almost exclusively by rich white men, whose interests are rarely consonant with those of women, poor and working-class people, be they white, brown, yellow or black. Now women who are willing to behave and want what men want, while retaining their 'femininity' are approved of and show-cased in the mass media. Hence, what appears to be an equal trade-off is actually a situation in which the cards are stacked against women.

Internal oppression and bad sex

As we grow from boyhood into manhood we internalize many messages spoken to us at home, school, in church and the media. These messages are injunctions, commands; the do's and don'ts of manly behaviour. (For a more elaborate list of sexual injunction for men and women see the SAR guide published by the National Sex Forum.) A sample list of do's for men include: initiate, be responsible, be in control, get it up, perform, give orgasms to women, know everything, make love to young pretty women only, be a great lover, score, have a big penis. Such messages not only regulate our sexual behaviour but influence our work styles as well. The don'ts for men include: fail, guilt, play, be passive, be childish, let go, accept pleasure, turn down sex, be vulnerable, be gay, feel.

Most of us have trouble with intimacy. It is no accident. Men tend to reveal less about themselves. We often equate self-revelation with powerlessness. We are taught to hide much of our inner life from ourselves and from others. (I am indebted to S.M. Jourard's essay, 'Some lethal aspects of the male role' in *Men and Masculinity*, editors, Joseph Plech and Jack Sawyer, for this train of thought.) Since men have the same amount of inner life that women do, we have more secrets. We hold feelings which make us tense. Holding is energy-consuming and stressful. This stress numbs our bodies and when combined with the injunction against feeling, it makes it very difficult for us to sense, to feel that all is not well. Not to be in touch with our own discomfort makes for bad sex.

Any kind of loving, and in this case between men and women, demands knowledge of the needs and the characteristics of the loved person and that comes from self-revelations. If we cannot let ourselves be known, women cannot love us because we are just abstractions; there is nothing particular about who we are that people can relate to.

For men, sex can work as a trap because it is the only place where we can get tenderness, warmth and intimacy. We often lack the skills to evoke these experiences in sexual transactions. There is nothing in the rest of our lives which trains us to do this. So we come into a sexual situation where we don't know how to get what we want the most.

For most of us everyday life and work is devoid of intimacy and sensuality for which we are starved. Because our experience is so limited we tend to miss sensual or intimate possibilities when they are available or we sexualize them immediately. This sexualization of experience often feels to women like pressure to fuck, which makes them angry. And the pressure is real. We feel it when sex becomes a goal to pursue. We want to get our penises inside them. When we go for that, the way we are trained to reach for any goal, we ignore the process, the sensual intimate possibilities with this sexual partner and concentrate only on one thing, getting off. Often we miss the person completely.

Sex therapy

Sex therapy is a relatively new industry in America, which often uses the issues discussed here to exploit people's unhappiness. I have tried to point out some of the ways our role training and the pervasive sexism in this culture robs men of the real (as opposed to macho) power of their sexuality. Though I am doing sexual problem-solving in groups, I don't believe there is such a thing as a sexual problem. We cannot understand sexual dysfunction separately from other issues between partners such as: unequal power, not talking straight, not asking for what you want, or sex-role assumptions, just to name a few.

One of the first reactions that men have to the women's movement is to withdraw. Everything you do seems to be wrong, every move you make is going to be sexist, so pull back. It's like a new game, like the new male game. The game is that I'm not going to be sexist and I'm going to be perfect in bed and I'm going to be perfectly in touch with everything, and it's like a whole other trip we're laying on ourselves.

Most responsible sex therapy in this country is based on some scientific research into sexual behaviour. The scientific method tends to break down phenomena and isolate activity from its environment in order to study it. Consequently, therapies which develop from this kind of research tend to view sexual problems as mechanical or as personal/emotional exclusively.

At the crudest level this stance towards sexual dysfunction stimulates the business community to create new commodities which offer non-solutions. A product has been created for men who ejaculate prematurely (i.e. faster than they would like). It is a gel which contains, among other things, a surface anaesthetic which desensitizes the penis. I used such a gel once and indeed it desensitized my penis. But it didn't help me deal with the nervousness I was feeling about being with that particular woman. In fact, I felt more removed from the emotional issues between us. It was not helpful in any satisfying sense. To use a gel is to give up your power to a commodity from which someone is making a profit, a profit from your discomfort, your emotional life. In this way capitalism penetrates the most intimate aspects of our everyday life. The personal and the political are connected.

Masters and Johnson's work is a more complicated example of the same problem. Their research has had an impact on the women's movement and our thinking about sexual dysfunction generally. They created permission for women to seek orgasms in ways other than fucking men. They made it possible for people to expect that sexual dysfunction could be demystified. They affirmed the importance of the clitoris in women's sexual pleasure. But to read their work one would think they worked outside history. There is no sense in their work of the relationship of sexuality to other issues. Their work has made an enormous contribution and they do help people. At the same time, those who look only to them for answers, are robbed of a deeper understanding of the power struggle going on between men and women and what relationship that struggle has to the large economic and social forces in this society. To not offer that understanding to people is to keep them from all of their potential power to help themselves and each other, and to change the society which generates these problems in the first place.

I would like to pass on some of the findings of Masters and Johnson which demystify much of the folklore about sexual behaviour that men carry around in their heads.

1   Seventy per cent of the men questioned in their research said they came quicker than they wanted to. A statistic like this takes this phenomenon out of the personal realm and makes it social. Often social issues become understandable when many people who experience them begin to share the details of their lives. Assumptions about sexual relating make it a pressure-filled experience for many of us. The pressure is not relieved when our competitiveness keeps us from sharing out experiences with each other and demystifying them.

2   The research showed the most effective ways for women to reach orgasm generally, are in order: masturbation, oral stimulation and intercourse. This information should be of interest to us. We often approach sexual relations with a pressure to perform which translates into panicked intercourse to give our female partner an orgasm. The odds are against it. Further, we make assumptions about what gives women pleasure without checking with them. There is no law that says we are supposed to know intuitively the particular way in which a woman comes to her pleasure. We can ask. They might be pleased by the question.

3   Because of the way vaginas are structured and because of their compensating nature, for most women, the size of a man's penis is not a factor in the elicitation of pleasure. The cervixes of some woman are pleasurably sensitive to pressure. In other women the same pressure is painful. The cervix protrudes from the back of the vaginal canal. Again, men with smaller penises may reach the cervix of a woman with a shorter vaginal canal. The cervix can also be stimulated with your fingers. The point is that anatomy is almost never as much the issue as our fears about it. If you are worried about the size of your penis you know now what most women go through all their lives worrying about their bodies' relationship to some male ideal of perfection.

4   Ten per cent of men questioned by Masters and Johnson experienced tremendous pain after orgasm and had to remove their

penises from women's vaginas. No reason for this has been put
forth, but understand, if you have this experience, you are not alone.

5 There is no difference, Masters and Johnson found, between the
sensitivity of a circumcised or an uncircumcised penis. There is a
myth I have heard that men with uncircumcised penises control
their ejaculations much better. It's not true.

6 Women are able to have multiple orgasms; that is, orgasms one
right after the other with almost no intermittent period. Some
women in the Masters and Johnson study said that they could
sustain orgasms for up to 60 seconds. We men apparently can't do
that, or don't think we can. It is important to understand the
limitations around men's sexuality may not be real. Myths may
have grown up that we all believe and because we believe them,
they become truth. Before women got into their sexuality, it was
considered impossible for women to have orgasms. Most women
never thought they could. It may turn out that men can have
multiple orgasms or can have orgasms that last 60 seconds. Maybe
some of you do. We know so little.

7 Men have a 'refractory period', a measure of time after a man has
an orgasm in which we apparently cannot have another orgasm.
For some men the period is 5 minutes, for others, it is half an hour.
Time varies. It has nothing to do with how masculine we are. We
need not feel bad if we can't fuck and then fuck again in 2 minutes
or 5 minutes. Some men get pressure from women to do this. We
have a right to explain ourselves and relax.

8 Arteries bring blood into the penis and veins take blood out. As
we become aroused, valves partially close down the veins in our
penises. This traps blood, which conjests the penis and is what
creates an erection. Research has shown that the valves are
connected to higher brain centres. I interpret that to mean our
minds control erection. Erection has something to do with our
minds, our feelings and our hearts.

*It's not just a support group, it's your whole environment. If you're
working on sexism and you're doing that in a situation where the
other people are into making out, getting laid and all that, then you're
really coming up against a hard place. For example, the image I've
seen created here is that women are really in tune and that they have
an idea of what's going on. That's true if they want to, but for the most
part they're into the game as much as men are.*

All of us should feel total permission to not be able to get it up. If we can't have erections it is a signal from our body that something does not feel right. Instead of seeing it as a failure, take it as a message to begin to look and feel what is going on with you and your partner.

It can get better for us

Why is it that some men have better sexual experiences than others? Men who think of themselves as less able to enjoy themselves sexually often attribute the problem to some unchangeable characteristic which the winners have and they don't ... it may be the size of their penis, some mysterious love-making skill, the right face or body. Clearly, the men who fit some media image of what is attractive have more access to women who respond to those images.

However, anyone who has conventionally attractive friends knows that good looks and access to women is no guarantee of happiness.

What follows are some thoughts of mine about how to enhance the possibility for more satisfying sexual experiences.

a) A man has to have been complimented some time by someone for his sexuality to feel good about it. When you sleep with a woman who doesn't offer the information, you might ask if you are pleasing her and how. Real information is useful.

b) Men who are not under pressure to perform from themselves or their partner have a better chance for enjoyment.

c) Men who feel responsible sexually for their partner and themselves and for what happens between them transform sex into work. Sex is a 50–50 proposition. Those of us who deal with this pressure by trying to give women their greatest sexual experience often feel ripped off, or uncomfortable later. We have been so concerned with the pleasure we are giving and how it is being received that we have forgotten about ourselves and what we want. To take responsibility for both people often makes it impossible for us to figure out what we want from women. Traditionally, women have complained that men only used sex to have orgasm and took no responsibility for what their female partners were feeling or what they wanted. Men are starting to experience feelings women have been having for a long time.

d) It is critical that men who want to have good sex like and respect women. That may seem obvious, but there are many men who don't like women, don't respect them and don't know it. Such feelings of anger and resentment often come from the oppression of our sex roles and we are afraid to admit to them because it will isolate us further from the one source of pleasure we are taught to pursue, women.

e) It is important that men be in touch with the part of themselves that likes to play, to be mindless, sensual, silly and open to experience and imagination. Playing is hard for us. Play demands that we ignore goals and just enjoy the concrete detail of the process we are involved in at the moment.

f) If you feel that the head of your penis is the location of all pleasure in your body then you are missing much of what your body has to offer you. The problem with such a limited pleasure experience is that it determines and structures everything you will want sexually and sex often becomes a routine.

g) Men who can suspend their self-consciousness – which keeps them distant and monitors their experience instead of being in it – have a better chance for pleasure. On the other hand, it is important for us to be aware of what does and does not feel good. We should know if we are doing more than our share of doing something we don't want to do. We need to be able to stop what is happening, explore it and not just go on with the movie in our head of how it is supposed to be. If you are feeling bad, she is probably feeling that way too or at least feeling that you are. As men we are supposed to want to make love all the time and women are always supposed to be available. Because we are lacking all the affection we need, we often get involved sexually and move full steam ahead and to hell with the feelings. Men who can talk about their feelings and who are interested in their partner's feelings can build intimacy. Such men want to know what the particular nature of that women is who they are with, how she is responding to what is going on, what it feels like to her, how she cares about you or doesn't care about you, what she likes and doesn't like. Some men are interested and willing to hear all that. Some men are willing to give up their movie, their mode, way of doing things to co-operate and create something mutually pleasing. If all our sexual experiences are the same we are controlling them.

What is really critical in all this, is that we understand we can change and there is something in it for us to change. It is difficult. There is no model in this society, no incentive to be any different.

There is no model for us to be vulnerable, open, and humane and powerful at the same time. We have to create that ourselves. And our sexuality is as good a place as any to begin.

Sexuality always has the potential to be one medium of intimacy for us. That is part of its power. We need intimacy, it gives us strength, it affirms our humanity and helps ameliorate our alienation. If we can enjoy our sexuality, give and receive pleasure, we deepen our links with each other. We are then less dependent on commodities for our pleasure. But when sex, like so much of our lives, is taken from us, packaged and sold back to us, we can be confused.

Conclusion

In the last decade the women's movement has succeeded in politicizing everyday life. One effect of this politicization is the attempt by many of us who want to build a revolutionary culture and movement in America, to scrutinize the conduct of our lives, our work, behaviour towards ourselves and each other. We want to understand the sources of our oppression. To the extent that we have responsibility for the oppression (for instance when we as men behave in sexist ways) we want to stop and know why it is in our interest so to do. When the oppression is outside our personal responsibility and results from the economic and political relations in this society, we want to change those relations. In order to do that we try to create a process of struggle which has within it the values we want realized in a revolutionary culture....

And I think most of all what's really critical in all this is that men understand what's in it for them to change around all this stuff. And this is very difficult because very often when we're talking to men who feel bad about all this stuff that's going on in their lives there's no model in this society to be any different. If you watch the Olympics, you know, it's all there. What wins out is this particular style of being in the world. There's no model for men to be open and vulnerable. You don't win if you're vulnerable or open. There's no model to look to. We have to create that ourselves.

To struggle successfully (to win!) we need love and strength. We need to generate our own power, a power which rests not on the oppression of others but grows from our ability to treat ourselves and

each other equally and with compassion, to realize ourselves as fully
as we can now in our work, in our relationships, in our sexuality.

Michael Singer
April 1978

'I MEAN, YOU CAN HAVE A MALE-CHAUVINIST FANTASY ...'

*Last summer, the tape of the original talk from which Mike Singer wrote
the previous article was played at the East London Men's Centre.
Twenty-five men from all over London turned up to hear it. It was a
strange experience, sitting around a cassette in a crowded basement
room in London listening to a voice from San Fransisco talking about
things so close and familiar. This is an edited version of the discussion
which followed Mike's tape. It was difficult to edit. Many of the men in
the room had never met before, the group was large and talking about
sexuality is hard at the best of times. Much of the content of the
discussion was about people sounding each other out, getting to know
one another and trying to deal with differences without dismissing or
putting each other down. We have tried to hang on to the feeling of the
meeting as much as the development of people's ideas. We don't
necessarily agree with everything in the version below, but we do identify
with the atmosphere of a men's group struggling to communicate as
openly and supportively as possible about their own sexuality.*

J: Could anyone explain to me what Mike was saying about guilt?
N: I was surprised what I heard him saying was that someone feels
guilty when they think they have power to change something, and
they haven't. They feel guilty when they cannot change things. That's
a long way from ways that I have thought about guilt. In the context
of sexism it seems easy to say 'Sorry – that's just the way I am'. I think
he should have said a lot more about guilt.
P: It's a bit limited, to say you feel guilty about not doing something.
You can feel just as guilty about being able to do something –
something you are really good at.
W: Guilt is very circular. If you can't change what you feel guilty about
you get even more guilty – and so it carries on.
H: Surely the thing is that you can do something about it Once you're
aware of your guilt, which has to do with ideas that have become
embedded in your life, once you understand why you feel guilty about
sex or about not being able to get an erection, say, or coming quickly –
you can even feel guilty about being exploited – you have to understand

something about that to do something about it. I thought the point that Mike was making was quite good really.

J: A lot of people though – including myself in certain situations lose any feeling of guilt and never feel it. You just smash something up.

H: It was news to me that when I'm making love I might be trying to achieve some sort of goal or ideal which I'm not aware of – an achievement idea that's situated in my head and I'm not necessarily aware of. I certainly feel that a lot of my guilt comes from feeling that I'm a failure in some way. I can feel that I'm not liked and I don't like myself.

J: That's based on the expectation that you shouldn't be a failure.

H: That's right.

N: I have difficulty with what Mike said about guilt. I think of guilt as anger that I turn on myself instead of someone else. I look for somewhere to turn that anger. Mike seemed to say that there's nowhere to take the anger, that you're stuck with it.

M: I found the thing about the 'performing pig' very interesting because you want the woman to get something out of it, right? He's saying the only way you will do it is if you're not worrying about it. But on the other hand if you're not worried about it you could come in 2 seconds. I find there's a big contradiction there.

P: Are you saying that if you don't worry about it the natural thing is to come quickly?

M: No, not necessarily. I can see it if it's to bolster up the bloke's ego. But if you want better sex.

N: I think what he means by 'pig' – or what I would say anyway – is not sharing the responsibility for everyone's orgasms equally with the woman, or whoever is involved. Both people are responsible for what happens not only one of them.

M: Yes, it could be the woman's fault. Maybe not that many women will take the responsibility. The roles just come out like that.

A: I have a whole load of 'oughts' in my head all the time. It's not just that I 'didn't ought to be sexist', it's much more in terms of, 'Oh, I ought to be enjoying this more, I ought to be letting myself go more'. Or actually watching an orgasm coming and reaching the point of wondering 'What's it going to be like. Is it going to be a good one, is it going to take me over completely or is it going to get stuck in my stomach' – monitoring all the time.

P: Yes, like watching yourself go through something rather than experiencing it.

J: I think there's a real tendency to do that if you're performing. It's

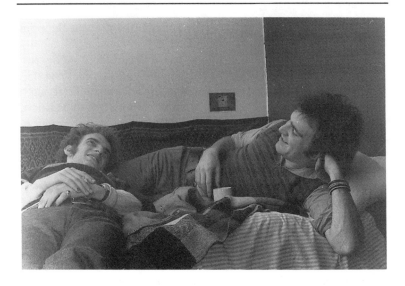

James Swinson

very hard to keep track of your own orgasm if you're trying to perform. It seems to me to be easier to enjoy an orgasm if you're relatively passive. That's my experience anyway.

M: I find it hard to enjoy anything if I'm trying to enjoy it.

W: The word orgasm is being bandied around as if we all know what an orgasm is, as if orgasms are the same for everyone and our own orgasms are exactly the same as everyone else's. I'm trying to think – like no one has tried to describe the process that goes on. It's just summed up briefly as orgasm. I was thinking that's difficult and I can only see it in terms of imagery. And the imagery is very interesting. Like one image that I always had was a rocket taking off, one's a steam engine starting up, another one might be a waterfall. But I was just wondering whether anyone was prepared to articulate their experience rather than just summing it up under the heading of orgasm.

P: I often find that I break into a fit of laughter or shakes or tension. Often it's painful laughter, sometimes it's good laughter. I never get this 'whoosh' rocket thing.

O: I get a great sense of release like taking a hot shower or something. It's just really relaxing. I don't necessarily laugh....

E: The waterfall is rather effective because it's downwards and has fluidity about it rather than force.

M: This guy that's just written a book called *Tao and Sex* he says the coming for a man's not synonymous with having an orgasm – and that's been corroborated by sexologists in the States. Everybody thinks you've just got to come to have an orgasm. It's not like that.

A: I think that's very important. It comes up in the questions on the tape after Mike's talk. That's very much accepted at the meeting that there is a difference between ejaculation and orgasm. And there's a male equivalent of the myth of the vaginal orgasm too. It's not necessarily the case that men have to come to get an orgasm. And some of the blokes on the tape talk about .... well, one bloke gets what I think is very superior about how wonderful orgasms he has without coming. But I think that there's a lot of truth in that and it's very important.

O: Yes, it's especially true if you've just had an orgasm – or rather with me it's likely to be half an hour ago – and you have another one. And when you come the second time and have an orgasm it's much more stimulating.

N: What occurs to me is a description of orgasm – which is an antidescription, because I don't know what it's like because I'm not there at the time. I was thinking what someone was saying about feeling competitive about orgasms; you can't be competitive about orgasms because they're not mine, they're the opposite of 'mine'. Does that make sense?

W: Do you mean that you're standing outside them?

N: No, I'm not outside them. I'm in them. And after a while all the pieces sort of drift back and here I am again.

T: But in a way that is saying you *are* having such an amazing time, isn't it? What you're saying is like a description of a spiritual experience – an amazing orgasm where you just lose yourself completely.

D: I feel quite competitive about that. I don't think I've ever.

N: I can count on the fingers of one hand the number of times it happened.

P: What I find very difficult here is the whole thing of dictating the conditions of your own pleasure. I think I've given women I've had contact with so little opportunity to know what I like, because I gave myself so little opportunity to know what I like. The women I know don't actually know how to turn me on, so I end up sort of dictating my own terms of how. So I'm permanently in control and I don't think I've ever had the experience of really letting a woman turn me on, and allowing her to be really creative in the relationship. To let loose in the way that you described I find just so hard to do. To not be on top of the situation all the time.

N: I'm conscious that when someone is trying to give me pleasure I can lose all contact with it and desperately hoping that some nerve in my body is going to feel pleasure.

B: When you raised the thing about 'performance pig' there was one thing that hit me forcefully (round about Xmas time I think it was) was the actual approach to fucking with another person. What happened to me, like most men in this room I suppose, the women that I fuck with are mainly feminists and so my approach is always to try and not be your typical male and always taking the initiative and going for a good hard bang – but being gentle and caring, because that's what I thought would be acceptable to a feminist woman. But then I met a woman to whom that approach was a fuck up. It wasn't what she wanted at all and it turned her off me. And we talked about it and it was a really big down for me. I was compared badly with this other bloke she was off with. In fact he's a bit of a male chauvinist but as far as fucking goes that's what she wants.

N: How about you? What did you want? You described both things in terms of the expectations of the other person.

B: Yes, right. And I feel that what I was doing was more in tune with my approach to fucking. And that is tied up with the question of performance – not only performance in terms of how good you are but also the manner in which you do it.

A: I think it's very interesting when you ask about questions the way you relate to people – which most of us to some extent have – there's a secondary stage or layer of ideology about how you ought to be doing things, about how you ought to be relating to women and men, how you ought to be fucking. I find this very ambiguous because on the one side you do need to be different, to be conscious of how you are and of how you want to change – and that works – but the other side of it is that you become more and more conscious of what you're doing and more and more sensitive to deeper and deeper layers of what's going on.

O: It's not that the oughts are secondary, it's the oughts of the new rules.

A: I think a lot of men start to set up models of what feminist women should be like, which gets them into very strange things. You can start accusing women of not being feminist enough.

E: Taking that point up, of thinking 'I'm holier than thou'. I find I get a bit screwed up if I'm trying to suggest to a woman how she should be. If you get a woman you like, who's liberal and friendly and quite giving but who you feel is, you know, too feminine in an unacceptable way, and you think 'Oh shit!' this is not my place to say anything anyway. What do other people think? Whether it's not their job to, whether it's too domineering of men to point these things out, whether other women ought to be doing it???

M: I can't see the point of imposing any sex morality on anyone. If a woman wants to be screwed by a male chauvinist, that's what she wants. There's no point trying to change that until she wants it to change.

N: Yes, except if JB is being oppressed by her saying he's no good.

M: Oh yes, but in that case I wouldn't go with her. I wouldn't try and change her. Maybe try and check a few ideas out.

P: That seems very harsh to me. In the sense that if you have an experience like that with somebody and you think that it's not quite right, to say 'That's it, I won't bother any more.' Rather than saying 'Right, you're doing it wrong' you could say 'Well, I like it different' and then see if they do change instead of the moralistic 'Well you haven't got it right.'

M: Well, by a chauvinist screw I mean you don't care about the woman. It's just 'I want' and that's it.

E: But in the end that's not very satisfying.

M: It's just a question of desire that's all.

E: How is it different from masturbating?

M: It's not really.

T: I mean, you can have a chauvinist fantasy. That's very easy. I do. I can get into looking at myself in the mirror and masturbating and looking at my body and my cock – seeing how it's sticking out – and my pelvis. That whole thing really excites me.

P: One thing he doesn't go into on the tape. There's the one argument as to whether you're chauvinist or not, there's also the argument of fucking being a central thing like a cure-all. And you might be very sensitive and the woman might be very sensitive, but you still see fucking that can substitute for everything else. So that when you feel you want to fuck, it could be that you want to fight or maybe sing or eat or change your job, or sleep. It's good that he stresses how we're fucked up about it, but still he doesn't say how that central role can be dispersed so there's less pressure on fucking as a way of working yourself out. It's like if you can sort out your sexuality with somebody else

then the rest of your life will just fit into place – which seems a bit....
A: He does talk about 'strokes', that there are a lot of other strokes.
When he talks about men's groups he's saying you can get a lot of
things from other men.
H: It's still in a very physical/sexual sort of vein, though. He doesn't
talk much about getting satisfaction from walking, talking, reading or
writing or doing practical things. It's still very much sensuality.
T: I think it's warmth and understanding, too, when you're talking
about men's groups. The fact that men usually only have that warmth
for women.
O: Oh yes. In my experience what he says is true. I feel I've got a great
deal from men's groups.
B: What I feel is that fucking – well let's go back a bit in my personal
history. If I were able (years ago) to live out my sexual fantasies, what
I would have been would be one of these compulsive, neurotic
promiscuous people who went around fucking as many and as often
as I could. And what I got in touch with after a while was the
realization that because of the way we're conditioned and that sex is
held up to be the fantasy was a search for a deep acceptance by
another person that I had been denied, and that I could find the deep
acceptance through sex. And I think for me that's what these strokes
are about – feeling this kind of acceptance from other human beings
at this very deep level, and that you can feel this in ways other than
fucking. Fucking is a physical and emotional acceptance of one
person by another. But I don't think necessarily it's the ultimate....

June 1978

'WHY MUST I BE A 30-YEAR-OLD TEENAGER IN LOVE?'

*A lot of us have had the experience of being at a discussion or meeting
where the gay question comes up; people go quiet for a bit and it feels like
they're uncomfortable about their heterosexuality/ homosexuality. Then
the discussion goes forward on a pro-gay line and we're all making
opaque assumptions about what we think and no one's strong enough
to question anything. Here's something from my own struggle to deal
with the gay/straight split in me, it's been hard to pull together but I think
it's come.*

Some notes about my sexual history

I started to write this article about a year and a half ago. At the time I felt unhappy at not fitting into either the gay movement or what I felt was the mainly heterosexual men's movement. I didn't feel I was 'bisexual' either. I grew up as 'heterosexual' in a relatively normal way. I fancy women. When I was a child I felt very scared and guilty about sex which I identified as being my desires for women.

Then 3 years ago I started to get to know people involved in the gay movement. Prior to that I'd hardly slept with anyone other than when I was married and I felt like I'd had hardly any sexual experiences. With gay people I felt, for the first time in my life, an ease about sex and an openness which felt an enormous contrast to my previous life. I was very deeply moved and sort of fell in love with my friends and their ideas.

I think I became very dominated by feminist ideas and the sense that homosexual relationships were the only non-sexist ones. I met women who'd apparently become gay by act of will and I started to explore my own homosexuality.

Looking back it feels like my motives weren't always so pure. I felt guilty about being a man. I felt oppressed like a woman 'cause I was a single parent and I hoped feminist women would feel solidarity with me. But later I was hurt deeply when feminists treated me as a man and gay people ignored me as 'straight' 'cause of my desires or involvements with women. At the beginning, a woman I felt close to said 'We're all gay really.' That gave me self-confidence in my homosexuality. But I misunderstood.

Paula Tree's anti-heterosexist contracts:
(i) admit any opinions that you have that women's (i.e. men's) lovings are not as good or as powerful as men's. Don't keep these opinions secret.
(ii) agree to actively fight these prejudices and ask others for support to do so.

Liberating Sexuality, Paula Tree,
Grassroots, Manchester

Today it feels like 'gay' and 'straight' are inadequate categories when it comes to dealing with our experiences. They describe, rather, social structures of exclusion and relating.

When I'm feeling good about myself (which isn't so often) I feel I can be close to men, that I *do* have real feelings of love which save me from facing unsupported the torments I get into with women.

My relationships with men seem to be like friendships with high spots of sexual emotional closeness. Whereas with women it's been more intense, I make a lot of demands and get into intense strange scenes. One of the contradictions of my homo/heterosexuality is that I feel my identity is different according to the sex of the person I'm involved with. I feel more free relating to men but at the moment that's not giving me the comfort I seem to need. I can feel guilt about that, but what this represents is simply that I'm getting more support from women. 'Until the next time.'

So the strength I have got from men has helped me to face involvement with women again and exploring my heterosexuality. I feel now that I can allow myself to get deeper in because ultimately I can exist without women, even though it might not always feel that way.

When I started writing I wanted my experiences public so that others might know they weren't alone. When I needed to share my experiences there was no one who could understand. The subject of men developing a new sexual orientation needs to be made more political. Of course this going through things alone is an experience many gay people have had to face and if one finds one's way through, it can give one a deep understanding of love and truth. But many of us get lost in traps of confusion and self-denial and get scarred by the process.

It happened to me and it need not have happened if there'd been people who'd understood what was going on.

Sometimes I've understood these sexual changes in terms of learning about men's bodies as opposed to women's. At other times it's been an escape from performing as a virile man or from depending on relationships with women in order to feel good about myself. Often I've hoped that I would 'discover my sexuality' and everything would start to flower again.

Then I've learnt that sex is only a partial separation from bourgeois reality – and that ultimately this reality gets through the walls of desire into the relationship by the back door. I still feel a failure 'with women'. 'Until the next time!'

I can see that your head has been twisted and fed
With worthless foam from the mouth...
...Yet there's no one to beat you, no one to defeat you
Except the thoughts of yourself feeling bad...

I can tell you I'm torn between staying
And returning back to the south.
            from *Another Side of Bob Dylan* 'Ramona'

Well if you want to make me cry
That won't be so hard to do
If you should say goodbye, I'll still
go on lovin' you
Each night I ask the stars up above
'Why must I be a teenager in love'.
            Dion and the Belmonts

Heterosexism in Mike Singer's article

Nine months ago as I pasted a photo of four men's bums onto a page of the last issue of *Achilles Heel*, it got up my nose that he could pontificate about men's sexism and sexuality and never even question the entirely woman-orientated nature of his experience. For example, he says: 'I want to acknowledge that the orientation of this article is heterosexual. I am one and do not pretend to speak about or for any other kind of sexual experience.' I want to open the cracks that heterosexuals paper over in order to avoid contact with their own homosexuality. If, as appears to be alleged, there is nothing there, then they have nothing to fear; but if it rests on fear of ostracism and conformity, etc. then one is oppressing oneself, gay men and, more pertinent to this discussion, people like me.

Mike's statement, 'I am a heterosexual' may, in part, reflect his legitimate wish to resist moralistic pressure from gays or non-straights to conform to the tyranny of *their* stereotypes. But the real question remains unaltered. Each of us has a choice – to see our heterosexuality as a social product in which one's self-identity rests at a deeper level out of which come in varying degrees heterosexuality, homosexuality and other potentialities.

> Although it can feel like a separate part of my life I can't help being struck, in retrospect, by the enormous influence on my sexuality of living with my child as a single-parent father. It's completely changed my involvement and dependence with my friends and has felt very contradictory with my friendships with feminist women.

Or we see ourselves as finally made and we paper over the cracks to change.

Rereading his article this morning I was again and again struck by the positive things he says, how little I've understood about my relationships with women, how insensitive and insecure I was with R yesterday afternoon. And saw more clearly, the struggle to avoid both irresponsibility and taking patriarchal responsibility for deciding the truth about what was happening. It takes two to tango.

And Mike reveals the inner nature of heterosexism so very clearly that he gets very close to demystifying it; I feel the force of what he says inside *me* in this paragraph:

> For men sex works out as a trap because it's the only place where men can really get tenderness and warmth. But they have no skills to evoke these things because there is nothing in the rest of our lives that trains us to do this. So we come into this situation where we want warmth and intimacy and we don't know how to get it. But it's the only place where it exists so there's this tremendous tension for men getting into bed with women.

But the central truth of men's politics for all of us heterosexuals is that sex with women both *is* and *needn't be* 'the only place where men can really get tenderness and warmth'. In addition to being a homosexual, I'm a heterosexual like Mike and I want to be my heterosexual self. I feel *more* freaked out than most men by the emotional blocks my family and society have placed in the way of relating to other men. But I also see that the 'warmth' that heterosexual relationships offer is often deeply distorted and bound up with accepting assumptions about oneself which make one less of a person and fuck up one's relationships. I don't see that we can draw a line between wanting, on the one hand, to be more involved in childcare and changing our relationships with women, and on the other, getting more involved with each other. Men sleeping together, looking after each others' clothes and bodies feels like men becoming more autonomous and *therefore* able to give more to women. But sexual relating between men seems to come more from feelings of love and care for other men's sexuality – how you touch your friend reflects strange feelings – our support for gay liberation can be a search for our own lost feelings and a denial of the gay/straight split which bourgeois society has produced.

It grieves my heart, love, to see you trying to be a part of, a world that just don't exist.

from 'Ramona'

The third principle of radical psychiatry is that alienation is the result of oppression about which the oppressed has been mystified or deceived.
(Claude Steiner: *The Radical Therapist*, Penguin)

Mike says 'Sexism creates guilt in men and women. Usually what we mean when we say we feel guilty is that we are feeling intensely self-critical because we have ... failed to do something right. We judge ourselves against some sex-role model ... rarely do we have the power to live up to our expectations of "good" behaviour. These role models oppress us. We feel bad. We grow to dislike ourselves and become difficult to love.'

And becoming aware of our sexism has made us even *more* guilty and we've created new stereotypes and new tyranny. But it's still true that the heterosexuality that Mike describes creates with one hand many of the problems his other hand is trying to solve. Once one says 'I am this, I don't need to question myself' over one thing, it leads to another. There's a tendency within the new 'therapy ideology' which has developed as a backlash to the experiments of the last decade, and which supports people in wanting to be male, monogamous, heterosexual and play traditional roles. Which is OK when these roles are games pursued in a self-conscious way – but to actually *become* them?

Women have tried to support each others' independence from men. Men's lives are also crippled by our emasculated emotional dependence on women's femininity – men, too, can take heart from the song 'for lovers may come and lovers may go but I only have what I am. And I'd rather be lonesome and free than ...' bound up by that heterosexist shit.

Collectively reconstructing our sexuality?

Faced with this kind of discussion people tend to fall into one of two positions. Position A says: well I think it's up to each of us to work out our sexuality and if you wanna screw with men that's fine by me but I'm a heterosexual.' I don't feel much political support from persons of this type. It's too much of this experience which made me want to paste arses on and reply to Mike's article.

I have heard you say many times that you're better than no one,
and no one is better than you;
If you really believe that you know that you have nothing
to win and nothing to lose.

from 'Ramona'

Position B offers at some level a real personal commitment to reconstructing one's own sexuality, questioning one's own monogamy and heterosexism. What seems more important is that people don't make rational choices about whether they are A or B.

But what if you're in a secure heterosexual relationship and there are children to be considered? I guess I'm not sure there are secure heterosexual relationships anymore. Also, to feel that one wants to offer support but that one doesn't experience the problem oneself is a bit like feeling one's a middle-class revolutionary. It's a problem we've had a lot of experience with, beginning, say, with the situationists and the student revolts in France in the 1960s.[1]

I don't want to deny my sexism – I want to get into my fantasies. This is why I'm into teenage rock and also 'cos it says a lot to me.

Three years ago I thought I was part of a movement and we were all personally and politically committed to a new life together. We said there was no 'essential' sexuality.[2] We thought we'd found an eternal truth. Perhaps we were also expressing the undefinedness of the new-formed sexuality we were exploring.

Today sex itself seems just a little less important, less bound up with my insecurity and things seem a little more open. For a time I felt less solidarity with gay men. I envied their clarity about the identity they wanted. This was partly to do with feeling rejected as 'not gay'. Today I've got better relationships with gay men. I accept I'm no better and no worse than they.

Often I've felt alone and only felt generalized solidarity with anyone struggling to get some autonomy from the scripts which our families and our society has laid down for us.[3] So although it's been sometimes hard communicating about these problems with other men in *Achilles Heel*, they've given me a lot of insight and support for which I'm grateful.

Twenty-eight years of confusion about sexual orientation and loneliness in a world that thinks so differently make it hard to live and make one very dependent on people with whom one can share experiences.

I've hardly started to grasp the ways in which images of one's own sexuality hamper one's freedom and sense of oneself. On the one hand I'm discarding old categories of 'homosexual', 'heterosexual', etc. and constructing my own sexual identity. On the other, I want to live and get into the sexual images which are part of our society.

Well the time I called my baby, tried to get a date;
the boss said 'No dice son but you gotta work late'
Oh well my momma and poppa told me 'Son you gotta make some
money
If you wanna use the car to go ridin' next Sunday'
Oh well I didn't go to work, told the boss I was sick;
'You can't use the car 'cause you didn't work late'
from 'Summertime Blues', Eddie Cochran

I went to a Garden Party to reminisce with my old friends. A chance to share old memories, play songs again. When I got to the Garden Party they all knew my name. No one recognised me, I don't look the same. But it's all right now, I've learned my lesson well. You see you can't please everyone so you gotta please yourself.
Ricky Nelson

My changes have been to do with breaking into a situation where I was close to men. I have a friend whose socialization was gay socialization and who later got close to women for the first time. We've helped each other come through a little. I'd have liked to have written this article with him. I might then have had the strength to have given you more personal details about my life. When I asked him for the names of some of the singers whose words I've quoted, he said they were his words. So are some of the others.

I'm split between my personal experience and a sense of what's happening all over society. For me and many of my friends there's been a sense of getting closer to each other that has come 10 years after we expected it. And I think this is happening in lots of places, too, as the beginning of a generalized process. I think we're wanting to create a new sexuality and a new collectively shared love between all of us as the last feudal bonds of kinship dissolve away into the anonymity of mass society. That's the real women's liberation and it will be a real revolution.

Steve Gould
August 1979

Notes

1 '10 days that shook the university', Strasbourg 1966, see discussion in *Leaving the 20th Century: The Incomplete Work of the Situationist International*, translated and edited by Christopher Gray (London: Free Fall Publications, 1974), p. 85n.
2 'Nothing Personal', Char Stanier, 1976, IMG gay fraction and (now defunct) personal and political group.
3 Russell Gavin sent us his *An Age of Dreams* and I found things I liked in the foreword, see the poems too.

LETTER TO A FRIEND

The last decade has seen massive changes in the way men and women think about each other and themselves. For many these changes have been liberating and productive. For others they have been deeply confusing and have involved, temporarily at least, loneliness and despair.

We print here a letter written by a man in the depth of such a crisis. The writer, Brian, feels trapped in sexual contradiction. He feels he cannot go forward; neither can he go back. Desire itself becomes suspect. He cannot move.

We have all been in similar traps. Even when we must, in the end, know they are false traps, we often can't find the way out of them on our own. Only by sharing them – by working through them consciously with other people – can we begin to move forward again.

We hope to print more articles from men who are prepared to talk about their feelings and their struggles in the way Brian has. By learning about each other, we learn about ourselves....

Today, at the 'office' where I work the secretary mentioned the response of 'the men' to an article she had pinned to a notice board – 'Confession of a lousy lover'. She joked that most of 'the men' had blushed when they had seen it. I would freely admit to being a 'lousy lover' in that perhaps it would be more truthful to say that my experience of sex has been so rare and my experience of love so much rarer that I do not even attain the 'status' of lover. Most of my life is led in the shadow of the unrelieved mental pain, depression that this brings. At least I assume that is the case. I do not really know how my mind/morale would evolve if I had developed emotional and sexual relationships to any length. Perhaps I would be just as miserable and prone to emotional collapse.

However, I think that this approach – the very notion of 'looking for women with whom ...' is already objectifying, is already calculating and manipulative. It is already seeing other people through the perspective of my own needs. However, I do tend to see women in this way. I do not act upon this and I suppress it but I am aware of it when I relate to particular women and the very unrevealed existence of such possibilities in my mind make me feel dishonest, make me feel as though I am hiding behind a mask and make me feel furtive and uncomfortable.

I ask myself, of course, if I am not being too principled, whether perhaps if I go round and see X or Y that would not, in fact, be justified by the extent to which I know them. That perhaps we could get to know each other better in an open-ended way and that I need not see or make my visit the prelude to a later 'seduction'. A year ago I was opportunist in this way. The woman questioned the sexually objectifying way in which I approached her, we discussed it and got on very well. Perhaps one should not rate sexual experience. But I have had a lot of pain because I have never repeated the beauty of the one night I spent with her. (This broke up a monogomous relationship so she began to relate sexually to another close friend. She couldn't then cope with three of us.) I wonder now whether something less blatant and more open-ended might not be the way again. In thinking about that I wonder whether what has actually happened is that I am imprisoning myself again sexually. Whether, in various subtle ways, internalized mechanisms of self-repression have not re-established themselves under new names and this is the real reason I have slipped into a repressed and depressed inertia. Perhaps indeed there is a 'principled way-out' or one that is not too unprincipled.

But I also doubt this. I have already stated a feeling of sensitivity about approaching women in a manipulative way. I cannot overcome the uncomfortability of knowing the option I am keeping open and which at this stage I am hiding from the other person. In any case I feel the women concerned can clearly see it written all over me in my attitude to them. In the interests of their own autonomy they are repelled by it. Perhaps in writing this I have convinced myself that the best thing to do would be to talk to them about it, not in the sense of seeking favours, but in the sense of mutually clarifying things and 'clearing the air'. Operating deception in relations to comrades – even for good motives – seems bad practice. It isn't cricket.

This still leaves me with the same problem. When I first read Reich, Laing *et al.* I became clear how 'sexual scarcity' leads to sexual objectification. One looks at others as potential sex objects because sexual scarcity creates sex as a separate and special part of life. Denial creates a tension, a perception of a need and other people are regarded in an instrumental way as potential objects to satisfy that need. Sex is no longer a part of exploring all sides of another person. It becomes something you buy from porno mags or prostitutes or which is taken violently in rape. When I first discovered Reich I found a reason to explain my past behaviour and became clearer on how oppressive and self-defeating it has been. Euphorically I believe I could change all that. More recently I have discovered in my new cell how sexual denial creates these kind of problems. I have become warned that if I did have sex, I might start premature ejaculation again. I catch myself sneaking glances at porno magazines. I wonder how to regard my own passion for non-objectified erotic art. I think I can make out a case for the existence of such art but, I wonder, and, in any case, my reasons for looking are not solely to satisfy any aesthetic sensibilities. As I've said, I cannot deny the way sexual scarcity distorts my existing relationships and conversations with people.

In these circumstances I feel nervous in the presence of women who are angry about sexist oppression. I feel they have a reason to be angry at the way men relate to them. It frightens me when they say in a matter of fact way, that relationships with other women are bound to be easier, less oppressive and more enriching. It seems to me there is logic and truth in what they say. Extrapolating it further it seems to put me, as a heterosexual, in an impossible situation. What if, when a year ago, I had approached Z in a sexually objectifying way (I passed her a note saying I fancied her) she had been rather more sensitive?

Of course this challenges me to question my heterosexuality and to consider gayness. I do not deny that I can remember in childhood turned-on memories of a gay character. I can also remember vividly the point my parents decided to force it out of me. I can remember that they really fought and they succeeded. Intellectually I can accept gayness. I feel I am more able now to talk deeply with other men, to develop affectionate relationships with them and, to a very little extent express that in touch and hugs. But there is still a deeper level I feel I cannot contemplate – or contemplate only with anxiety and tension. That repression really has me tied down.

In these circumstances I reflect anyway that I have rarely and but little felt 'sexual' desire for any men and in any case the same problem of objectification would arise.

So I return to heterosexuality – or more accurately to masturbation. And I get more afraid as I get older.

Brian
June 1978

HOW I GAVE UP PORNOGRAPHY

Over a year ago I wrote an article on heterosexual pornography for this issue. It basically said – 'I hate sexism but I like pornography – isn't that curious?' – and it went into a lot of personal detail about my history. The collective rejected it and suggested I should read more of the feminist literature on the subject. I felt very hurt by this rejection, which affected me so strongly just because the article was so personal. I went very quiet and licked my wounds for a while. That was phase one.

But I did go and read a lot of the feminist material, and found out a lot more about how offensive women can find pornography.

> *We were then able to look at pornographic material not as entertainment in any sense of the word but rather as a kind of political media published by men and for men to perpetuate male authority and female submission.*
>
> (LaBelle)

And so I wrote a second and quite different version of the article, which included a lot of quotes from the feminists, and went into quite a full discussion of the slogan of Robin Morgan – 'Pornography is the theory; rape is the practice' – using the latest research on rapists. But my conclusion was that in spite of all this, I still liked pornography and still responded to it in much the same way. Again this was rejected by the collective, who thought that the quotes were great, but the rest of it was pretty thin by comparison. And the personal element had almost disappeared amid a welter of quotations and statistics. This time the rejection didn't hurt so much, because the article wasn't so personal, but it was still a disappointment after so much work. That was phase two.

> *... pornography functions to perpetuate male supremacy ... because it conditions, trains, educates and inspires men to despise women, to use women, to hurt women.*
>
> (Dworkin)

It seemed that I was stuck, I'd done the thing two ways, and I couldn't think of a third way. The collective was concerned, and called a meeting to discuss what could be done. But before the meeting took place, I was able to get into a situation where it was made possible for me to split into two, and have a dialogue between my two sides – the side which opposed sexism and the side which liked pornography. Let us call them PRO-porn and ANTI-porn. The dialogue went something like this:

ANTI: How can you look at porn when you know it's so demeaning to women?

PRO: I like pornography. Like that joke a few years ago with a man saying 'Pornography is getting worse, isn't it?' and the other man saying 'That's funny – I thought it was getting better.' I use pornography to masturbate over – I think that's what it's for.

ANTI: But don't you see that there's something hostile about pornography – it's a real putdown for women to be spread all over the page like goods to be bought and used? It's painful and degrading.

PRO: When I was 15 or 16, I wanted girls desperately, but I was never able to fuck until I was twenty. It was intensely frustrating to be with them and never to get what I really wanted. What was so precious about their cunts, I felt, that I couldn't get access to them? I felt convinced that they would enjoy it as much as I would. It was a kind of competitive thing: who was going to win – me with my Yes or them with their No? But they won all the time. I did all the work, I felt, and got all the excitement and all the frustration; they didn't have to do anything, but they won all the time. If I had dared to admit it, I was angry with them and would have liked to punish them. When I see women in porno magazines opening their legs and pulling their cunts apart, it's as if somehow I am getting my own back on all those girls who wouldn't open their legs for me when I was 16. And these women are better-looking anyway. 'There – you see – it wasn't so hard, was it?' It's as if I was proving that I was right all the time.

ANTI: But there's something sick about that, isn't there? You must admit that it's quite indefensible to hang on to those feelings for all that time, instead of just dumping them as you grew up.

Tom Weld

PRO: Well, in my therapy I found that my resentment at young girls for not giving me what I wanted was tied up with my resentment at my mother for not giving me what I wanted, back when I was a baby. When they said 'No' it was extra painful because of what I had made of my mother saying 'No' back then. But I didn't know that at the time.
ANTI: That's no excuse. People often blame things onto their mothers, but if you really have been in therapy, you should have got over that. How dare you use that as an argument! Haven't you got anything more convincing than that to offer?
PRO: When I was forming my critical opinions about sexuality, we talked about being pro-life, and being sex-positive. We saw the

majority of culture as being sex-negative and anti-life. So being in favour of sexual freedom was not only agreeable and exciting, it was also ideologically correct. Reich's ideas would have fitted into this very well, if only I'd known about them at the time. I still think there is something in this – the people I see in therapy are often still suffering from anti-sex distortions which they acquired in childhood.

ANTI: That is using a partial truth to back up a total lie. You know very well that 'sexual freedom' turned out to be a con trick played on women, by means of which they were told that being really free meant being exactly like a man, with a man's responses and a man's reactions and a man's assumptions. And pornography repeats that con, in an even more deceptive and offensive way. The most oppressive thing about pornography is that it's a stereotyped man's world, where stereotyped men's wishes and whims are one-sidedly played out at great length, with no concessions at all to the idea that there might be a woman's world, or a human world, where women might have different wishes or whims or where men might be less stereotyped and one-sided. It is a boring and repetitious world, where men really do 'only want one thing', as the old taunt has it. Pornography reinforces the myth that there is just one right way to be sexually – perpetually randy. It feeds just one set of fantasies, instead of somehow doing justice to the variety of ways of sexual being in the world. It's telling you the way it's supposed to be – but only one version, the version that fits best with a patriarchal society.

PRO: But lots of fiction does that – and not only fiction. The whole culture picks up on the normality of sexual relations where men do it and women have it done to them. Why pick on pornography? The stories in magazines are sometimes very good. I prefer the modern stories, which are often told from the woman's angle, and generally respect the woman's right to an orgasm and not to have babies, to the Victorian stories, which are generally very exploitative. The old stories are very male-dominant, the more recent ones much less so.

In real life, men are very reluctant to give women orgasms, other than with the prick. In pornography men are only too ready to do anything and everything to encourage women to come. I like that and I wish it were more widespread. Obviously some pornography does reduce women to objects of pleasure. But the pornography I like best shows women as *subjects* of pleasure – owning it, often initiating it, certainly participating fully in it, getting satisfaction from it. Being an object is bad, but being a subject seems fine to me.

ANTI: But can't you see that it is all so conditional? Women are only admitted to pornography on condition that they like having sex with men; there are lesbian and masturbation scenes, but the women involved always like men too. So it's not only predictable, boring and repetitious, it's totally deceptive too. It pretends to be about freedom and pleasure, but it's actually about compulsion and money. It's men who profit from the magazines and books, men who publish and own them, men who basically despise women – look at Linda Lovelace's *Ordeal*, for example.

PRO: I admit that there's something distasteful about the money that is made from sex. When I buy a magazine, that seems OK, but when all those other men buy so many thousands and millions of magazines, that's not OK. And men making huge profits – the women get fees, but the men get the fat profits. There's something gross and suspect about it, it makes me feel unclean by association. Prostitution even more so. In itself it's not bad, but the money and the men who tend to own and control it – that's all horrible. The in-fighting over the vast profits to be made – something disgusting about all that. The unacceptable face of capitalism – and a half.

ANTI: How can you admit all that and still like pornography?

PRO: Women without clothes on are sexy. If I saw one in the street I would look, if I saw one in the park I would look, if I saw one on the beach I would look. It's natural to look, it's instinct, anyone would look. So now here's a magazine giving me a good look. I'm grateful to it, and to the women who take part.

ANTI: Women don't like to be looked at in that automatic way. It's the machine-like aspect of it that's so suspect. You're like a robot – you see a tit and your eyes swivel – you see a wet cunt and your cock goes stiff – it's like a programme. And it's a programme which goes against women and their interests – it actually freezes women into a fixed role which they can't escape from – it's so incredibly narrow. It stops you seeing so many other things.

PRO: What I do know is that I just respond so positively to naked women. It lifts my spirit, not just my cock. I remember a film of Bob Guccione's which I saw once, with women doing various things, including running about in the country somewhere. And I just remember the grace and power of one woman running – it was a beautiful sight, an inspiring sight, not anti-woman in any way.

ANTI: But it's a *man's* version of women. It's still got this one-eyed vision. It may make you feel good, but what does it do to women?

Does it make them feel – 'That's what I am aiming for' – or does it make them feel – 'I am inferior by comparison' – or 'That's not *my* idea of women' – or 'I don't like her doing that for men' – or what? The point is that a woman's reactions are not predictable, but your reactions are all too predictable. You talk about being sex-positive, but what you really mean is being prick-positive; you talk about being pro-life, but what you really mean is being pro-cock. It's not the same thing.

In pornographic books, magazines and films, women are represented as passive and as slavishly dependent on men. The role of female characters is limited to the provision of sexual services to men.

(Longino)

And at this point a strange thing happened. I had been using a red cushion for the PRO character, and it had a certain red glow about it up to this point. But now I had what amounted to a full visual hallucination: I actually saw the glow go out of the red cushion, It became dull and ordinary. And I realized that I had been investing the PRO character with a lot of idealized charisma. Or something like that. I had been seeing it as standing somehow for real biology and common sense; a sort of foundation of healthy animal instinct. And really it was nothing like that: it was a false male story, put about to serve the interests of the patriarchal system.

No, the feminist objection to pornography is based on the belief that pornography represents hatred of women, that pornography's intent is to humiliate, degrade and dehumanize the female body for the purpose of erotic stimulation and pleasure.
(Brownmiller)

And from that point on the dialogue simply consisted of the PRO character giving in more and more, and agreeing in the end to give up pornography.

Now what does this mean? It is not that I have stopped responding sexually to women or pictures of women or to erotic stories. It is that I have decided to give up buying and reading and supporting pornography, on the grounds that this will make me a more consistent anti-sexist man. A better fighter for the cause; a lesser embarrassment to my comrades and friends; a more consistent and coherent person.

Normally I am very suspicious of decisions like this: they often represent a moralistic and unrealistic commitment which lasts about as long as a New Year's resolution. But in this case I feel as if I've really learned something about my overevaluation of the 'healthy male attitude' to sex. I have seen through it; I can't be taken in by it any more. And this is what really makes the difference for me, and takes away my defences.

I remember, about 10 years ago, how I used to say to people – 'All I really want is one good fuck a day, and I'll be happy'. I can now see how absurd that was. It was nothing to do with the other person involved: it doesn't even *mention* the other person involved! It is a robot–ego type of remark. But at the time it seemed the epitome of robust masculine good sense. And now I can see that it's just as stupid to ask for one good wank a day – there's nothing particularly basic about that either.

We are unalterably opposed to the presentation of the female body being stripped, bound, raped, tortured, mutilated and murdered in the name of commercial entertainment and free speech.

(Brownmiller)

There are lots of different types and styles of pornography. In this article I have mainly been referring to the commonest and most overt, easily obtainable stuff, in magazines like *Whitehouse, Park Lane, Escort, Fiesta, Club International* and *Men Only*. The vast majority of pornography available on the open market is not violent, and contains little overt suggestion of violence. It was not until I visited Denmark that I even saw any pictures of women being bound, chained and whipped. I remember how upset my 10-year-old daughter was when we brought the magazines home and showed them around. We had to explain that the lady was not really suffering in the way she seemed to be, that she was an actress pretending to be hurt – but her natural reaction did make a strong impression on me. It seems obviously right to oppose this kind of thing, which is very much a part of the whole world of pornography, and it seems to me that we have to accept the feminist case that there is a connection between this kind of violence and the more ordinary porn I have been writing about.

> *Pornography is a hate campaign; make no 'liberally sophisticated' mistake about that. It is a campaign to humiliate and brutalize all females, women and children. If it continues to succeed, we will be back at the bottom of the barrel – all of us – and for generations to come.... this is not a pretty time. If my assessment is correct, it is a time of war.*
>
> (Lederer)

My own experiences in therapy lead me to believe that most men hate most women, deep down; certainly some of the psychoanalysts have found this. For example, Robert Seidenberg says:

> In the unconscious of men as found in psychoanalysis, there is a deep-seated fear and loathing of women. All the songs of love do not displace this underlying contempt for those 'unfortunates' with gaping wounds where a penis ought to be.

I don't to labour this point at length here, because it doesn't really connect with my own experience as I have been describing it, but it comes pretty close – just another part of the same wood, perhaps. So I think that those women – like Andrea Dworkin, for example – who do see a deep connection between violence towards women and seemingly innocuous soft porn must be right.

Perhaps it is too easy for me and other men to dismiss accusations of rage and sadism, and maybe we do have to go even more deeply into this troubled area. I feel as if I've made a definite step in the direction of opposing pornography, and I feel good about that as far as it goes. But I wonder how much further I have to go.

John Rowan
21 June 1982

References

Brownmiller, S. (1976) *Against Our Will*, Penguin.
Dworkin, A. (1974) *Women Hating*, E.P. Dutton..
Groth, A.N. (1979) *Men Who Rape*, Plenum Press.
Lederer, L. (ed.) (1980) *Take Back the Night*, William Morrow. (Contains most of the quotes used in this article.)
Seidenberg, R. (1973) 'Is anatomy destiny?', in Jean Baker Miller (ed.) *Psycho-analysis and Women*, Penguin.

Chapter 4

Sexualities
Identities and relationships

MOTORWAY CONVERSATIONS: SEX IN LONG-TERM RELATIONSHIPS

It was hot in Nottingham's University Park. Andy rolled over and started to do press-ups in preparation for the long drive back to London.

'I am putting on too much weight,' he said as he began the exercise.

'Yes, you are,' Paul was quick to reply.

'Now, now. I'm still pretty fit.'

As they approached the car, to their right from behind high privet hedges, smoothly clipped, an Edwardian vista of surreal significance opened up: a ladies' bowls match was occupying all the greens. Each player was dressed in white, the teams distinguished by the colour of the band circling the hat on every player's head.

They had been planning for several weeks to tape a discussion about sex in long-term relationships for a magazine article. Now the moment was upon them. By the time they had got to the M1, Paul had worked out the levels required to record the ideas and generalizations of their present phase. Holding the microphone in his hand, he started it off:

Paul: 'It seems to me that what happens in your sex life, usually has a lot to do with what is happening in the rest of your relationship. For example, if you are not prepared to listen to one another's sexual needs, the chances are you are not prepared to listen to one another about a whole lot of other things. Or if there are issues of power between you, if one person is pushing at the other, the chances are it will not only be in your sex life there is that pushing, but in every other way too.'

Andy: 'I think that's true, but I also think that things can happen in your sex life which are separate and autonomous from other parts of your life. What I am thinking of is the way in which sex – because it is

about intimate, sensual contact, stroking, caressing and touching –
can bring out strong infantile or childish feelings and desires. It is
easy for me to see sex as the only place where I can get that kind of
caring attention. In that context certain issues become highlighted.
For me, these issues have sometimes revolved around who's giving to
whom ... that's one of the most important ones.'

Paul: 'What do you mean by that?'

Andy: 'Who's giving the pleasure: who's doing the stroking; who's
turning who on. I think I am particularly sensitive to being given to –
and not being given to – because of becoming more aware of this as
an issue in my childhood. This can be a difficult area in relationships
because sexual sensuality – that almost infantile ease of contact – can
reinvoke those questions which occurred in childhood about getting
enough, about being given to enough. I don't think gender defines
this, or that this is an issue just for men. Writings which come out of
a feminine psychoanalytic practice have emphasized this point about
women's sexuality.'

Paul: 'There are some quite similar things which go on in my
relationships. Stuff about fairness and wanting to be given to in the
same amount that even runs over into at the same time. It seems hard
to get to a point of understanding whereby one partner can give
something to the other for a period of time, and then the situation
can reverse with the receiver becoming the giver, without either
partner getting anxious that they are going to get left behind in the
race to get enough.'

Andy: 'Get stuck with the giving role.'

Paul: 'Right. Get stuck with one role or another. But that can also be
an issue in other areas of people's lives: being fair, getting equal
shares, for example, of spending money, leisure time or food. Getting
enough, having enough.'

Andy pulled into the fast lane and overtook a line of lorries, and
then responded.

Andy: 'For me it is difficult to ask for what I may want emotionally.
While I have been becoming aware of my relationship to my parents
in my childhood, through therapy, I've found that that has washed
into my sexual relationship. It has become easier for me to be aware of
not being given to, and so become – in a subterranean way – surly,
sulky and resentful; often having an undercurrent emotion of wanting
to be looked after. I think I still find it difficult to reveal I am upset to a

woman or reveal the depth of my need. Sometimes I can say the words that I'm upset or I can talk about what's happened to make me feel upset, but there's no real emotional content in my communication. And that has some connection to sex, but I'm not sure what.'

Paul: 'What I thought you were going to say when you started off, was that it's easier to get to the point of being upset because your needs aren't being met, it's easier to do that than to ask for what you want. There can be a build-up of dissatisfaction. I find it terribly hard to be clear about what I need as well ... to actually say what I need. I also know that if I can express my needs, there's a chance they'll be met even if they aren't met in full. Also my needs become a lot less dangerous to my woman friend. I know that she can feel quite terrified that she may not be able to fulfil this well of unexpressed needs, and then I'm going to get angry at her. Because it's unexpressed, because it's unknown, the well seems enormous. It seems much bigger than maybe it is if I actually get it out. Connected to this is the fact that I often think more about a woman's sexual needs than I do about my own. That's one, classic, male pattern: feeling responsible for another's pleasure. I suppose for a woman there is a similar pattern which is to do with pleasing the man and this can be just as self-denying. I feel that these tangles in long-term sexual relationships can be eased if men express their needs, say what they want, and then there is room for a woman to move in that – to say no or yes, or to say what she wants.'

Andy: 'Go on.'

Paul: 'This in turn connects to the whole issue of separateness – in ourselves and in our relationships. Being sure of who we are, of our identity as men, helps with the feeling of being swallowed up or with the concern of another's enjoyment. That's to do with the whole issue of being separate people, knowing what our limits are, where our boundaries are, where we end and the other person begins.'

Andy: 'I relate to that in that sometimes I can get into a state of anxiety about the other person's enjoyment of sex. It's not so pronounced in the early stages of the relationships I've been in. Then there is a much clearer sense of this being two quite distinct people who are getting to know each other and are able to let the other person have responsibility for their own pleasure, and be able to take their own decisions. I think in a lot of long-term relationships, sex becomes part of the joint enterprise, part of the business of the relationship, fitted in between washing up and work. Somehow there occurs an erosion of each partner's identity, in an everyday way, and expressed in sex.'

Outside the windows, noise of the tyres, rubbing into the tape, fills the silences. Drivers in their cabs look down, calculate times of arrival, load deliveries, Yorkie Bar consumption. The lanes stretch on, each vehicle a capsule, interaction only possible in disaster and accident.

Andy: 'Maybe there's a kind of added male thing in there which is that it is very easy for me, and maybe for a lot of men, to translate an anxiety, an insecurity or an unusual feeling, an emotion, raw and stark, into control. So that what then becomes experienced is male responsibility rather than the reality of who I am, who is this person, what are we doing here and what do we want to express together. That becomes translated into am I being a good enough lover or am I giving her what she wants, etc.

'One of the things I have become aware of – in myself and in other men I have talked to about sex – is that wanting to have sex a lot, feeling a great need for it, is quite tied up with misery. There's no direct link between feeling sexy, feeling erotic, having desire for somebody else – and – wanting sex. Sex can be experienced very easily as being separate from, removed from, eroticism. I think sex is a vehicle for many needs and feelings: making things better, when you're feeling anxious, tense, maybe a bit depressed. Feeling out of contact with somebody and out of contact with yourself. It's the easiest way to connect to someone else and to yourself. Nowadays I think I feel this less, but one of the things that comes interestingly out of the Hite Report on male sexuality is that the reason most often given for men's desire for sex is the sense of affirmation they get as a person from sex. In other words it is not necessarily pleasure, sexual sensuality or erotic gratification that is most important but a sense of affirmation.'

Paul: 'I suppose affirmation in the sense "I am a good lover", but also in the sense that "I am a loved person", and "I am a person worthy of love".'

Andy: 'That's right. That's the most important aspect. Gender division in society is so profound that the maintenance of love and affection between men and women in long-term relationships is very difficult just because of these negotiations which take place between the world some men inhabit – of work, sport, rationality – and the world of some women – connected as it is to emotionality. And also there are all the issues of projection, of dependency needs, which men and women project onto each other. This means that the simple sense of being loved, of being cared for, and of being wanted for oneself is actually not all that frequent. It can be quite absent in many men's lives for periods of time.'

Paul: 'There is often a feeling of wanting to have sex and then going into it with a lot of energy. It can be like going into sex with a feeling if desperateness – in a rush – "I've got to get the most out of this". And then at another level there's a feeling of "I'm going to get this over quickly". A fear of getting into it and enjoying whatever goes on.'

Andy: 'It's a fear, I think, of that form of deep, intimate communication where the rules are not like verbal communication. The rules are a bit unknown or there are no rules.'

Paul: 'Except that people make rules very quickly in order to cope with the insecurity and there's often this feeling of disappointment which comes afterwards. Like you were looking for something you didn't know you were looking for and you weren't necessarily going for what you were looking for, or even asking for it. So the feeling of disappointment is almost inevitable.'

Andy: 'Because you don't know why you're actually engaging in any kind of activity, because it's not necessarily coming from erotic needs.'

Paul: 'Right.'

Andy: 'I think that's very important – that kind of rushing. It's interesting the sex manuals concentrate on this What they do, though, is never touch on the root cause. They always talk about it in terms of a failure of technique. You've always got to have more foreplay and you've got to be more loose and relaxed about it. It's a technocratic solution to the problem of sexual misery. It never questions why it is that men find it so difficult to be so loose and relaxed and go wherever it goes – to express, to be involved in a process, rather than an act.'

Paul: 'To not actually penetrate necessarily when it comes down to it.'

Andy: 'Right.'

Paul: 'So that is all right if you only end up talking.'

Andy: 'Yes. It's very difficult not to feel denied in that situation, to somehow go through that feeling and to come out somewhere else.'

Paul: 'I think it's quite hard for men, and I include myself, to make love lightly. To not invest a whole lot of other other things in it. To ...'

Andy: 'Have a quickie. Do you mean have a quickie?'

Paul: 'I don't mean have a quickie necessarily. I mean not make a big deal of it. Have fun. Now that's a contradictory thing, because on the other hand there's some ideology which says: we're only in it for a good time ... the swinging sixties ... the sexual revolution ... but I don't actually believe that is what it says it is.'

Andy: 'What do you think it is?'

Paul: 'Oh, just a lot about ego and status, and ...'

Andy: 'Notches on your cock.'

Paul: 'Yeah.'

Andy: 'In having fun, or treating sex with lightness. The problem arises that for men, and possibly also for women, sex does have all those different meanings. It carries a very heavy load. It's going to affirm someone's essential worth, carry love that somebody wants to receive, be a vehicle of personal growth and development, and have personal pleasure. That's an awfully big package.'

Paul: 'It's also a big burden to go on someone else. It's like saying you don't love me unless you want to fuck me when I want to be fucked. It's a big number.'

There is a pause. Where to go next? Paul glances at the list of topics scrawled down on a piece of paper.

Paul: 'What about boredom in sex? The most common phenomenon?'

Andy: 'Well I have a line on this.'

Paul: 'Let's have it then.'

Andy: 'I think many people feel that the fact that their sex lives settle in a somewhat boring routine is inevitable. It has to happen because you have discovered everything there is to discover about the other person. What more that is new and exciting can happen? That's obviously true at one level, but I think it's quite a superficial level. The word boredom can stand for a lot of other words: kids often use the word "boring" to express the negative feelings they have about themselves or the situation they are in. That can be true of sex too. Boring is the word you use, but it may be antagonism, anger, fear that you are feeling. Another way of coming at the question is to understand that in long-term relationships, there can be an identification of the partner with a parent – and this makes sex taboo; and therefore unwanted, predictable and unexciting if it occurs. Sex can also be experienced as boring because of that phenomenon we've already touched upon: whereby in a long-term relationship, two people's separate identities merge into one couple unit. And then it's very difficult for erotic desire to flourish because there aren't two different distinct individuals for desire to spark across. There's this one blob. This one boundaryless mass.'

Paul: 'It's a lot to do with stuckness. Things not being said or done – or frustration – so there is always potentially somewhere to go.'
Andy: 'What's that?'
Paul: 'Where there is to go may not always be to do with sexuality. The answer to a love life that's got boring may be not be to read up the manuals and to think of new ways of doing it.'
Andy: 'Fucking under the kitchen table.'
Paul: '... the other things that aren't happening, the need to get unlocked before your love life can get unlocked.'
Andy: 'I think it's to do with being able to let go into yourself with somebody else. And that can be very hard in long-term relationships.'
Paul: 'You've got a lot to lose. You can feel the other person has a lot of power over you, potentially.'
Andy: 'And paradoxically, the more secure the relationship, the harder it is to take risks. You define a difference between you and your partner – whatever that is, food, taste in films – and it can be perceived not as a difference but as a threat by your partner.'
Paul : 'There's something about recognition which is very important in there. You were saying about not being able to fancy your partner because you are so wrapped up in one another that you can't see your partner as a separate person. It takes two for the act of recognition to happen. Someone to be enough inside themselves to see what's going on in their lover. It also takes the other person to express where they are at, to let out something that can be recognized.

'Allowing themselves to be seen. I think a lot of blokes have difficulty in allowing themselves to be seen. I think that's what you were saying. It isn't just that blokes need to be active, don't let themselves see their partners. They don't see what's happening to their partners. Also they ride over parts of themselves and don't show anything that anyone else can get into, get excited by, get involved with, engage with. We are very frightened of engaging.'

Newport Pagnell approaches.

The car pulls into the inside lane and slows down for the exit. Climbing out of the car they hear each vehicle's roar as it ploughs past. It is time to change drivers, and continue the discussion. They stand for a moment on the tarmac, immobilized, bound up with the terror of the orgasm, shaky from feelings brought up that are unresolved; they wonder if they have any words left.

It is Andy's turn to start this time:

Andy: 'What we've been talking about connects to many of the concerns of *Achilles Heel*, and of the inner life of men's groups in the sense that the idea has grown that men need to have space to themselves in order not to rely on women to service them emotionally – to have their support network, friends, maybe to live separately from their lovers. That has been part of a whole critique of the way nuclear families are organized. It can seem that living in separate houses is the most desirable and most politically right-on thing to do – because it recognizes the autonomy women demand but also the need for men to break their dependence on women. But I think this way of separating out men's and women's lives physically can also have negative aspects. Men find it difficult to retain a sense of themselves and be intimate. There is something disturbed about our boundaries. Maybe this comes from being brought up as a male infant by women in a patriarchal society. I don't know. Inasmuch as all men have problems with having an emotional language of being able to be very close but still knowing who they are, to have these boundaries secure, so that you are able to show yourself to somebody so that they can engage with you, really meeting someone else isn't just difficult, it can be actually threatening. This connects to what I was saying about men's groups in that if I live separately and get the space I need from my woman friend somehow that will all be all right, but it won't actually touch the root of the problem which has nothing to do with whether you live together or not. But it is about how do you stay close to someone and not get threatened by the intimacy. It is to do with very interior, intrapsychic male processes. I'm saying this in a rather polemical way, but I think that some of the preconceptions of those involved in sexual politics are a bit glib about all this.'

The transcript here indicates there is a long pause.

Andy (restarts the conversation with a question): 'Have you any thoughts about active and passive roles?'

Paul: 'Only one thought really. I recognize a certain transition ... men's movement ideology says you shouldn't be only active in sex but also passive, able to receive as well. The way it's posed is a dichotomy – either one or the other. I find I can switch from active to passive, but to move easily between the two is something I am learning. In a long-term relationship it is easy to take another for granted. It's easy to not put energy into keeping the relationship alive, into making it work. The priorities you make reflect that. On another level men don't prioritize in their own lives, pleasure or sense of wellbeing. So sex tends to happen as an afterthought, late at night or in some habitual way or time. It's hard and feels risky to make a priority of it – to put aside some of your best time for one another. And that's part of the work system we live whereby we give our best hours to our work, the rest is recovery time. We don't give our best time to pleasure. It would be nice if our work was all pleasure but it ain't, you know.'

It was getting harder and harder to talk. Twenty-five miles to London. They continue to talk for a few miles more. Later, whilst editing the transcript, erasing personal disclosures they do not want to make public, they omit the last 15 minutes of discussion. It seems flat and ordinary. Reading the lines they recall the feeling of coming into London, spent, exhausted, with no more words to come.

Andy Metcalf and Paul Morrison
September 1982

Acknowledgement

Many thanks to Neil Martin, who laboured hard to transcribe a tape full of traffic noise. Andy did the editing and wrote the story of the journey.

BOYS AGAINST SEXISM

These are edited extracts from an extended interview originally recorded for the film True Romance etc., *made by the Newsreel Collective. Gary and Dave were in the fifth form of a Hackney boys' comprehensive at the time. A lot of the girls that we met making the film were angry and had clear ideas about what was wrong and what they wanted to do. But most of the boys were stuck with the old ideas – or were plain demoralized and confused. There were a number who knew some of the 'right things to say' to us about girls because they'd got it in a social studies class. They accepted ideas about women's equality intellectually, but they didn't see what meaning it had for their own lives. We met very few boys who were developing such understandings. Gary and Dave were exceptions: they impressed us because for them 'sexual politics' was becoming more than ideas; whole sides of themselves had been legitimated by girls' new assertiveness. And they felt the strength to reject much of the power of 'boys' world'. It was inspiring and encouraging to talk to them.*

True Romance etc. *is available for hire from The Other Cinema, London, and the Concord Film Council, Ipswich.*

True Romance etc,
A film by the Newsreel Collective

Paul: 'What is it that gives boys status?'

Dave: 'It's different things. Some boys have got a reputation for violence. Like there's a boy in our school who used to be a skinhead, and he's got a reputation for causing a hell of a lot of violence, beating up Pakistanis, things like that.

'Some boys get it through girls, being able to chat up a lot of girls, being very handsome, physically attractive. And some boys by being comedians, lunatics, doing hilarious things like playing practical jokes on teachers, or – I don't know – bringing contraceptives into the school and showing them to the teachers, things like that.'

Gary: 'Some boys accept the fact that if they want sex, why shouldn't a girl want it, right? But the majority of girls feel that if a girl gives it away to them, then after a while the girl becomes a tart. A funny thing, at school a few days back a guy said – now this guy is always boasting that he gets girls easy and he likes one-night stands and things like that. He contradicts himself by saying he likes a girl who doesn't give it and who it takes a while to get. In other words, he wants a girl that can give it easy. And yet he wants a girl that'll fight for it as well. That boy is uncertain of what he really wants.'

Paul: 'He wants the process of conquest, or whatever it is.'

Gary: 'Yeah. Another thing, a lot of guys want to go out and sleep with a lot of girls. But when they get married they want to marry a virgin. Which is silly really, because if you can go out there and sleep with a lot of girls, why can't the same girl you're going to marry go out and sleep with a lot of boys?

'It can't work on this way much longer. If it does, it's all going to be a shambles, really.'

Dave: 'It is all a shambles, what do you mean?'

Gary: 'Society teaches us that if a girl feels she wants to sleep with someone she must kill that feeling. "This is bad. I mustn't think this." A boy if he feels that way must go out and get it.'

Dave: 'If a boy sleeps around he's a man, but if a woman sleeps around she's a tart.'

Gary: 'It's funny, but if you go to a party, a guy's meant to get a girl. A girl's meant to stand around and let the guy worry about it and chat her up. But don't let him get nowhere.'

Dave: 'If she was to break the unpardonable sin and chat up a boy, then she would be labelled a tart.'

Gary: 'That's silly as well, 'cos I tell you and this is a fact: a lot of guys would *like* a girl to chat them up. Because they're basically shy, right?

'Girls should be independent, same as boys are, right, and they should be able to do exactly the same things as boys are able to do.'
Paul: 'How would you describe boys' relationships with other boys, in general?'
Gary: 'That's a funny thing, really, because if a boy is close to another boy, it's sort of said "No, man, this is a funny thing. Them two are too close, you know. They must be gay or something." When two girls are close, they could walk down the street holding hands, everything's fine.'
Dave: 'But if two boys did the same, their names'd be mud in the school.'
Gary: 'Yeah, because ... if I went into a room, right, the acceptable way to greet my friend was to punch him on the shoulder, or shake hands, you know. But if a girl went into a room, they'd kiss each other on the cheek or something like that.'
Gary: 'If you've got a friend, it doesn't matter how long you've known him, you keep him at a distance, as a man. But you let the girl get close to you. I just don't see it as right.

'The only way you're meant to relate to a boy is if you're boasting. 'Cos you come into school and if you wanna say something to a guy you boast about it. You don't talk about your failures to him. You're not meant to do that. Your failures are meant to be kept in yourself.'
Dave: 'You don't talk about your failures or shortcomings with girls either. When you're with a girl you're supposed to be Superman. Like I know a lot of boys, when they're on their own they're friendly to you, when they're with a girl they try to take you on or something – put on a veneer of super-hardness, try and pick a fight or something.'
Paul: 'What is it that blokes don't talk about?'
Gary: 'Their failures. That's basically it. Their failures.'
Dave: 'They don't talk about girlfriends they've failed with. Or times they've been too shy to chat up a girl, they don't talk about that. Or girls who said no ... they might cover that up.'
Paul: 'Is this "they" or "we"?'
Dave: ' "They", "we", everything. Basically a lot of guys, if a girl does say no, then they'll tell their friends they dropped her, not she dropped him.'
Paul: 'What happens if you try to talk about something you feel vulnerable about?'
Gary: 'Guys behave differently. They think you're weird and you're silly. If you stroll into school one morning and you said, "I went to bed with this girl and I was a 3-minute wonder", or something like

that, they'd say "Man, you're crazy, you're useless, you're hopeless", 'cos you're not Superman like they are or they pretend to be, they think "OK, I can do this. He's no good, he's not worth the trouble."

'You just get put down. And being put down ain't a pleasant feeling really. That's understandable. So no one comes into school and just ... discusses it.

'There's a lot of guys who would sit down and listen, but the majority just crack jokes about it and take the mickey.'

Paul: 'What about being attracted to other blokes?'

Dave: 'That's the last thing you can tell another man. I mean, you can joke about it. "Oh, I fancy you." But if you meant it, you'd never be able to show your face in the school again.'

Paul: 'That's in your school.'

Dave: 'Yeah.'

Gary: 'I know a few guys that ... a lot of the white skinhead blokes go queer-bashing, deliberately. They go to a gay club in the West End and follow them out into an alley way and then beat them up.'

Dave: 'A lot of boys do go through a phase where they wonder if they have feelings for another guy. But they are too scared to admit it. And anybody who is a virgin. They get the mickey taken out of them.'

Dave: 'Sex is supposed to be a great thing, with bombs exploding and thunder and lightning and the world being rocked and everything. You know it's built up a big fantasy image about it. And when you really have it you think "Is that all?"'

Gary: 'Yeah, that's true, 'cause if you go in there expecting too much, you're going to receive very little.'

Dave: 'You think that when you have sex you're going to walk into the bedroom a boy and come out a man, deep voice, big chest sticking out and muscles all over you. And you can go round and spit the world in the eye and you know, you're god.'

Gary: 'If that was so, man, would I be here?'

Dave: 'Yes.'

Gary: 'I suppose if you place too much importance on it ...'

Dave: '... it messes everything up.'

Gary: 'I'm not always trying to be hard, get into fights, stuff like that. Sometimes I like to be sort of different, sensitive, in a sense, right? And people think that 'Ah, you're soft' and they call you girl because that's not the way a boy's meant to be.'

Paul: 'So you get called girl?'

Gary: 'I have been, yeah. Not in school but sort of outside school where I can be more myself. I hang around with lots of girls and because you hang around with a lot of girls and because you're not screwing them all the time, "What are you ... feminine?" '

Paul: 'What difficulties come up for you in relationships?'

Dave: 'Sex, usually. Sexual pressures from your friends. You know, you've been going with someone, they start going at you, "Well when are you going to screw her?" And her friends put pressure on her. "Have you been to bed with him yet?" and all that.

'Even though you might want to wait and she might want to wait, her friends and your friends apply pressure. Sometimes as you meet a girl your mates say "Go on, ask her! She'll go to bed with you." They start immediately.'

Gary: 'If you've been going out with someone 6 or 7 months, and you don't sleep with them, guys will go "What are you doing? You're wasting your time. If she doesn't want to give it, leave her."

'OK, it doesn't affect you consciously, but subconsciously it does have an effect on you. It sort of makes you feel, "They're sort of right, you know man, I shouldn't be looking like this. I was taking my time, I should be up there having more fun with someone else." It causes your relationship to get sort of edgy.'

Gary: 'Sex is the sort of thing that can make or break a relationship, you know. All right. Because, if you've got a good relationship and you start to sleep with someone and it doesn't work out, it puts you down, right? And if you can't talk about it then that's the end of the relationship, really.'

Paul: 'And has that happened to you?'

Gary: 'No, not yet, but I've seen it happen and it's come close to happening to me, sort of thing.'

Paul: 'But you did manage to talk about it?'

Gary: 'Yeah, 'cause I'm an open sort of person and I like to talk about sex and stuff like that, especially with the person I'm going out with. And, man, I brought it up, I said, "I want to talk about it, right?" And OK we sat down and talked about it, 'cause she wasn't used to talking about that sort of thing, wasn't sort of aware of herself. After a while when you get used to it it sort of eases everything.'

Paul: 'That's the thing about men in general: sex is something you just do, but you're never supposed to learn – you're never told how to do it. Or ... there isn't something to talk about, it's just supposed to happen by magic.

'Can you describe that a bit, your sexual education, or non-education?'

Dave: 'Basically we were just taught about the mechanics with none of the emotional things ... as if it was switching on a television or something. You know, you just get into a woman and you go up and down and a baby is born or something. We were just taught that.'

Gary: 'See, and your expectations are "that's brilliant, you know, let's have fun". It's not as brilliant as you hoped.'

Dave: 'It's more complicated.'

Gary: 'And when the crunch comes, especially the first time, you think, "Right, I've got it now, I'll do it this way." But when it actually comes to it you find out that it's not as easy as you thought. There's another person involved. As I see it, it's harder to sleep with someone you don't know than with somebody you do know. Because the situation will be tense, you'll just be too tense for it.

'But someone you know, you'll feel relaxed, and it'll be OK, you can guide each other through it.

'But when you're with someone different, you expect them to know, they expect you to know.'

Paul: 'Have you been able to talk about that to other blokes?'

Dave: 'If you show any doubt about the sacredness of the great sexual act, the almighty penis, and all that; or if you question it, then there's something wrong with you. If you question, "Why should I? Why should I chat up a girl? Why should I go to bed with a girl?" then they think there's something wrong with you.'

Paul Morrison talking to Dave and Gary Channer
March 1983

CAN'T YOU GO SOMEWHERE ELSE!

One particular act links all these places: The stairs leading to the balcony of the Adelphi Theatre, the side wall of Old Scotland Yard, the stage behind the cinema screen of the St Austell Odeon, a forest near Bury St Edmunds, the top deck of a Bristol bus, Southern Region railway carriages between Waterloo and Clapham Common, the Southbound platform of the Northern line at Charing Cross, the 25th floor landing of a block of flats in Deptford, a Sussex multi-storey car park, Portishead Library at night in 1973, the Royal Box at Covent Garden, the courtyard of a block of flats off the Kings Road during 1968, a mansion entrance in Essex, Clevedon golf course, a lane in Kilburn behind the Gaumont cinema, a disused quarry, a South London cinema, the lift in a London YMCA, a

Cambridge car park, the entrance to a field in Suffolk, Chelsea Embankment, the National Film Theatre, the Israel Museum, motorway service stations, dance studios, golf courses, tube trains, woodlands, roadsides, dustbins, cinemas, beaches, cars, vans, lorries, boats, gardens, parks, heaths ... the open air at any time.

These are some of the places that myself and five men I know have had sex with other men.

Sex can be immediate. You see a man, you smile, he smiles, you hesitate, he hesitates, you whisper 'Do you have anywhere to go?' He says 'yes'. You leave, together. Or you have sex where you are or near where you are. If it is a popular place other men may join in. Or you may seek in vain, spending hours looking and waiting, finally going home. It can be short and fast or long and slow. You may arrange to meet again or just say goodbye.

Memory: Midnight

I was having sex with him in the urinal, three other men were also there, one was sucking his cock, I was fondling his arse, he was squeezing my cock. We heard someone coming in, adjusted our clothes and stood at the urinals pretending to piss. The new man stood next to me, I hid my cock in my hands, he pissed a long time, shook his cock, put it away and left. I turned to the man next to me, we began having sex again, sucking each other's cocks, rubbing nipples, kissing. I felt very excited. Another man came in. I turned to the man next to me and whispered 'How about going somewhere else?' He said 'Let's go outside and talk'. We left the urinal and walked across to the pub opposite.

'My name's Tony.'

'Mine's Martin.'

We shook hands.

'Would you like to come back to my place? I live in Kilburn', I said.

'I'd like to come back, but it's too far and I have to be home soon.'

'Well, can I come back with you?'

'No, my lover's in.'

'Doesn't he know you have sex with other men?'

'No! ... I don't know ... I hope not.'

'You don't talk about it?'

'No.'

'Why not? Doesn't he have sex with other men?'

'I don't know ... I suppose he does.'
'So you don't ever take people back?'
'Only when he's away ... why don't you come back inside?'
'No, I think I'll go home', I said.
'OK. Well I'll just get finished off ... see you again maybe.'
We kiss and move off in different directions.

I walk home feeling dispirited but when I get to bed I wank off thinking about him, his body and the excitement I felt with him.

Most public sex takes place between consenting men, as such it causes disapproval among heterosexuals and some gay women and men but remember, as we suffer from lack of social environments to meet, we are extending ourselves our right in using what is available to initiate contact.

I have never lost the pleasure of the sweet moment of sexual sharing with another man. Sometimes lust is involved. Sometimes escapism. Sometimes wanting to be with another man, wanting affection, wanting shared pleasure.

I have been having sex with other men in 'public' since I was 16. I used to skive off school, take a bus to Bristol, hang around the cottages until I met someone and then go off with them. Often the men were married – I knew 'cos they had babychairs in the car, or articles I identified as belonging to women, wore wedding rings or because they told me (there is a confessional element involved in public sex, that of sharing pain with a stranger after you've been intimate) – or said that they had relationships with women. Often they would ask me if I had sex with women and look uncomfortable when I said 'No, only men'. It was through meeting gay men like this that I discovered the few pubs and the club where gay men met. I liked it best when the man I met would take me back to a room or into the quiet countryside, a place where we could eventually discard our clothes and enjoy our bodies. Usually the sex was/is sucking, fucking, mutual wanking but sometimes other things too. Sex in public didn't only happen with casual partners but also with my lover (oh yes, I had a lover, he was older than me and had had other sex partners).

We used to meet when we could, sometimes this was difficult as our relationship was secret and always it seemed we had sex at some point of our being together. Once I was helping him prune trees in his garden and we went into the garage and fucked in the wheelbarrow. At the times I wasn't with him I went looking for casual sex. Only once did I have a nasty experience in which I felt threatened, most times I felt that being younger and a seeker I had power.

It wasn't only sex, partly it resulted out of oppression for it was the only way I knew at first for meeting gay men, but it became fascinating as the variety of men of every race, age and class seemed endless. I still remember some of these men. They inform my sexual fantasies. I wank about meeting them again or remembering the time we met. I re-experience what I know of them in my bed.

Memory: Night

What, I wanted to ask him, is your wildest fantasy? This to a half-clothed man surrounded by other semi-naked men in the bushes of the Heath. I saw the glint of pleasure in his eyes and the question slipped away as I reached out to touch his chest. I was aware of breathing men, his body, his face illuminated by the moon as I came. Afterwards I wondered who he was, what he did and would he be there again if I returned? I did not wonder why he was there. For the pleasure of those moments, the excitement of sex in the open air was why.

When you think of the oppression directed against sex it is stunning that so many men have so much sex in the open, in public. That men actively create the privacy to be intimate within public spaces. This fact is contained; for the thought of men indiscriminately having sex with other men in public eats into the image that straight society creates and when it does enter the media it is presented as an unwholesome activity. Indeed sex freaks straight society out – it is OK to be gay as long as you don't have sex! Little do people realize but this is only the tip of the iceberg.

Imagine what might/could happen if more women and more men revealed their sexual thoughts and behaviour....

> In the open
> under the moon
> under the sun
> round the corner
> you can sense it
>   taste it
>   touch it
> open your eyes
> you'll see us
> everywhere.

Martin Humphries
September 1982

HEATH OR HOME

I have a fantasy about a perfect world. It is a vague and varying fantasy but among its more consistent aspects is the hope that, while freedom of expression would be possible, people would not have the desire, either individually or collectively, to express power.

I have other fantasies: many of them involve either the assumption or rejection of power by me, within a sexual context. I feel very ambivalent about these fantasies, especially as Crowley's motto 'Do what thou wilt...', with the comforting addendum that everyone you are doing it to is consenting, seems to have become a battle cry of gay sexual politics. Not only is it a very appealing motto but it also conforms to one of my criteria for a perfect world: freedom of expression. My ambivalence stems from the perception that much of the gay world seems to be expressing itself in ways which involve the assumption of power. Power obviously does have great sexual appeal; much of gay male imagery and behaviour is testament to this appeal. Should this relationship be accepted without question? As gays, we have long been denied power by a heterosexual world, and it is understandable that we should want to assume it, but instead of using it against the conventions that oppress us we seem to be using it, in a specifically sexual manner, against each other.

I fantasize about sadomasochism, but I feel it is 'wrong'. I'm turned on by pornography, but wish I wasn't. I enjoy the idea, the anticipation, indeed the actual, anonymous, act of sex in public places, but feel debased and dissatisfied afterwards. Replace 'sado- masochism', 'pornography', and 'sex in public places' with 'being gay' and this was the position I was in 15 years ago. This is, for me, a real dilemma. Am I sexually repressed, unable to enjoy the sexual diversity that lies within and around me? Or are these very options themselves symptoms of sexual oppression?

Perhaps these options are a valid part of current gay life and, as such, should be defended against attack from those who do not understand them. Certainly, having rejected the mores of hetero-sexuality we are in an ideal position to explore our own sexuality. Our bodies are after all, our own. Let us do with them what we will. But what are we doing and why? I question the support of much gay sexual politics for sadomasochism, pornography and what David Fernbach, in 'The spiral path', calls the 'butch shift', because they could be compensation for perceived loss of power. The proponents of the 'Do what thou wilt' argument would say that power does not come into it

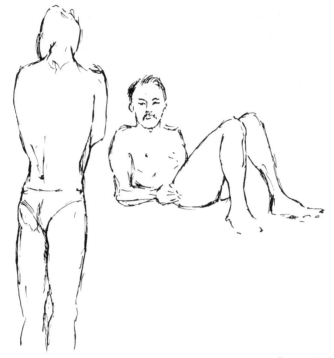

James Swinson

because consent is a crucial corollary to this freedom. Consent is, however, usually compromised. If I had absolute freedom of choice then my actions, made with full understanding and acceptance, would be consenting. That is, unfortunately, a rare situation. If I buy 'Him', then I am consenting to do so, but it is a compromised consent. I see too clearly the exploitation by such magazines of my insecurities and their creation of images, desires and, ultimately, frustrations. How can any of us reach the airbrushed perfection of the models depicted? Why should any of us want to? If I put my sadomasochistic fantasies into practice I would again be consenting to do so, but am I exploring the full range of my sexuality or am I indulging my own and other's wishes for punishment and abasement? When I go to Hampstead Heath I am consenting to do so. Once more I cannot do it without questioning why. Do I want to be prey or predator, or does the anonymity, the objectification of such situations allow for the assumption of roles that I would not want to assume in a less impersonal setting? Dennis Altman in *Gay News* No. 223, suggested that public sex was 'an affirmation of sexuality'. The only way it affirms my sexuality is by all-too frequent visits to the STD clinic. If it is a 'yearning for community' as he also suggests, then that is all it is; a yearning. It is not my idea of a community. Pornography and S & M imply consent. Rape and fascism do not. Where, though, does the borderline between the symbol and the real lie? Where does consent stop? A sadist may justify his/her sadism by claiming that the masochist consents, but what if the sadist is in a position of such power that it becomes irrelevant whether an individual consents to be a masochist or not? The power of the user of pornography cannot be that far removed from the power of the rapist.

Are my doubts self-hatred; a conflict between conventional moral standards and sexual desires? Or do I recognize the power games of objectification and violence in myself, and wonder what fears produce them? I do not know. I know that I have no desires for such conventions as monogamy. I would hate my sexual options to be more restricted than they already are. I do not condemn aspects of gay life because I fear they may hinder heterosexual society's acceptance of homosexuality; I see nothing in conventional heterosexual mores to admire, so such acceptance is of no importance to me. But does this mean that we can act without exploring the motives for our actions? In a review of 'The spiral path' in *Gay News* No. 223, Jeffrey Weeks countered David Fernbach's criticism of the 'butch shift' by saying that 'it is a crucial element in the emergence of a distinct gay identity'. If so, it looks like I'm going to miss out on my identity again. Is it heretical to suggest that the current macho imagery is an attempt to compensate for a feeling of not being sufficiently masculine? Surely the fact that we do not possess the conventional trappings of masculinity is our saving grace.

I am not trying to lay down any laws, only to voice my own confusions. I do not feel that political justifications of personal preferences are enough. We must first understand those preferences.

Jonathan Greveson
January 1983

SOME OF MY SEXUALITIES

> Isn't it strange
> that in times like these
> I have such trouble
> in finding one voice?
>> Andy Metcalf

What does it mean to you? Bisexual.
Two-sexual. Two sexualities (in the same person?)
or a sexuality divided into two (or more),
perhaps further subdividing like a
bacterium.
Polymorphously perverse
or warped, or endlessly in conflict, or
locked in perpetual indecision, at an
arrested state of development, or getting
the best of both worlds.
Someone who doesn't know (admit) what
their 'true' sexuality is? (Read
heterosexual.)
Someone who is (should be) in transition
towards accepting their 'true' sexuality?
(Read homosexual.)
Me?

A version of my history. At public school I had sex with myself and other boys because there was no other sex, because I was bored, because of the pressure within me. We did not become close. I had sex even with people I hated. We did not identity as homosexual. Queer was the word to use to damage others. It said 'not me'. But after I left, it seemed obvious to continue having sex with men. They wanted it with me. It was fun. It was easier than getting sex from women. It was exciting because it was illicit and illegal. Sleeping with men felt normal enough to me; didn't matter much that it was abnormal in society – just made it more exciting; I liked the image of the outsider with a secret life. A double life, no point in confronting. Gay Liberation? – nothing to do with me. I used/was used by these men. We did not become close. I didn't want to believe that I could love men. At the same time, I was involved with women and eventually drifted into living with them. This, after all, was 'the Real Thing': women I fell in love with; men were just for sex.

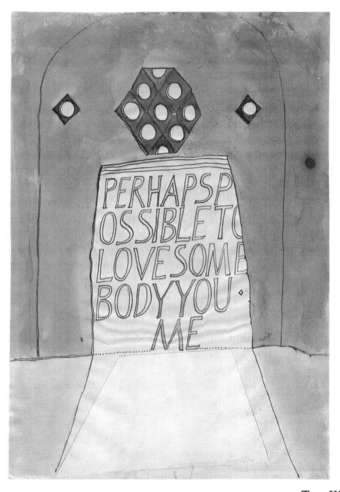

Tom Weld

Then things began to change. I could not prevent myself becoming close at some level to the men I slept with. I made a break. I decided that it was abusive to have sex without feeling, and I felt more for women; I was living with a woman; where I was living, I lost contact with any gay men; so I chose (did I really choose?) the heterosexual option. When I moved from Leicester to London, contact with the gay and men's movements opened up the politics. Anger replaced the excitement I had felt when I remembered how I had been treated (attempts to poison relationships: 'Don't go out with Chris, He's queer, you know', nauseating apologies for hostility: 'Sorry, Chris. We thought you were queer'). Therapy opened up my denied needs and feelings, focused the vague stirrings. I met one man, then another. I have found that I can love a man.

So who am I? What can I relate to? The heterosexual family? My life – my feelings mock it.

A gay life? I don't live it. I can't be gay because I live with a woman. So I don't exist. My sexuality doesn't exist. It can't. Everybody there *is* only homosexual and heterosexual.
and bisexual.

That word again, a by-pass of understanding, giving the illusion of explanation. Something with which to dismiss me. The old duality. Heterosexist, male world view. Virgin and whore. God and devil. Jekyll and Hyde. Fire and water. The Steppenwolf. Which box are you in?

A sexuality. My sexual feelings do not differentiate genders. Desire is all. A glance, a bodily posture, an intonation of a phrase that melts me inside. A moment in a long friendship, an intuition of a kindred spirit, a suddenly open sensuality, a whole personality, a texture of skin. I have desired someone in the street without knowing their sex. I have reached for a woman's penis in bed. Sexuality is just part (a special part) of my way of relating to people. The same feelings. A question of degree, of intensity. An important part of being with myself.

A sexuality. I have needs from each relationship which are not the same: my needs from men and women are almost separate. They conjure totally different images and fantasies. There is no hierarchy between them.
Woman?
Strong, sane, direct, needing support; giving and receiving, safety, warmth, engulfment (fear and desire at the same time), piercing perception (scared she will see through (to) me), mysterious power, otherness;
sensuality of wood (warm hardness, organic, life-affirming) and clay and earth (pleasant dampness, moulding to fit, creative, yielding), a softer emotional flavour;
relating in relaxed intense closeness, like moulding two immiscible clays together, other to other, antagonists;
penetration as a means to a unique sensual/emotional closeness.

Man? Devious, reserved, harder; drier emotional timbre; sensuality of wire (sleek and lithe).

There's a barrier between us; a potential of intense empathy; risk (of the unknown, of complication); once broken, it floods me with feelings. Not more intense than feelings for women, but more desperate, tense. A different kind of sexual tension. An emotional closeness of like to like, a sexual closeness of narcissism, of giving and receiving penises.

I live with a woman. Most of my closest friends are women. It is not that I desire men because I hate women. My closest male friend was another man like me. He has chosen to identity as gay and lives with his lover in New York.

My sister?

Our relationship felt different to those I had with straight men, and from my observation of theirs with each other: it was more like those that I have with women – closer in fact in some areas. I feel cut off from straight men. I fear you.

A fantasy. You have knives in your shirts. You take our money to suck cocks and then cut us, stabbing the heart of your sexuality, ritually killing your suppressed desires. But it is us who die, while you go on to penetrate another of us in the only way that you can.

You seem dead to my needs, dead to understanding. There's a whole dimension of experience missing between us, a humour, and a potential. I am angry at your viciousness and deadness. I am impatient and angry at your liberalism. DON'T ask me to explain what 'camp' means. DON'T try to sleep with me. *If* you want to 'discover your gayness', to 'explore the possibility', do it with each other. DON'T abuse my body, entangle my emotions that way. I am not a gateway to your gay liberation, a free counselling service on the right (on) way to fuck men. DON'T fuck me to validate your politics. I feel sick at the thought. If you do not truly desire me, STAY AWAY.

I am angry at gay and bisexual men who attempt collusion with me in setting up a new boys' club. 'What do we need women for? We've got men', at gay and bisexual men who cover your misogyny with knee-jerk accusations of homophobia, projecting my rejection of you onto the woman I live with in a sexual relationship. I can't stop desiring women just because I desire men. The personal is political doesn't make the political personal.

A lot of anger. Finally I am angry at me because I recognize parts of these attitudes in parts of me.

A sexuality. My closest love is a woman. We live together because we want to. We are closer to each other than to anyone else. That's taken hard work. We are married.

I have never lived with a man. I have tended to live with women. (Who taught me that?)

Why? Support, service, all the traditional reasons, or free choice. (Was hers as free as mine?) Fear of loneliness, of myself? Did I learn my needs? I have privileges (there's guilt here). I know that my marriage, my apparently heterosexual lifestyle oppress gays – monogamy oppresses me too as a (gay) man. But isn't exercising my freedom as a man to hurt a woman oppressive to her? How am I any different to bisexual men deceiving 'their' women by having 'a boy on the side', or straight men looking for a 'newer model'? Men justifying deception on the grounds of preventing hurt. The screw tightens. The spiral turns. After all, compulsory heterosexual monogamy oppresses women too. Coming out is no cure for pain.

Contradictions are equally true. Nothing remains static. Needs and feelings change. Sexualities ebb and flow. Emotions steadfastly refuse to obey political theories.

In an instant, in the twinkling of an eye ....

Christopher Poke
May 1982

LOVE AND SEX: IMAGINATION AND REALITY

At the end of April 1971, three weeks after my 16th birthday, I enjoyed my first physical sexual experience with another man. It has taken me many years to realize not only did this man physically resemble the men who inhabit my fantasies, but I attributed to him facets of character he may not have possessed. Facets I want all my lovers to have.

Before we picked each other up in the afternoon of that day in April 1971, I'd often dreamed and wanked off to fantasies of dark-haired, hairy-chested, physically well-built men who were older than I. I'd read the graffiti in every cottage (public toilet) I visited and the occasional newspaper reports of men caught soliciting. I knew that being gay was dangerous, in that being found out could cause

POEMS BY MARK TOLSON

BROTHERS

(For John)

Our closeness
has kept us
fenced apart.
Our shame
and timidity
hemmed round
our lives
haunting every
communication.

Shared childhoods
resonating
with joy and pain.
An endless song
echoing through
dreams and
lingering in our
averted gaze.
Eyes sheltering low
now reach out
and touch

and a cocoon
of many withheld bruises
trembles and
slinks away.

The last of my habits,
cling like freaky limpets.
So much crap was swept
             away
by the turning tides and
              burnt-out winds.

This weather
torments my compromises.
Under cover
love creeps in.
Uninvited,
casual as a stray cat,
purring through my bones
and clawing at my heart.

Suspended tears
gush forth, like
a faulty fountain,
into the towering black void
of night
as I rejoice with our love
             and
cry with this vulnerability
that thrusts
my masks out of reach

Two men
naked together,
aching
alone.

---

problems, and having sex with other men was dangerous, both
physically and legally, but that didn't stop me. That day I left school
at lunchtime, caught the bus into Bristol, the nearest town,
determined to have sex.

I got off the bus at College Green and nervously approached the cottage. There was no one inside. I waited. Someone came in. I began to shake. Standing at the urinal in my school uniform, cap in my pocket, pretending to pee. I looked up and saw a dark-haired man in a white jumper. Was he? How could I tell? I looked again. He was about 5 feet 11, 30 years of age and wore jeans. He was looking at me. I zipped up and left. He followed me out. What should I do now? I started to walk round the block. He followed. When I stopped, he stopped. I caught his eye. He smiled. I went back into the cottage. He

James Swinson

followed me in and this time stood next to me. My heart was beating so hard. He said 'want to come with me?' My mouth was dry so I nodded. He zipped up and I followed him out. He went to a small blue van, got in and opened the passenger door. I got in. He said 'I know somewhere safer than this'. Drove out of town and stopped at a cottage underneath the flyover.

We got out and I followed him into a cubicle. I'd had a hard on since getting into the car. He seemed nice, calm, assured. In the cottage I felt his prick through his trousers, it was hard. We began to kiss, I felt under his jumper, undid his shirt, felt his chest and nipples. He undid my trousers, I his. He began sucking my cock. It was wonderful, better than I'd imagined. I sucked his, he must have been turned on by inexperienced youth for he didn't complain. He asked if he could fuck me. I said, yes, as this is what I'd been dreaming of for years. He turned me round, greased his cock with spit and pushed it in. It hurt, but not so much that I didn't want it. I came whilst he was fucking me and he came soon after. We tidied up and he offered me a lift back. I accepted and back in the car told him it was the first time I'd had sex. He didn't believe me, saying 'how did I know what to do if I hadn't had it before?' I replied that I imagined it all many times.

Looking back I can understand he didn't want to accept the responsibility of being the first person a 16-year-old boy had had sex with. Whilst he probably realized how young I was before we had sex he only took in the implications after he'd come. Later, whilst thinking about it he might relish the fact that he had broken in a virgin but he didn't want to end up in a potentially compromising situation. For all I know he could have been married with kids of his own. He dropped me at the end of my road. We didn't make any arrangement to meet again (another seed sown). I walked to the house positive everyone could tell just by looking at me that I'd had sex with a man. The first thing I did was to have a bath, only later would I relish keeping the smell of a man on me.

Although I went back again and again to that cottage and many others in Bristol I never saw him again. A shame, as I am eternally grateful to him, for he made my first sexual experience very enjoyable.

Whilst he was not, perhaps, my ideal man, he had enough of the physical attributes that turn me on and which I have consistently looked for in men ever since. Of course, these qualities of desire formed much earlier in my life. Despite the fact that I have had sex with a wide variety of men – gay, non-gay, black, white, with disabilities and without – I am surprised at how rigid my internal fantasies of physical desirability are.

I clearly distinguished between the men I only have sex with and the men with whom I have sexual/emotional relationships. I would have sex with practically any man who showed sexual interest in me unless (ironically) he was clearly much younger than me. I have always been more interested in older men. My first lover, when I was 17, was 11 years older; my second, when I was 19, was 10 years older; my third, when I was 20 (this relationship began when I was with my second and continued alongside my relationship with my fourth) was 47 years older (he is now 81); my fourth, when I was 26, was 17 years older (this relationship is still ongoing emotionally, and has managed to survive infatuations with other men); my fifth, when I was 33, was the first time I had an intense sexual/emotional relationship with a man of my own age.

Keith, Larry, Stanley, Ronald and David. What similarities other than age unite them? Well all are men who need nurturing. Four have been taller than me. All are dark haired, though none possess the hairy chest that inhabits my dreams and I sometimes find on men with whom I have casual sex. And the sex. Well all have fucked me – Keith and David particularly well. I have fucked them all. Now I only get fucked in imagination, which is due more to the times than desire. My relationship with David was sexually exclusive. This, on my part, was due purely to the realities of HIV infection. I find sexual monogamy difficult but with this particular health issue I had no wish to jeopardize his health or my own. So, for once, I remained sexually faithful for the entire relationship.

All are men who can, in time and with trust, reveal their inner hearts. None have been easy – what relationship worth its salt is? All have been, and are, rewarding. But I still have that itch called lust, promiscuity, wantonness or delight. I have an insatiable curiosity about men: as I go about the streets, parks, tubes, buses I see men about whom I wonder what their chests, buttocks, toes, feet, cocks, balls and minds are like. Let alone the taste of their skins on the tongue. I always see at least one man who I would want to caress. Sometimes I see men who would return such a caress.

Reciprocity – that is what I want most. Sex, to me, is always boring when its one-sided. I remember picking up a handsome hunk, 6 foot something with a muscular body and gravelly voice. We went back to his flat. He stripped off in silence and lay on the bed, said 'suck it' and closed his eyes. I stripped off and began to kiss and lick his cock. 'I said suck it.' So I did, in a few minutes he came, took it out of my mouth, stood up, started putting on his clothes and asked 'want a cup of tea?' I refused politely, left, went straight back to the cottage, picked up a delightful, slightly overweight, man in his mid-30s who I saw several times.

One-sided passion can also be a bit much. I have been cruel in my time to those who wanted me more than I've cared for but also I've had men who have found my ardour hard to take. I remember a dustman who would occasionally ring me up and visit. He was shy and sexually inexperienced. I found him exciting, partially the fact he was a dustman, partially the fact that he had very smooth skin and reddish hair everywhere, and partially his inexperience. Once after I'd sucked him off but not come myself I began to suck him again whilst wanking. He said it was too soon, that he couldn't get a hard on. I said that I was happy sucking his delicious soft cock whilst wanking off. This was too much for him, he became uncomfortable. I stopped. He left. I never heard from him again.

I'm fortunate in that I have had years of sexual freedom in which it was possible to go out, pick up a man and have unconstrained mutually satisfying sex. I've spent frustrating afternoons and evenings when I didn't find anyone. Times when to go cruising was displacement activity. Having sex with a strange man was delightful, delicious and also meant I didn't have to think about anything else except being there with him, experiencing whatever was going on between us. During the last 10 years many of us have re-evaluated our sexual practices.

After initial strictures about limiting our sexual activity it is clear we can enjoy safer sex with a variety of partners. Yet constraints of AIDS mean it is early days in terms of feeling easy about multiple partners because either fear determines minimal sexual activity, or because imaginative safer sex seems to demand a degree of trust that is almost impossible with people you don't know.

Awareness of AIDS forced me to reconsider my sexual playing. I follow the guidelines to excess. (No fucking, even with a condom.) This may well change, nothing remains in stasis so who can say what my sexual practice will be or who my partners are in 10 years' time. Sex and death are for us gay men closely linked at this time. *Petit mort* has turned into the possibility of *grand mort*. Death, which has always surrounded us, is now in bed with us – or could be. Or could have been and is now inside us ticking away, growing. A seed implanted in the past that is beginning to flower in our cells. From the first medical reports AIDS has been associated with death and it is only in recent years that the realization of living with AIDS has supplanted the idea that AIDS = gay = death. A lesson which is slow to be picked up by other affected communities, particularly the heterosexual ones.

My first experience of death was when I was 10 and my father died. I can see you now nodding sagely and saying, 'ah that's why he fancies older butch men, he's father seeking'. It may be. In fact I'm sure that much of my early sexual cruising was to do with finding a man who would be tender and loving towards me, who also reminded me of the man I had lost. After all how much closer can you get to a man than fucking or being fucked by a man you love – even if you only met him 3 seconds ago?

Culturally, gay men experience death all the time. We are constantly told that we don't exist. We grow up as though we don't exist. We all have to come out. 'I thought I was the only one' – don't we all experi- ence this? We are denied, scapegoated and killed all the time. Inside we all have a fear of the pogrom. Some gay men never recover from their upbringing. How many gay men do you know who've committed suicide?

It is only now that many gay men, for the first time in the history of the world, accept ourselves as complete beings, appreciate our gayness as the beautiful, glorious, enriching, life-enhancing thing it is. Yet, in this time, we also have to accept death as a part of our lives. A whole generation to whom death was something in the distant future, or something that happened to other people, must come to terms with the fact that people they know, people younger than themselves, or that I, you, us, may die because of a virus that is spread through blood and spunk. Two secretions that are associated with life. This experience will fundamentally change us. How, it is too soon to say.

Already patterns of our sexual behaviour have changed. Mine have, have yours? Will our desires also change? Men, as a gender, have always wanted sexual variety and have ensured that for men it is not condemned by society. Straight men have envied gay men because we could have so much guilt-free sex with so many different partners. Will the fact that we cannot do this in quite the same way mean that ultimately straight men will also be affected with a behavioural psychological change? It isn't so far fetched. Gay male behaviour has often led to changes of male perception and behaviour. Who knows. Carl Morse may be right in *The Curse of the Future Fairy* when he says 'and the 23rd century is full of faeries!/For all the commands to alter and delete did not print out,/and they have survived...'.

AIDS has re-focused our attention on issues of power and oppression in sexuality in ways that no one (including most gay people) wanted to look at. Gay men offer not solutions but a vocabulary. Our naming the realities of safer sex offer not prescriptive sexual activities but an enriched way of defining what we find sexual. My imagination survives. My fantasies may disproportionately rely upon memories of past fantasies or past realities to reach an orgasm that sends ripples through my body. But a part of me still creates new fantasies: 10 years ago I would have laughed at the suggestion I would find condoms erotic but now the act of enclosing a cock in a sheath can be exciting. I understand that every time I make love it is not only my body that is participating, it is also images that inhabit my mind, my past and my possible futures. Within all this it is possible to focus on myself so that only the person I'm with is of importance and the ghosts we all carry, who form a part of the baggage of hopes, needs and desires that we bring to all relationships, to all actions, are for that moment taking a back seat.

Accepting that being with one person and thinking about another is okay sometimes is important. Accepting that making love is different emotionally and physically at different times in different places is important. Love is, sex is, whoever we are, whatever we are at that given moment. The other person may not be the person they are, they may be a composite being who I have invested with trappings from my imagination. That can be okay. What isn't for me is for it to be the same all the time. Love has its pinnacles and its valleys. Sometimes I do it for the other person, sometimes they do it for me, sometimes we do it for each other, together in mutual needs and desire. Sometimes we connect, physically, emotionally and mentally (sometimes we only think we do – self-delusion is a commonplace event in human lives).

I know what I want in my head and what I want in reality are not necessarily the same things. That what I want in my head isn't necessarily what I want at all. Sometimes it can only be found in the doing of it. That's the beauty of other people, they can give you what you cannot give yourself. You cannot ever imagine what someone else can bring, you only think you can. Men, it would seem, don't need to give themselves permission to have sex but we do need to be told that it is okay to love – love in the sense of giving ourselves freely.

I, of course, want it all. Love and the whole damn thing. But I have learnt that what I imagine I get, and what I get aren't always the same thing. Sometimes what I get can be better than what I imagine. Then it's bliss. Bliss because the unexpected bringing of beauty is always a gift which brings its own joy.

My imagination has always affected my experiences of sex and love. It has never ruled them, or at least my memory won't allow that it ever did. It has always allowed for the intrusion of other experience. Allowing the imagination totally to control behaviour would result in limited experience. I feel my imagination is limited in that I use a series of stock characteristics to trigger sexual fantasies. In fact, the men I conjure up in my imagination as sexual turn-ons are invariably boring in real life because there isn't enough. When in reality the person who fulfils the imagination turns out to have more than I ever dreamt, then it becomes totally other. This is a rare experience. With my lovers I have found that they have so much more in them than I can ever imagine.

When I'm alone and feeling sexy I start to play the magician, conjure up a man of my dreams to play with. But given the choice I would always want a flesh and blood man with a life of his own and his own dreams beside me. Wouldn't you?

Martin Humphries
July 1991

NOTE

1 Thanks to Steve Cranfield for allowing me to paraphase from a letter he sent to me.

Chapter 5

Male violence

THE COLLECTIVE DISCUSSION

During recent months the issues of male violence have become current within the national media. Feminists have become more vocal and visible in their demands that male violence be stopped. This has been crystallized in the Women Against Violence Against Women demonstrations and in the media response to the atrocities committed by the Yorkshire Ripper. We in *Achilles Heel* unreservedly support the women's movement's activities against male violence. But for us to be able to take our place as men in the struggle against male violence we need to be able to understand the roots of it. What has emerged for us out of our discussions in the collective during the preparation of this issue is an awareness that the violence within ourselves is a result of the process of learning to be men. We hope that these articles will enable us, both individually and collectively, to be involved in that struggle.

We have found it hard to explore these issues. We felt paralysed and confused; it took us a long time to move beyond that state. In our initial discussions we came to realize that it was important to spend time exploring our own aggression and being on the receiving end of it. Whilst our experience of violence is not wide, all of us had a range of experience deeper than we had imagined. It was difficult to own up to the ways we are aggressors in our lives, particularly in the face of the horror we felt at the depth of male violence both historically and in our society. It was painful to recognize the battering we have received at the hands of other men in reinforcing the male power system. We couldn't shoulder the burden for all men's violence through the ages. Yet we do want to take full responsibility for our own violence and take steps in the struggle towards stopping, dissolving, subverting and ending male violence in general.

James Swinson

The heart of the matter

At the heart of the male condition is the contradiction that we learn to fear other men as part and parcel of learning to be men. Fear – and its shadow, violence – are integral to the process of being a man: the father, that absent figure of power, the ultimate court of appeal and dispenser of justice; the other boys at school, with whom we all too often had to compete to be 'hard'; the authorities – the upholders of male standards of behaviour. And as we internalize the daily lessons so we come to despise women for being all that we have lost. Validation is never there for the expression of vulnerability or pain. Put simply: big boys don't cry! Anne-Marie Fearon in an article in *Shrew*, 'Come in Tarzan, your time is up' summed up the process succinctly:

> You frighten the child – with a monster mask, perhaps, or a cap gun. In the case of a girl, you don't let her retaliate; you tell her that girls are pretty and nice, they don't put on ugly faces or play with guns; but you let her feel frightened, cry and run to mother. Chances are mother will say: 'Never mind those nasty boys, you can stay and help me make the scones'. Thus the girl learns her role in life; she is to be frightened, helpless, tearful and in the kitchen. In the case of a boy, you forbid him to cry or run to mother (if he does, he will be called a 'wet' or a 'drip'); and you teach him to deny his fear and hurt. This is very hard and puts him under constant tension; so you give him a gun and a monster mask, and now whenever he feels that tension he can channel it into aggression, and project his fears on to someone else. He is now ready to frighten the next generation of little ones, and so keep the whole system going.[1]

Our understanding of this system is that it is based on both patriarchal and class oppression. As we write we find ourselves seesawing between these analyses, searching for the links between them. Whereas both men and women are exploited by virtue of their class, the whole system is maintained and reproduced in part by means of a male monopoly on violence. This monopoly operates at the state level and also at a personal one. As men learning to accept a violence in our relationship with other men as a 'natural' commonplace we become the unwitting/conscious accomplices of a system dependent for its survival, in the last instance, on the violent suppression to all threats to its existence. As men we are taught to expect violence from the time we are born; it is a fundamental part of what makes men 'masculine'. We learn to be violent in all areas of life, with wilful aggression against others as part of the collusion in the preservation of male power through the denial of rights to women and gays. Theories have been developed justifying male aggression as a natural state. At the same time as learning some of the most positive aspects of our existence from fathers, brothers, heroes, we learn how to oppress others; that the easiest way to express pain and anger as a man is through physical rage(?); that to compete with men is 'natural' and that 'success' and status are worth denying ourselves and others for; that violence is a necessary currency for men to use.

It is clear to us that under capitalism and imperialism the majority of women and men suffer much violence and degradation. With this comes frustration and rage which men do not always direct at the source of oppression but take out on individuals – especially women and children. We recognize and support the popular armed struggles of those peoples suffering the brutalizing regimes of imperialism. But, it is because violence has become an essential part of man's relationship with the world and himself that a violent response to oppression cannot always be accepted uncritically. Throughout the world popular movements to overthrow oppression (which we support) contain within them the contradictions of the old order. In Cuba, following the revolution, all manifestations of gayness were suppressed. In Iran, the process of removing the Shah has established a more entrenched and archaic form – in Islam – of male dominance. In Ireland, many of those fighting British imperialism, have set their faces against the struggle of women's rights. In Britain, much of the left has ignored the mounting violence against women and the media's treatment of it; and it is an open question how seriously many male socialists address these questions.

A price to pay

In this society a sexual division exists – not as necessity rooted in biology – but as a structural system of inequality which men resolve both ideologically and materially to their advantage. However veiled and uneven this distribution may be and however much individual men may feel that they don't resort to violence in their day-to-day lives, it remains true that men derive benefits and power – economically, socially, sexually, politically – of which male violence is an essential part.

We have to realize though that whilst men derive benefits from the male monopoly of violence, there is always a price to be paid. Partaking in, and retaining the image of, being a 'man' involves the loss of our sensitivity, vulnerability and capacity to love. We have become so good at deceiving ourselves that even though we feel the pain we are paralysed by the complexity of a reality we have colluded with. Imprisoned like this our violence and anger often emerge as substitutes for other – disallowed – feelings. Of weakness, fear, and pain. The appearance of physical strength or a dominating social presence is so often a mask for inner weakness, confusion and underdevelopment. Men rage because their vulnerability is touched and they have no language to express it. So perhaps one of the ways of confronting male violence will be by encouraging other kinds of emotional expression. Men don't know how to be assertive without being violent because so often they are deeply unsure whether there is a 'self' for them to assert.

The politics of the present government have introduced a new urgency into this discussion. It is a government with an ideology which accentuates patriarchal standards and practices; its path is one of governing by fear. Its attempts to discipline the workforce through mass unemployment (and to impose masculine values of authority and competition) have led to a dangerous situation where men – increasingly isolated and unable to fulfil their male roles in work – are liable to take out their frustrations in forms of violence against women. Thatcherism has laid the ground for increased attacks on those who stand outside the bounds of its severe normality – white, heterosexual, patriarchal.

What can men do about patriarchal violence? We can discover the ways in which to unlearn what it is to be a man and not become the most powerful and deadly creature of the species. As men we can work with each other in counselling and therapy. We can learn from the writings and experiences of women and gay men. We can challenge the violence of other men in all areas of our lives; we can publicly demonstrate against male violence. We can insist that within the struggles we are involved in, questions of women's oppression are not relegated and subordinated.

The articles on violence in this issue explore at greater depth some of the issues touched upon in this editorial. We are aware that we have only touched upon an enormous area; and that we would not have progressed to producing this issue were it not for the work already done by the women's movement and gay men. We would also be interested to hear from and include writings from men who are already involved in counteracting male violence.

June 1982

Note

1 *Shrew*, 'Feminism and non violence', 1978.

MASCULINITY ACQUITTED

Tony Eardley looks at the implications for men of the recent trial of Peter Sutcliffe.

Behind the legal ballyhoo and the column yards of prurient media 'revelation' the real significance of the Sutcliffe trial lies in what remains obscured. One could scour the pages of cross-examination and defence, psychiatric judgement, family gossip, and pious editorializing and not find one man asking the real question – what is it about our society that causes men to go around murdering and mutilating women?

It has been left to feminist commentators to expose this evasion. In her *Guardian* column Jill Tweedie[1] suggested that men's apparent silence on this question means that we are complacently resigned to some sort of biological determinism – that violence against women is encoded in our genes, always has been, and always will be, amen. Psychologist Anthony Storr, writing about Sutcliffe in the *Observer*, certainly fell back on this explanation, harping back to the old story of our hunter past.

Many men would dispute this, feeling that the complicated and varied elements of their own life experiences deny this reduction to biology. Many men also resent being automatically characterized as rapists and murderers by virtue (?) of their gender. But it is precisely men's overall silence and the apparent lack of any widespread disquiet amongst men about male violence which makes women justifiably suspicious that even those least personally violent amongst us secretly enjoy the benefits that accrue from the violent actions of others.

The Sutcliffe murders have provoked confused feelings of anger and shame for many men; for some of us, anti-sexist and socialist men, who see ourselves as potential allies of feminism, it feels a responsibility we cannot accept but somehow must. As one friend I spoke to said: 'I don't want to feel that it's part of me, and yet it is.' The problems we have in articulating any kind of political response seem to spring from a deep-seated reluctance to uncover the roots of our own masculinity and the construction of our sexuality.

For, of course, it is the construction of a masculinity which requires a violently enforced power over women which is in question, as the Sutcliffe trial makes clear, if by default. 'Not mad, not bad, but MALE' – the trial graffiti is succinct and to the point, but disquieting for those of us who feel uncomfortable with the idea that maleness is some kind of hereditary disease. If we can't believe this then we have to face this question ourselves.

To find a way in to what the Sutcliffe affair means for us it is instructive to look at the trial as a kind of institutional cover-up job – a public exercise of the individual self-evasion which most men habitually indulge in. The fact that all the institutions concerned – police, judiciary and media, are largely male-dominated and were in this instance represented almost exclusively by men makes this all the more apt. But more than that, they are the institutions of the state which are responsible for invoking the 'criminal process'. This is the basis of the bourgeois justice system and by its approach to criminality which treats offenders purely as individual 'deviants' it has the function of reflecting and upholding the dominant ideologies. In this case the process moves on from the assumption that the forces which shape masculinity are in themselves beyond reproach and that a problem occurs only when an individual does not fit in, or acts in some excessive way. Thus, as Lynne Segal points out,[2] Sutcliffe was tried from within a value system which could only see him as an 'aberration' rather than an expression of the consequences of this very value system. This approach makes it possible to ignore all the other 'sexual' murders of women, the thousands of rapes reported every year, the overflowing women's aid refuges around the country, and the daily abuse and harassment of women on the streets; not to mention the porn shops stuffed with magazines of sexual violence and the steady flow into mainstream city cinemas of films depicting the sexual murder or terrorization of women.

This individualization of Sutcliffe's crimes is the first stage of the cover-up. Any responsibility which might fall on society (i.e. other men) is sloughed off and the way is paved for Sutcliffe himself to be partially absolved through the plea of 'diminished responsibility'. It is significant that the Attorney General accepted the defence plea,

Ronald Grant

backed up by the full weight of the psychiatric establishment. If the judge had not overruled him and insisted that a jury had to decide on Sutcliffe's mental state, he would have been packed away quietly in some mental hospital with very little fuss. *The Times* described the trial as 'a public catharsis, an exorcism' and it's true that it was a show trial, but not quite in that sense. What the judge's decision meant was that the public conscience needed to be assuaged; by invoking the full criminal process of trial and punishment we can reassure ourselves that we are a sane society in a situation which begins to provoke some doubts.

Then there is a plausibility in the 'diminished responsibility' argument which serves only to mystify the whole process. The role call of psychotic symptoms sounds convincing. They add up to the classically recognizable picture of the 'over-controlled' character – capable of violent outbursts under provocation. But it is presented as though mental illness develops entirely outside any social context, and none of the doctors had any words to say about what sort of society we have that creates people in that mould. It might be more possible to take it at its face value if the 'over-controlled' character didn't sound uncomfortably like a description of the end product of 'normal' male socialization. But in the end, in the trial's own terms, it becomes meaningless to ascribe total responsibility to Sutcliffe, and so, in the absence of any willingness to look at the social construction of masculinity, one is left with a moral void into which can conveniently be dragged the classic deus ex machina or 'God told me to'.

Women to blame

With the question of responsibility fudged, everyone now sought 'reasons' for Sutcliffe's actions and for his mental state in the behaviour of the women around him. Nothing demonstrated more clearly and disgustingly the complacent commonality of values between prosecution and defence, murderer and media. We hear that Sutcliffe's mother had had an extra-marital affair, that 'the happy marriage was destroyed and so the father became unfaithful'. By implication the mother's callous betrayal of the marriage led to Sutcliffe's instability. Sonya Sutcliffe looked well set up for blame once the papers discovered that she herself had a mental breakdown some years earlier: 'The mania of ripper's wife!' screamed one tabloid. The Attorney General listed her 'impossible behaviour':

> He had to take his shoes off when he went home, wasn't allowed to use the washing machine and had to do his own washing. She was obsessed with cleanliness, cleaning the carpet with a brush and pan. She pulled the plug out and shouted at him.

After all that, we are to suppose that it was hardly surprising that he went out and killed thirteen women!

We were told that the first time Sutcliffe went to a prostitute she cheated him out of £10 and mocked his impotence with her. Havers again:

> It was a reaction which, you may think, was not altogether surprising, the reaction of a man who had been fleeced and humiliated. It was the sort of loss of control which you don't have to be mad for a moment to suffer.

This theme runs through the whole saga: that is somehow 'natural', if a little excessive, for a man to suffer a 'loss of control' when cheated and mocked by a prostitute and to brutally kill her. It is made clear that it is altogether more understandable (and excusable) when the woman is a prostitute by the constant distinction drawn by police, journalists and lawyers, between the prostitutes and the 'respectable' women. The Attorney General again: 'Some were prostitutes, but perhaps the saddest aspect of this case is that some were not.' What he is saying, and this attitude is shown to be broadly shared by the police, the press and the defendant, is that prostitutes are fair game, they are outside of society and part of a filthy underworld which society must defend itself against. What we are invited to be really angry about is that, unlike that other folk hero, the original Jack, Sutcliffe broke the rules and killed 'respectable' women – 'our' wives, mothers and daughters. This is certainly backed up by the kind of remarks I have overheard men making. And, of course, it is not the first time that prostitutes have been officially recognized by the courts as fair game: the London police officer who suffocated Pat Malone and cut up and concealed her body was eventually prosecuted not even for manslaughter but only for 'unlawful burial'. But then she was lesbian, too, which puts her even further beyond the pale.

What comes over so clearly in this trial and others involving prostitutes is men's total sense of a-responsibility – as though it isn't men who demand their services, who control their incomes through pimping and 'protection', who then prosecute them for soliciting. Those images spring to mind that give the word hypocrisy its meaning: the politician who fulminates against vice in the House and slips off to the call girl, the judge who jails the whore and pays another to whip him. The issues raised by the Sutcliffe case may have been instrumental in encouraging the introduction of the private member's bill to decriminalize prostitution which fell in Parliament in June this year. The government's official reason for opposing it was that they preferred to wait for any recommendations from the forthcoming report of the Criminal Law Revision Committee, but since the arguments used by organized action groups like PROS who support decriminalization are directly those which challenge this male hypocrisy, we can expect other attempts to sink similarly unless backed by massive support.

There is of course a danger in overplaying the importance of prostitution as such in this case. What distinguishes prostitutes from some other women more than anything is their particular vulnerability to attack by men. That's why Sutcliffe chose them – because they were available. And when other women found themselves in the same position – alone in a secluded place at night – they became equally vulnerable. Nevertheless, the institution of prostitution is central to the development of male sexuality both historically and at present and Sutcliffe was obviously part of a northern 'brothel culture' and a frequent visitor to the red-light districts with his male friends. So it is not insignificant to look at what light the existence of prostitution sheds on the nature of male sexuality.

Sexuality and male power

But why do we talk about 'sexuality'? Surely most acts of violence against women, most rapes, have little to do with sex but are to do with asserting power? This is true, but in a world of enforced inequality between the sexes, sexuality becomes inextricably bound up with power. Men are brought up to expect women to cater to our needs, physical and emotional – to be bringers of comfort, reassurance and delight. But in this process we are lucky if we ever learn to look after ourselves. It is a terrible weakness often desperately concealed behind insouciant machismo. Women generally recognize it but are expected to pretend not to, and we dread its exposure; marriages (and other relationships) are rooted in this fear – we exchange a share in our economic and social power for the emotional and physical services of women. Under these circumstances any sign of autonomy in a woman, of independence, is a terrible threat and one which many men have no resources to deal with except by violence. Yet somehow we expect in the act of sex a dissolution of this power structure in a free exchange of love and tenderness, and when this is not forthcoming our security collapses under the weight of its own coercion. One of the most abiding and seductive myths that all of us, men and women, are instilled with from our first understandings of love and sex is that the bed, the privacy of 'freely' exchanged sexual love is that one place where we cast off the world with our clothes and become anonymous, essential, lost in one-ness with our partner. When in fact the opposite is the case. Angela Carter, in the preface to her book, *The Sadeian Women*,[3] describes it thus:

> no bed, however unexpected, no matter how gratuitous, is free from the de-universalising effects of real life. We do not go to bed simply in pairs; even if we choose not to refer to them, we still drag

there with us the cultural impedimenta of our social class, our parents' lives, our bank balance, our sexual and emotional expectations, our whole biographies – all the bits and pieces of our unique existences.

And so the moment of apparent equality is the moment which most harshly exposes the inequality between men and women, and economic and social power become crucial elements in our lovemaking. The alienation from ourselves that this causes at the moment when we expect to feel most integrated, affects both men and women, but this is when men expect women to make it all right for us and when they do not or cannot our frustrations are once more unleashed. The fantasy of the prostitute gains its attraction from this unexpected collapse of our power. I have never been to a prostitute but the fantasy is one I have learnt among others growing up as a man. The attraction of the prostitute is that with her we can buy entry to a controlled environment, a playroom – a 'rumpus room of the mind' (Angela Carter q.v.) – where we do not have to acknowledge the undermining reality of women's lives, but instead can purchase complicity in an elaborate simulation of love unshackled by domestic realities. But the prostitute must remain excluded from society, secret, illicit. Not just to maintain our illusions, but also because she is dangerous in that, seen too clearly, the purely economic nature of the contract with her may expose that same reality which exists, mystified, in marriage or romantic love. This exposure may threaten that very basis of our powerful and our security.

I am not in a position to talk about Sutcliffe's childhood, his socialization, but I have no reason to suppose it was remarkably different from that of most men. Where men are not taught at an early age to cater to our own needs but instead to use our power to obtain others to do this, violence becomes at once the ultimate sanction and a front behind which to conceal our insecurity. We all become 'over-controlled' and go around with inexpressible needs, only really knowing how to demand compliance. To recognize this is not to excuse the consequences but only to open it up to question. The institutions which have grown up perpetuating and legitimating male dominance only serve to mask the truth that this domination is based not on any intrinsic superiority but on brute force, and the Sutcliffe affair, for all its publicity, was an evasion of this truth. People hoping for a private reconciliation or accommodation of power and sexuality within individual relationships are doomed to failure because that private retreat is an illusion. It is up to us to find public and political ways to uncover the development of our own masculinity and to challenge the presentation of this masculinity as given, natural, and inevitable.

Tony Eardley
October 1981

Acknowledgement

Thanks to Steve Gould for the development of some of the ideas in this article.

Notes

1 *Guardian* Women (21 May 1981).
2 'God, the Ripper, and the Prosecution.' *Big Flame* (June 1981).
3 *The Sadeian Women* (London: Virago, 1979).

STONY SILENCES: A DISCUSSION OF ANGER AND VIOLENCE

This article is based on transcripts of tapes of two evenings of discussions in the Achilles Heel *collective, and was put together by Andy Moye and Tom Weld, two members of the collective.**

These discussions gave us a focus for exploring our own experiences of violence – both as perpetrators and victims – as a crucial step to demystify and understand the meaning of what we all know and feel to be so much part of ourselves as men.

We felt it important to explore these experiences as honestly as we could, whilst recognizing that the violence we talked about doesn't define or delimit ourselves as men. We took it on trust from one another that when we spoke about violence in our relationships, past and present, we were attempting to disentangle the negative from a whole range of feelings and consciousness, positive and negative, which lay outside the scope of the discussion. The focus on violence was a means for us to get through to some of its roots in order to understand it better.

At times it was a demanding and painful process, speaking of experiences we have kept hidden from others and often from ourselves. But through sharing those experiences we began to uncover common threads and consistencies in our anger and violence. We began to see

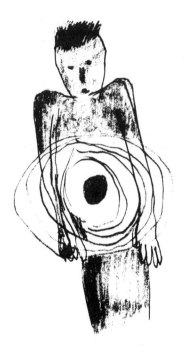

Tom Weld

that as men we have learnt a language of anger and violence in fantasy, and in practice, as substitutes for an emotional language and the expressions of needs which we have learnt to deny and suppress. All of us have learned this language, even the 'gentlest' of us.

We have divided the discussion into four sections: violence within the body; 'temper' and anger; with women; and, finally, schooldays. All of these sections overlap to some extent, although the final section on our experiences at school stands apart from the others in the sense that it is about a specific situation in our pasts.

There are many situations and experiences of violence and anger which we didn't discuss. But we hope that by publishing this piece despite all its omissions and inadequacies more men will be encouraged to confront and explore together their own aggression as a step towards discovering a masculinity unburdened by the latent threat of violence.

Within the body

All violence has a bodily aspect. Whether we are overtly, physically violent, verbally violent, or boiling inside, there is something happening in our bodies. How the emotion gets there in the first place is one thing which we go into elsewhere, based as it is on a variety of situations; what we do with it from there is another matter, with tendencies learned early in childhood. The results range from nervous illness caused by extreme internalization, to external physical violence towards another person.

The language which comes up again and again is descriptive of direct physical experience – 'gulp down/back', 'turning in on oneself', 'holding on', 'gritty-faced'.

There are ways in which we *need*, in a physical sense, to hold on to our anger, as though it gives us a warped kind of security. If we do hold on (gulp down, turn in on ourselves), we are at least in familiar territory. Everything is under control inside us. If we let go, on the other hand, get angry, come out with it, even though we might know in our heads that we would feel better in the long run, we risk a new and threatening situation.

The turning inwards of anger can become hatred. The image of the stone held inside us. Almost as if we could point to the place in our bodies where we 'hold' it. It is one of the many physical pressures which lead to stiffness and aches.

What happens to us over a number of years if this is our pattern?

Mike: I went to the ironmongers and the two people were taking orders over the phone. I wanted to buy something. I could see it, I could actually have got hold of it. They could see me, but they just went on with these phone calls as though I was invisible. I felt this anger rising, rising, rising ... more than 5 minutes, nobody else in the shop, they knew I wasn't being served, and they just went on with these phone calls.... I saw these two choices; either screaming at them, or walking out. I knew I was going to walk out. That's just what I do in that kind of situation. And then at that point, having made that choice, I started wondering had I actually done myself damage, had I internalized this fury; and was that another nail in my coffin? I happened to need to go into the same shop later that day ... apparently without any anger at all, and I felt as if nothing had happened. I felt on the one hand bad about not having let my anger out before, but on the other hand maybe it *had* all disappeared. But then I'd been saying to myself 'it's all disappeared' for years, and I know really it hasn't because I do feel these fantastic wells of fury around quite a lot of the time. I find it no easier to get angry at the time in an appropriate way than I ever did. At least, I have occasionally been able to, but it's very hard ... although it's always worth it.

On the other hand, Mike also mentioned one possibly healthy area of release for those emotions:

Mike: Smashing things can be quite therapeutic and does actually release something because the very action, the very physical action is, in bioenergetic terms, exactly what one needs to be doing. That's why I love playing squash, and probably partly why I was mostly even-keeled when I lived in the country, because I cut all my own wood and it involved an enormous amount of chopping each day.
Kevin: That's right what they said about cold showers and chopping wood!
Mike: I was realizing the other day how many things I do with my fist clenched, which all relate to anger and holding my anger in. Other things which are open and the anger's gone, like massage or dancing or swimming, are all things which I love doing but somehow I find difficult to build into my life.

Boy, has he got a temper!

We talked a lot about anger – about how we found it difficult to be plainly, honestly angry, without a surge of rage and violence sweeping through us. Much of our 'anger' seems very abstract, without a real context or point. So much of our experience is about bottling up all kinds of fears and frustrations which can then be unleashed in 'appropriate' situations and 'appropriate' ways – with women friends in particular, even if not directly aimed at them, but displayed in front of them, for our benefit.

This abstractness to our anger and the ritual ways in which we all display it (and it was noticeable that we each have our own rituals) establish us very close to violence. It would be pointless perhaps to mark the transition from one to the other. They are inextricably bound up together, with a logic which we became increasingly aware of.

'Big boys don't cry' is a violent imperative which we have all experienced in one form or another. This amounts as a matter of course to a pressure stifling our emotional life at source. What *is* allowed, and given subtle encouragement, is precisely male anger, as a socially acceptable safety valve for everything else which is not allowed. A pejorative pressure is put against our expression of an emotional language – especially expressions of that which hurts as – a father's contempt or lack of interest, say. But there is validation and legitimate space given to 'anger', 'temper', etc. as 'natural' characteristics for a man.

As men we come to know the power this validation gives us. It is readily and controllably expressed. We all noticed how we retold tales of our own 'fits of temper' (how archaically biological that phrase is) and the amount of physical havoc we had wreaked in our displays, with a distinct, if subtle price. In this sense, even anger becomes detached, another dislocated element in an emotional dyslexia we are encouraged to take for granted. We have all learnt this lesson and become our own best bosses, bullies and petty tyrants.

Mike: I had a 'temper' – I have a temper. I'm wondering though about this notion of 'temper'. I remember in our family there was a big thing about which of us had bad tempers. My mother's father had a bad temper, and there was this myth that if your eyebrows join you've got a bad temper. He had this bad temper. And she used to say, you're just like him, you've got this terrible temper. And his eyebrows joined like mine do. Really I was given a certain kind of validation – that it was alright for males to have a temper. When they gave me a travelling clock two Christmases running and I broke them both within two days of getting them, the story was related with a certain amount of grudging acceptance or even admiration as though it was alright, though it was fucking stupid. And I still smash things, or slam doors, or break things, or tear clothes to bits. I do things which are almost uncontrolled but at the same time I've never actually smashed my fist. I have put my hand through a window and cut it, but not at all badly. In a way I knew I wouldn't. It's only just controlled but it's controlled, nevertheless, or nearly always.

I've thought about my son a bit – he's 5 – and he shows his anger in a very immediate and full way, in a healthy way. In fact the only people I can think of who do this are children. Adults find children's anger hard to accept in the same way we find their tears hard to accept; and the reason we say 'shut up, be quiet, stop crying' is partly because they are showing up the difference between them and us – they're showing us that we can't do this anymore. In a way what we're feeling is envy.

Nick: I think you get to a stage where people start saying 'Come on now, be grown up – you're big boy now. You can't behave like that anymore – throwing tantrums.' That word 'tantrum' at a certain stage becomes very pejorative, doesn't it? Something which you should shake off when you get older. I know the way I express my anger has a lot to do with my childhood. My brother had 'a temper' and he used to flare up at things which seemed unrealistic ... unnecessary. He was very sensitive to a lot of things. He would flare up and have these huge rows and storm out of the house and disappear for hours on end and my parents would get all freaked out. There was this whole ethos in my home where things like that were seen as really indecent.

Unlike my brother I was always characterized as being even-tempered, even-keeled, and I tended to have to mediate between Andrew and my parents. I feel it's left me for years with a real fear of violent scenes and angry scenes. Any anger I did have became bottled up and I didn't know how to use it.

Kevin: Was your brother ever given any validation for those scenes of anger? Was he ever asked why he was angry? Was that ever worked through between your parents and him?

Nick: Well, a lot of it was to do with these real difficulties he had in his life. He had this very bad speech impediment, he used to get bullied at school. He was very unhappy really. I think my parents recognized that and he used to go to speech therapy. It was all kept very hidden from me – I was younger ... it was never talked about openly in the family anyway. But on the one hand, although they recognized the objective reasons why it happened, they couldn't deal with it themselves. When it did happen my father's reaction was to be really angry with Andrew for disturbing the peace in that way. My mother would be more upset than angry. No, I don't think he ever was given much validation for it even though they recognized on an 'objective' level that there were reasons for it. When it happened, he wasn't acknowledged; he was seen as a problem.

Kevin: So, they could manage when everything was externalized onto speech therapy and 'problems at school', 'bullying'. Those were 'his problems', but when he actually flared up....

Nick: ... *he* was the problem....

Kevin: Yes, he was the problem – 'Stop making a scene, stop being stupid!'

Nick: Exactly that, I can just hear them saying that and him stomping out.

I was talking to Sue the other night, telling her about our discussions, and I said, 'Do you think I'm a violent person?' And she said no, and then she said, 'Well, yes, I think in some ways you are. My experience of your violence is always in relation to things going wrong, and frustration with machinery and with inanimate things.' And that's really right. I don't know whether it's a transference from feelings about people but definitely that's what makes me most expressively and physically furious. It can be a car or anything. I start cursing and swearing – 'Fuck this fucking thing!' and (thump, thump on the chair) like that ... you know. It's the only time it really comes out, in that kind of situation. But the thing is the only person who sees that very much is Sue, and it often happens when I'm with her. And that's partly to do with a feeling of licence that I can let things out. It's also something else as well, which is while I feel I can let things out, at the same time I feel that somehow exposing myself to her means that I ... I have less power. It means I feel more vulnerable. And that makes it worse. It means I feel more frustrated and more angry about it. And end up being increasingly uptight.

Mike: I don't really think smashing things is appropriate because it usually is a substitute for smashing the person – which does happen in my relationship with Ruth. I get into situations where we do hit each other. And that's not 'appropriate' either. It's wanting to annihilate the problem. It's not appropriate because when I hit her I want to smash my way through the problem rather than be angry with her or with the aspect of whatever's happening. It's like a total rejection of the problem rather than coming to grips with it.

With women

In many relationships between men and women, there is an underlying threat of the man's physical violence towards the woman. This may not be based on any actual violent act ever having taken place between them, but rather if the man is physically stronger and bigger (or even if he isn't, as long as she feels he is), he has a sanction over her. 'Just give in quietly, will you? I don't want to hit you, but you know I'm stronger than you, and that it will hurt if I do hit you.'

Holding in; smashing things; hitting a person. A spectrum of ways we deal with our anger, all usually inappropriate. Here are some accounts of how some of us behave, specifically with the women we live with/have primary relationships with.

Ian: It's always been important in my relationship with Judith, though gradually less so, that I'm physically bigger and stronger than she is. That's frightening. That gives me power and a confidence that I don't like. I can *insist* on things. Assert myself. We're going to the pictures: what film to see. And with issues that carry more weight.

Rick: Sounds more like power than violence.

Ian: Behind it there's a threat of violence. I've very rarely actually been.... We've fought fairly frequently; but there have been times when I have been in a rage, when I've thrown things, picked up chairs. I've never actually done anything violent; but there's been that threat that if I really let go, I could do it. I don't know if I actually would do it. Judith's rage is pretty terrifying too. It would be good to get to grips with what those moments really are.

Mike: It's only in relation to Ruth that I've ever been, and am continually really, really, angry. I can scream with my entire lungs at her, as I've hardly ever been able to do even in a group-therapy situation. Sometimes it just stays at that 'pre-violent' level and it's very good. And it's a great release for years of repressed anger. But then she also gets a kind of backlog which isn't even about her.... But sometimes we get into a state of total frustration, often when we put each other in a double bind, where the result is physical violence. On occasion we have punched each other quite hard in the face, hit with various weapons, and thrown heavy objects. We fear each other then: and it's quite equal in the sense that we are well-matched in strength.

In my previous long relationship, I was very aware that I just held the sanction of greater strength. Having seen my 'temper', she was aware of that. She said she was afraid of me. After we parted, I felt totally sickened by that. It was just there, more or less whatever I did or didn't do.

Kevin: Often I experienced a sense of self-denial and feel 'un-together'. I haven't cleaned up and the place is a mess, and I feel depressed with that. She comes and says the place is in a mess, and that reminds me I'm depressed, and I'm immediately hostile, and angry with myself because she's exposed me to myself. I feel frustrated that it takes her to remind me that the place is in a mess. I don't want to be reminded and ... it's really painful. And so I get all gritty-faced.

Rather than saying, 'Yes, I've been silly not to deal with myself emotionally and open myself up before', it's more 'Oh fuck, I've *got* to deal with it'. That's where the resentment comes in. The other part of that is 'And *you*'ve made me. It's your *fault*.'

Nick: I get angry when someone – particularly the women I'm involved with – starts probing away at things I want to leave covered up; or when I'm forced to try and open up emotionally, or relate to something I find difficult. I get filled with this frustration which turns into anger and is directed towards the person who's making me do it. It happens quite often. I can't get to grips with what's happening inside me in a way that I can relate to the other person. That makes me really angry. With myself, but also with her. It's a self-perpetuating thing – I'm afraid to show my anger as well. I can only show my anger with someone I feel secure with, yet showing my anger makes me feel insecure ... showing a side of me I don't want to reveal, which in turn makes me feel more resentful towards that person who's forced me to do it. It builds up in that way.

Rick: In the early days of my relationship with Hilary she was emotional and I was unemotional. She would get really angry about things, and I would withdraw. She was very frustrated because I never responded. Then when I got into the growth movement, we started getting in touch with feelings and emotions, and I started to get angry back. She got scared, that the moment I got angry I would completely beat her up. I couldn't get it right. If I withdrew it was wrong; if I got angry back, that was wrong.

Later I decided to take it in a different way. If she was angry, she was angry about something. There were two things there: one, she was angry about something and the other, she was angry. Before, I concentrated on the something, got angry back at that. Later I began to say,'How about this person who is angry? There's something about that, something I haven't done justice to.' So I got more able to deal with her being angry, and what that was actually about; what had happened, and what my part in that had been. That worked a lot better. I learned a lot more from that.

Schooldays

In our discussions one institution had a special place – school. All of us at some stage went to boy's schools where all the teachers (or nearly all) were men. Our first taste of institutional life. Several things emerge from this experience. At one level we became part of a struggle with the other boys – a struggle always present, sometimes cruel – to be better, harder, stronger, more powerful than the 'others'.

One man talked about the hierarchy that existed in his school, with the 18-year-old school monitors at the top, with the power to beat the younger boys. Perhaps it is no coincidence that this was a public school. The power the school monitors had to bully and control was entrusted to them by the 'masters' in the name of 'the school' and its shadowy traditions of courage, excellence, leadership. For this man that hierarchy was fostered to initiate all the boys into the acceptance and practice of authority. A case maybe of 'torturing the future torturers'.

The rest of us went to state schools of one sort or another, where such a clear-cut story does not emerge. But we were all in a struggle for respect from our peers, a kind of authority in itself. None of us competed successfully in this struggle, but we all competed none the less to a greater or lesser degree. The memories of pain and fear and resentment are our testimony to this and remain part of us.

Kevin: For me secondary school was an initiation into the most violent society I have ever been in. I remember from the first day I was at school, the older boys, particularly those in the next form up, but a few older ones as well, duffed up the first-year boys – not badly, just terrorizing us. It set a pattern. (I remember talking with my father about this, then. He was doing his best to console me. I remember him saying things like,'It'll be over soon, the novelty will wear off for them, just give it time.' I feel fond of this memory of him.)

Nick: Some people went through that, and grew up in some way to relish that, and became really sadistic. You'd go up in the hierarchy, starting off at 12 years old completely terrified of these school monitors, who had the power to beat you. Some people rose and grew into it and some didn't at all and ended up being really terrified of it.

Kevin: This is really the first time I've talked about school. It is still painful and it still frightens me. It seems to me that a boy had to assert himself to take his place in the classroom and that usually involved violence of one kind or another. It did for me, but I couldn't cope with it. I was nearly always 'non-violent'. But I didn't get out of that trap. I internalized all the violence. I remember being jeered at for not retaliating and that being as wounding, or more wounding, than getting a punch in the face. The contempt that some of the other boys showed for me was horrific – it outweighed the little support I got, the little gestures, from some of my friends. It was something I started to believe about myself in a very big way. That really paralysed me. I've tried to erase it from my memory.

Ian: I wasn't actually bullied a lot, but I was frightened. And I definitely kept out of the way to avoid being bullied. And that was a deep experience for me. But since then, I've gone on to feeling that I've got to prove myself, or ought to prove myself in that sort of context. Especially in a working-class group. I was very aware of the possibility of not knowing how to respond to the word 'tough'. And I wonder what I did with that in relation to my younger brother and my cousin. I'm fairly sure that I tormented my brother. It all seemed to be a question of being better or not better than someone else. I remember that sense of shame. Shame – that sounds a better word than guilt. There's a kind of shroud around guilt.

Together with these memories stand those of the school itself, its rules and regulations, the official authority exercised by our 'masters'.

Ian: There's something about the whole school administration that seems ruthless – utterly ruthless. I think the main thing about institutional violence is not what people are made to do all the time, with the obvious punishments and all that – it's the balance of what is denied that's really important. Nobody cares, nobody respects you as an individual and that builds up – you know it's building. I think this leads to an incredibly deep self-hatred, a sense of loss; and it's that which often spills out, and what's often underneath the punishment of violence, which is mostly to keep all that down.
Charlie: There's a fascination about violence – a kind of perversity – there's so much bottled up. I mean the headmaster at my school – I'd have liked to have destroyed him, quite slowly and tortuously – that was my total fantasy for a couple of years, because of things like getting caned for things I didn't do. I was put in detention by a schoolmaster who didn't even tell me I was in detention. So I didn't go. And next morning I was hauled in front of the headmaster and I was standing there trying to explain this to him. And while I was trying to explain it, he was just writing my name in the punishment book for four strokes of the cane. And I was left bottling up pure hatred.
Mike: A thing that happens for me is internalizing, fostering, almost nurturing this sense of defiance and indignation. In situations at school, like breaking completely petty rules; instead of raging at them, I just held them in, and they became hatred, because there was no way of being angry or violent about them. I held on to that like a stone inside me, and I still do that; it's horrible. It has a physical reality.
Rick: How does that turn into hatred?

Mike: Just knowing in yourself the reality of the situation, and that you were punished wrongly and that the thing was ridiculous by your and any reasonable and good standards and just knowing it:

> I can't do anything to you – The Authority – but I know my values are better than yours, and I *hate* yours. I can't do anything – you are too powerful – and I don't know how to be angry, how to get together with other people and do something about it. The only thing I can hold onto is this hatred of it.

Andy Moye and Tom Weld (eds)
September 1981

* The names of all those involved in the discussion and all those mentioned have been changed.

LIVE DANGEROUSLY: HOMOPHOBIA AND GAY POWER

> This your anger and sadness, your shame to hide
> that father's gift
> paternal line of hatred and fear
> handed down in clenched fist, a loud-mouth aggressive stance,
> blows struck
> for more violence and hard bitterness
> against women, gays, the gentles,
> who your despair and confusion turn to enemies
> to rape, beat and humiliate.
>> (Anonymous poem in the anti-sexist
>> men's newsletter, No. 11)

This article is written by a gay man and is about gay men and homophobia. Lesbians also experience homophobia (lesbian-phobia?) along with all other forms of male violence – see the attacks against lesbians by men at the lesbian conference earlier this year – and gay men (like all men) can and do show signs of phobia towards lesbians but in this article I'm speaking of my own experience as a gay man.

Be prepared

Whenever I'm on the streets, in a pub, a park, a cottage,* or a shop I'm aware of who is around me and how they are reacting to me. If it is during the evening or at night on the street I'm aware of who is in front, is someone behind, why are they walking so fast, what are those men doing on the other side of the road? I try to keep alert and not fall into daydreams, to be prepared in case I'm about to be attacked physically or verbally. This may sound like paranoia (try wearing a gay badge and then see if it's our paranoia or yours) but such safety precautions are necessary as the incidence of attacks on gay men makes clear.[1]

This is not a new experience for gay men, we have always been attacked. I knew this from a very early age. My life at school was a balancing act between not letting it be known I was gay for fear of the consequences and still being open to myself as much as possible – which involved not expressing clearly the gender of those with whom I was having relationships or fantasies about. By the time I was 15 I led two lives: at school I was a 'straight' guy (I was occasionally bullied by those who saw me as a sissie and were upset by it) who liked drama not football, whilst outside of school I spent hours cruising cottages looking for and spending time with men like myself. This involved a large amount of self-deception and went on until I was 17 when I met an older man who showed me other aspects of the gay scene – though I didn't and still haven't stopped cottaging – and from whom I realized that it was possible to be openly gay with other people who were gay but not outside of that small circle. This awareness was reinforced when he lost his job as a social worker when his boss discovered that he was gay. I knew that the barrier erected by straight society to prevent them knowing about gays was maintained by threats of physical violence and it took me several years before I rejected and challenged this threat and came out. Then and only then did I discover that the dangers of being out are more concrete and easier to deal with than remaining in the closet. Rather than the threats being intangible and heightened by silence, they can be faced with a self-confidence previously unknown. This is not to say that all is easy, especially as attacks on gay people are increasing. For me this awareness is brought home by the fact that two of my friends were attacked within the last year, eleven men I know slightly, an old friend/lover committed suicide last year and society's hatred of gays was a contribution to his despair. With this personal knowledge of how we are put down, discriminated against, oppressed and denied, street skills readily develop. The root cause of this street sense is the homophobia which surrounds us.

Cultural and personal homophobia

Homophobia has a number of definitions ranging from: 'the revulsion towards homosexuals and the desire to inflict punishment as retribution'[2] to the 'allowance within oneself to the belief that one is able to excise or control gay desire'.[3] Both are interconnected for we live in a dominant culture of straight patriarchy which is homophobic and expresses this phobia through those who accept its values – it is hardly surprising that those men most homophobic are also those most sexist. It is often said that those most outwardly violent towards gays are those who fear gayness within themselves, whilst this is sometimes true it is also too simplistic. Closetted[†] gay men, whilst often verbally aggressive about other gays, are rarely physically violent towards them, though these men collude with straights to exclude us they do so under the mistaken allure of safety. Not-out gay men will participate in the putting down of gay men in order to keep up a 'straight' facade. I was once eating a meal with friends of my mother's, towards the end of which one man told an anti-gay joke about where faeries come from. I joined in the laughter forgetting I was gay or that hours earlier I had said goodbye to my lover in order to be there.

The homophobia engendered by church and state through control in order to maintain dominance gives licence to all, including those who are aware of fears of gay desire within and those who are readily violent towards any 'minority' group. Racism or sexism not only involves fear of the loss of power, but also pleasure in the retention and showing of that power; the same is true of homophobia.

So what happens?

An organized gang of at least four thugs were reported to be beating up and robbing men on Tooting Common. The police were operating on their own account during the same period, arresting gay men on the Common for importuning.[4]

The direct effect for gay men is physical violence from individuals or groups who claim to be heterosexual. Homophobia is created and lives on through the family, the media and education – a continuous process of reinforcement to straights that gays are not to be tolerated and to gays that to be gay is awful. If we are aware of this we can fight it. We can fight the learning process which separates men from women as they grow into a 'straight' world. We can fight against the attitude that a man's cock makes him superior to women, that the only way in which men can relate is through aggression and competitiveness, that a man showing emotion is a weak man, that men loving men are sick: 'Heterosexuals are what they are because they deny the homosexuality that is latent within them, sublimating it and/or converting it to aggression.'[5] But what is it that unlocks this aggression? It is being unable to deal with the reality of men loving each other sexually and enjoying it. Straight men and closetted gay men are so freaked out by the fact of men openly declaring enjoying each other sexually that they will do anything to deny it. I identify as a gay man and openly and proudly acknowledge that I have loving pleasurable sex with other men. An open declaration is important in affirming ourselves and is supportive to each other. Coming out is the first step in dealing with the violence presented as our due.

What do we do?

That all gay men are at risk is undeniable, but what can we do about it when our homes are entered, the streets unsafe, when we are beaten or killed, when we have little or no help from those who enforce the law? We have several options all of which relate to being openly gay and supportive to each other. If we are 'out' and have a network of friends/lovers, we can demand that the law acknowledges that we are under attack and pressure agents of the law into doing something about it. Every time we are attacked this means telling everyone we know, attempting to get media coverage and using gay lawyers to contact the police.

Individually we can take care not to get into situations which may lead to violence. This caution related to awareness of how and when a situation may become potentially violent and does not imply that we should stop confronting or provoking the straight world, for the skills of provocation may be the very skills necessary to deal with the violence we continually meet.

> when epithets are hurled at one in the street, it's best to shout epithets back; trying to ignore them with dignity or responding with overt fear seems only to intensify the hostility. Although I am open to correction on this, I have the feeling that the safest response to physical assault is fight back; the bruises one may incur seem to me preferable to the corrosive rage that follows from helplessness.[6]

Continuing to demand our rights to space may be seen as initiating conflict but I refuse to accept that hatred levelled at us. We are constantly being attacked by straight society which positively encourages its adherents to destroy us. How would straight men feel if they could often read this:

> Funny fellow, Alfred, he thought. Bright, decent, possibly even extraordinary. And there must be other heterosexuals like him – scientists, public figures, teachers, artists. Killing someone like that would certainly be judged a waste. And yet. There's always that and yet. They can't possibly be that good.[7]

The original passage uses the word homosexual and expresses an attitude we often encounter, an attitude we must continue to challenge through presenting positive alternatives to each other.

Collectively we can learn the arts of self-defence, which is a practical way of building confidence and abilities. In London two gay self-defence groups have been exploring the issues of violence through practical self-defence workshops running since the begin- ning of this year which developed out of the discussion groups and stimulated by the work of gay men in Canada. It may appear negative to be organizing as a group to counter violence but learning in a group situation gives confidence to deal with attacks when one is alone – the time they most often happen – and the strength to be openly gay on the streets.

What can anti-sexist pro-feminist men do?

I expect to give and receive support from lesbians and other gay men. I also expect support from non-gay men (or men who do not identify as gay) involved in anti-sexist politics whatever situation I'm in and especially when that situation is potentially dangerous. Non-gay men need to learn an awareness of homophobia from us.

After an *Achilles Heel* meeting we decided to go for a drink in a local pub. I was wearing a badge with the word gay clearly readable on it. Immediately I was picking up hostile reactions – men staring at me, nudging their friends, talking about me knowing that I could hear them. I became very tense, standing taut, staring them out if I caught a man's eye. I felt very uncomfortable and intimidated. I stayed close to the men I was with. I wondered what they'd do if something happened. Chris held my hand seeing my tension and asked if I wanted to leave. I said that I was feeling threatened by the reactions of the men around us but that it was our space as much as theirs. We continued talking. We finished our drinks and left. Outside on the pavement we all said goodbye, hugging and kissing as usual, at the same time other people from the pub were also leaving and moving past or around us. I was glad that I was travelling home with Chris, two felt safer than one alone.

In this situation I expected these men, my brothers, to be aware of the hostility that was being presented and to be supportive to me. It is important that gay men know that non-gay men sense the hostility that we receive and support us in dealing with it. A clear definition between those who shun gays and those who support us needs to be discernible. Those who shun gays share a number of unstated assumptions of which the most important is that something is wrong when a person diverges from the usual (to their eyes) pattern of existence. Some express their attitude with ugly open hostility, by jibes, insults or physical attack. Those who support us should work on any doubts or fears they have and be prepared to consider sharing gay experience and openly express their support of us, for homophobia will only fail to exist when straight society sees it as their problem which they must eradicate.

Not all gay men
have hair on their chests
shave regularly, work often
and whilst walking through the streets
spit like a virile male
to clear the throat
of last nights/early morning cum.

Some
dream in falsetto
naked under sheets
curled in foetal position
wear eyeshadow and lipgloss
leather boots with denim
purse lips like movie queens
or sprinkle sunshine smiles as they pass
strangers who think pleasurable of
the variety of men.

> (with thanks to Paul Mariah whose poem
> 'Misrepresentation' stimulated this one)

Acknowledgement

I would like to thank Ronald Grant, Tony Landsberg, Noel Grieg and the *Achilles Heel* collective for their help, advice, love, support and criticism during the writing of this article.

Martin Humphries
September 1981

Notes

* A cottage is a public lavatory used by gay men to meet for sex either there or elsewhere.

† Closetted men are those who acknowledge that they are gay to themselves but not to others.

1 See CHE report 'Attacks on gay people'.
2 *Society and the Healthy Homosexual* by George Weinberg.
3 'Being Gay and Jewish' by Martin Kriegar.
4 *Gay News*, 1 May 1980.
5 'Homosexuality and liberation – elements of a gay critique' by Mario Mieli.
6 'Gay politics: sixteen propositions for the eighties' by Michael Denny.
7 *Cruising* a violently homophobic novel by Gerald Walker which is also sexist and racist containing examples of every anti-gay attitude I've ever met.

SEXUALITY AND MALE VIOLENCE

> Every woman adores a Fascist,
> The boot in the face, the brute
> Brute heart of a brute like you.
> (Sylvia Plath)

I can think of no culture which does not, in some way, confront the issue of violence: sometimes by eulogizing it; sometimes in an attempt to banish it. The west, at least since the advent of capitalism, has sought to control and channel violence to its own ends, largely through the development of oppressive sciences of a military, or paramilitary kind.

A weighty literature has arisen around the issue, yet only in the past 50 years or so has there been an attempt to discuss violence in the context of sexuality, where it has, nevertheless, an important historical place. Most importantly, the women's movement has dealt explicitly with the relationship between sexuality and violence. At the moment, with the worldwide media coverage given to such public displays of violence as the Yorkshire Ripper murders, there is an atmosphere of tension and urgency especially among those who have been, or fear being, victims.

While men inflict violence on each other, and women sometimes initiate, or participate in violence, it is usually the case that in the context of our private lives it is men who are violent and women who are the victims. In the sphere of organized, 'legitimate' violence, for example in war or sports like boxing, violence becomes a contest between men (often with women as the prize). But in life as it is experienced from day to day, that is not the case.

This article is an attempt to redress an uneasy balance. For the most part it is women who have made painful attempts at unravelling and understanding what is involved in violence. Men have remained, on the whole, conspicuously silent: not that in our various roles as doctors, psychologists, sociologists, politicians and teachers we haven't spoken and written reams about the phenomenon of violence and frequently acted as though we had some special access to the experience of victims of violence. What we have done is to distance ourselves from violence through professionalism or exclamations of horror, and evade the crucial issue which women cannot confront for us: what it is to *be* violent, and what that violence means for our existence as men.

I have chosen to concentrate on sexual violence since it is here that there is least understanding. In the argument I am putting forward there is an attempt to establish a crucial link between violence and sexuality. This will involve an outline, first, of the way in which the historical conditions for the kind of violence we experience at the moment is supplied by the relationship between patriarchy, the family and the state. Then, I want to concentrate on what I see to be the reason why so many men resort to violence, which resides in a sexual conflict of language and perception at very particular personal levels.

The most recognizable form of sexual violence is rape. But I want to get away from the habit of discussing rape as a singular event and look more at the distressing range of violences which are sexually related and which, it seems to me, make rape not simply a possibility but a logical outcome of what our society generally sees as 'normal' sexual relations. Not only is that the case, but the very act of ascribing normality to particular forms of sexual behaviour – heterosexual fucking – sets up the conditions for violence. The reasons for aggression towards gay men and lesbians are very complex, but in this context I shall see them as stemming from the arrogant reduction of sexuality to the power of the phallus: this allows men a sense of justice in the intrusions they make on homosexuals, yet ironically is tied up in the threat and danger posed by non-heterosexual relationships and behaviour.

While I am convinced that in various forms the entire range of human relationships is sexual, I shall confine my arguments to behaviour which at some point becomes recognizably sexual, involving some form of sensuousness and the expression, however directly, of desire. Similarly, I shall limit the sense in which I understand violence. It can be argued that in subtle ways all kinds of manipulation and control are violent in that they operate against someone's will or against their best interests. But I will be particularly concerned here with acts which, through physical power or verbal coercion, inflict an immediate damage on the victim. That damage may be emotional or mental as well as physical, and may be inflicted through verbal abuse, threat, imprisonment (whether in a state institution or in the home), or physical assault.

Patriarchy, the family and the state

The history of the capitalist state, the fundamental importance of the family within it, and the new exercise of patriarchal power that has resulted, are important for any discussion of violence and the possibilities of resistance to it. Yet they have also provided a form in which the left has been able to depersonalize its account of violence. Central to my argument is the importance of violence in reproducing, at grass-roots level, the coercive power of patriarchy and capital. To avoid analysis of the individual exercise of such power is to miss the boat entirely. For this reason I have started with a briefly sketched outline of that history before looking at a number of ways in which individualized violence both expresses and generates it.

Since the sixteenth century, the development of capitalist commodity production and its necessary organization around large stabilized workforces and markets has meant the development of wage labour and a consequent fragmentation of personal *and* work life. Where once it was possible for the majority of people to live and work together in community-based families, sharing to some extent (though not completely) the work involved in producing necessities, capitalist production has made such a structure impossible to maintain. With fewer men in control of the larger scale of productive activity, families have been forced to release members into a segregated workforce for a large period of the day, thus entrenching already existing dominations of women by men and drawing a harder line between their accepted spheres of operation.

Together with this change in the productive life of communities has come the development of professional, scientific institutions and ideologies whose position in the managerial and technological organization of industry has given them the power to determine what most of us perceive as normal, good, or inevitable. Thus, through filters of education, media, legislation and the sharing of these in private talk, we come to take as our assumed starting point the relationship between work and the family, and true respective roles of men, women and children in it.[1]

Patriarchy predates this history, and an extensive discussion would analyse the importance of patriarchy in making such a history possible. Patriarchy is a system of governance by which all men have some stake in determining the lives and histories of the women and children assigned by whatever system to their care. The hierarchy which operates within this structure of governance is thus shared out among the men, rather than including women who are reduced alike to their reproductive and domestic roles. Those women who break out have, at least until the recent advent of the women's movement, done so on male terms and individually.

The difference which capitalism has made to patriarchy is to take it out of the hands of individual men or communities and place it in the more scientific, professional hands of the state. Men are still invested with the dominant role within the family, and are encouraged to exercise the power they have developed over the history of our 'civilization'. (A discussion of the nature of this power comes later.) Yet this power has been narrowed considerably. State control say, in Britain, has taken over many of the functions once attached to the position of an individual patriarch. Education, the public care and welfare of children, taxation, and various forms of legislation around divorce, contraception and so on, are now secularized concerns handled by a professional bureaucracy. To that extent, the state has become the supreme patriarch. The extent to which individual men still exercise their power seems to depend on the intrusive power of the state in a particular society. Under fascism,

Ronald Grant

in both Germany and Italy, (though with remarkable differences occasioned, e.g. by the dominance in Italy of Catholicism) men exercised their power not as individual patriarchs but as compliant agents of a state crystallized in a single patriarch: a Hitler or a Mussolini.

Throughout the history of capitalism there have been significant periods in which we can see clearly and intensely both the individual and the collective expression of power through violence. For my purposes, the advent of fascism under Mussolini and Hitler raises questions which I think can help our understanding of violence in the context of sexuality without our falling into the conservative trap of laying the blame on individual pathologies, or into the left-scientific trap of blaming a ruling-class conspiracy. In the discussion which follows I am offering not a general analysis of fascism, but extracting a number of questions which are relevant to my topic.

Fascism and patriarchy

Under fascism, the key points of patriarchy are exaggerated. There is an increase in 'legitimate' institutional violence, organized and sanctioned by the state: men are forced, institutionally and ideologically, not only to accept without struggle the class positions they are thrust into, but to make a determined, enthusiastic ritual of it in the interests of a disciplined sexual and racial supremacy. While women are further isolated in the home through national and familial policy, there is an increase in violent sexual practices. In what appears to be a quasi-mystic brotherhood, men share out the power among themselves. Through a hierarchy of leadership culminating in the heroic figure of the dictator, there is a vicarious satisfaction of pleasure in power which seems to me sensuous as much as it is intellectual and emotional. The massive tyrannies of Hitler or Mussolini are reproduced by men, and exceptionally by a few women, in private form.

Such vicarious pleasure in power is not, I should add, exclusive to states which have gone all the way toward fascism. The fascination of the case of the Yorkshire Ripper is an interesting phenomenon here: not only has the case allowed men (in and out of the media) to express a paternalistic indignation at the public magnitude of Sutcliffe's violence, but to use the case to disguise our own collusion as well as taking from it whatever vicarious satisfactions are appropriate to our own personal misogynies and desires.

In the context of sexuality, one of the most interesting aspects of fascism is the way it reveals how willingly and easily men band together in this brotherhood to ritualize and extend the power historically vested in them. This occurs, I should add, in a way which at the same time strengthens and cuts across class structures. To explain this fully would need an analysis of the intricate relationship between class, sex and race which I'm not in a position to give. But I would like, at this stage, to confront a popular position on fascism and sexuality which seems to me rather dangerous.

It is consistently argued that there is some intrinsic relationship between the political form of fascism and what has been called 'pervasive' sexuality, most notably homosexuality and various forms of sadomasochism. Even in the work of some socialist film makers I admire, like Bertolucci and Liliana Cavani (*The Night Porter*), it is not merely assumed but actually pointed out that men and women with a tendency towards 'perverse' sexual desire develop, under the right conditions, a tendency towards political fascism. In an otherwise excellent film, *1900 (Novocento)*, directed by Bertolucci, there is a crucial scene in which a young fascist man and a woman rape a young boy. Then, with the woman participating on the sidelines with smiles and cries of encouragement, the man takes the boy by the legs and swings him around the room until his head smashes against the stone walls several agonizing and horrific times. It is a powerful scene, disturbing for its illumination of the terrible power of fascism, yet dismaying for its stark, unexplored equation of fascism with 'deviant' sexuality.

The truth in this common position needs to be flushed out. First, we need to disabuse ourselves of the assumption that sexual practice in relation to fascism is somehow present in our biology as though deviance, so defined, were genetically determined. Second, we need to efface the positivist ideals against which we measure sexual normality and deviation. Sexual violence is no more a part of homosexual practice than it is of heterosexual practice within the family. And third, it needs to be said that the argument developed in the episode from *Novocento* is no more plausible, but also no less dangerous, than the argument that rape is enacted by men with 'personality' problems giving vent to unfulfilled sexual desires. Susan Brownmiller's *Against Our Will*[2] is just one of many studies which points out clearly that rape takes place not as an extraordinary event but frequently within the family by men whose sexual life would be regarded by our society as perfectly normal.

It needs to be argued then, that as rape is an extension of male-dominated heterosexuality, so the development of patriarchy reaches its most extreme and recognizable (transparent) form in the kind of national fascism represented by Italy and Germany between the wars. The harnessed violence of that period was legitimized and nationalized by the violence inherent in patriarchy under capitalism at all levels: from the violence of power relations in the family, to that of the language in which heterosexual relations were, and still are, conducted. The extermination of the Jews, which we take as the representative expression of fascism, can be seen as a eugenics based on a highly selective, reproductive model of sexuality. To commit

Ronald Grant

genocide in the name of such a model does not seem to me extraordinary. It fits neatly with the model of the Holy Family developed by the Catholic Church, and in so far as the programme included homosexuals, it can be seen as a monstrous enactment of the kind of social vilification of homosexuals in so-called democratic societies like Britain and the United States.

Another important aspect of fascism is the way in which it sharpens and exaggerates the degree to which women often collude in the violence which assaults both them and others whose sexuality (and in some cases ideals) is regarded as abnormal. For fascism to triumph as it did in Italy and Germany, women's collusion is necessary. The most compelling argument I have read on this is an article by Maria Antonietta Macciocchi[3] where she claims that: 'The characteristic of Fascist and Nazi genius is their challenge to women on their own ground: they make women both the reproducers of life and guardians of death, without the two terms being contradictory.'[4]

The position of women, as Macciochi continues, is enshrined in a 'mystical femininity' whose two poles are administration to national and military heroes in the tradition of Florence Nightingale, and a reduction of sexuality to the model of reproduction on which eugenics is based. This means, for Macciocchi, the elimination of a sexual energy for women: '[Fascism uses] the skeleton of a language or a particular metalanguage to address women. The body of fascist discourse is rigorously chaste, pure, virginal. Its central aim is the death of sexuality.'[5]

While violence, like patriarchy, predates capitalism, it has developed new expressions and generated new forms of control and channelling. It has also, as I have already mentioned, generated new forms of analysis and explanation. It has been argued, by Sartre and Marcuse among others,[6] that violence occurs because, as men, we, too, are victims: of the aggressive alienation of work, of the constant bombardment of our senses and egos by capitalist media (including advertising). Our isolation in the work place and the frustrations and schizophrenia induced by the lack of control that goes with it – so the argument goes – supplies ripe conditions for individual aggression. And – it continues – because we eventually return to the home the most available object of aggression is the woman. Where work becomes scarce (as in Britain now) violence is more readily enacted on other men as well as women, and becomes more of a public show, gang-based rather than simply individual. We could add that racial and class tensions also become involved at this point.

Now at one level that is a convincing argument, and one that I would offer limited support. Yet it remains both descriptively evasive and non-explanatory. It doesn't confront the issue of why, after all, it is men on the whole who are the victims of that violence (though, as I have said before, this means neither that women are passive as victims, nor that they don't have the capacity to strike back with their violence). Because to the extent that we are victims, we still hold a power – *as men* – to enact rage and authority on those who have no power, or who have struggled for it against enormous odds. And despite the authority vested in us as men – as husbands, fathers, professionals – we still choose, deliberately or otherwise, to enact that power with the hand, to communicate not in a language of gentleness but in and through the skin.

The language of sexual violence

I am interested in the way we, as individual men, use violence and develop something of a habit of it. In a general sense the will to violence and the enactment of it depend on an inheritance of the dynamics outlined in the last section. But there is still a complex process by which we learn its use and become, according to or against our will, agents of the power of patriarchy. I should stress here that even the most apparently gentle of men need consistently to deal with violence, either their own or that of others, and to recognize that even if we do not ourselves behave violently we bear the threat to women and a variety of minority groups.

How do we learn, in the first place, to speak a language of domination? There are many reasons, some of which can be seen if we look at what happens as we go from birth to what we have learned to call adulthood. The language we speak to our mothers moves, in that time, from the most intimate and sensual – the shared utterances of skin and first speech – to the tyrannical, the instrumental and the dismissive. At some time between birth and, say, 20, we learn to recognize our mothers as servant, nurse, giver of birth – that is, as socially inferior beings from whom, by a process we learn to ignore or disparage, we have somehow sprung. In this conflict between recognition and denial we lose the language of intimacy and the knowledge of our mothers we must once have had. The reality of the woman who gave birth to us and brought us up is reduced in our perceptions to its physicality.

This is the first violence, the severing of intimacy. We learn to identify with the father, real or absent, either through his example and teaching, or through the powerful indoctrinations of the media and education. Ironically, as sons we are in a position both to dominate and to be dominated. We dominate because, as male children, there is some special status attached to us and our development. We are encouraged to demand from our mothers, and later from other women, the nurturance and physical care that our early helplessness made necessary. We learn quickly that there is no need for us to produce the minutiae of our material or emotional lives: it will be done for us while we get on with the job of becoming men.

Many of us, I think, become little tyrants in the course of this development. A conflict arises, however, between our sense of the power thus given to us, and the everyday position of the mother in the home. While it is generally the case that discipline is ritualized in the province of the father – that is, we are dealt with when He comes home – the small and seemingly inconsequential disciplines and controls are enacted by the mother, especially at the early stage. While the generalized and dramatic discipline of the father engenders respect and in some cases, awe, partly because of his physical presence and partly because of his continual absences from the home, the littler disciplines of the mother come into conflict with our sense of her as servant and nurturer. I can remember early expressions of my own violence being 'caused' in this way by the indignant resentment I felt at being punished by someone who was simply a physical presence and one who, at the same time, was clearly scorned and not respected by my father. Even as an adolescent the bitterness and rage I felt at my father's unjust tyranny of discipline didn't make me as indignant and resentful as my mother's more desperate and less damaging methods of discipline.

It seems to me as well that the father, seeing the naked conflict between the dominating and the being dominated, challenges his own intimacy with the mother and sides with the son. This is what happens in the film *Ordinary People*, in which the director takes the side of father and son, seeing them as the 'natural' allies against the mother and eventually forcing her out of the script altogether. That didn't happen in the same way to me, but I recall as I think about it an ongoing struggle in which my father attempted to enlist my support against my mother, usually in terms of my intellectual development. My refusal for a variety of reasons to comply with this engendered its own set of violences, which operated through a kind of rage and fear at the power over me of this distanced, petty man.

The violence we enact first against our mothers is sometimes physical: we push them away, or hit out, or 'terrorize' in our boyish games. Or, as we grow older, it is carried through a look, through silence, or through tone. As we become adults, have girlfriends, lovers, wives, and mates, we have already learnt the habits of violence which, to my mind, become almost so automatic as to be inevitable *in some form*: whether the violence is enacted on someone else or turned inwards in self-destructiveness, it is still there, part of the abrasive conflict between ourselves and the world.

James Swinson

One way of understanding this I think is to look at the languages of men which precede violence against women and to a certain extent against other men as well: languages which, as I have already discussed with reference to the article by Macciocchi, reduce women to their physicality while organizing their sexuality around a reproductive or passive model, and release men to determine the range and variety of their own sexuality. I don't, here, mean language merely as the spoken or written word, but as the range of means by which relationships are communicated and articulated. As words are a way of organizing thought and perception, so fucking, for example, is a way of organizing desire. If our desire is tied up with the kind of attitudes to women discussed so far, then that will become apparent in our fucking. If we are challenged by the women we desire, then it is inevitable that fucking in some way becomes violent, involving the display of physical power which is the most concrete basis for our domination.

As agents of patriarchy, reproducing it to a greater or lesser degree as individual men, we have developed a language of what I would like to call determinations. This, I should stress, is a language which cuts across class and racial boundaries and is present in educated and illiterate speech alike. The articulate language of academia is just one example, albeit a very powerful one, of this 'language of determinations'. Because it is limited and to a certain extent fossilized, it can be learnt by passing through endurance tests in the development of specialized vocabularies. What I mean is something more basic: it is language which, on the whole, is removed from the minutiae of private life and which reflects a concern with broad, assumed categories of behaviour and perception.

Our daily needs

We learn such a language during the process discussed earlier of growing into adulthood. But it doesn't stop there. Most of us, as men, have not on the whole *had* to attend to the satisfaction of our daily needs. At work, these are supplied by the employer and frequently administered by women and low-paid workers – especially non-white people – such as tea women, secretaries and cleaners. This will vary according to class position: bosses have secretaries, workers don't. But the structure of the patriarchal–capitalist work force is such that even the worst-paid male workers can be sure that there will be someone, usually a woman, less skilled and less well paid and doing more shit work. If not, then there is the home where our needs are supplied by mothers, wives, girlfriends and daughters. What is most extraordinary is that it is not just a single, narrow set of needs that is satisfied by women, but a majority of them. Our subsistence is supplied, our egos are cosseted either by a tactful woman companion or by some victory in the war for possession of women as objects, our frustrations are soothed and our desire received. Where work and the family, as two separate domains, do not supply these needs, they can be obtained from women in other ways. Most significantly, porno-graphy and prostitution have taken on the dual roles of catering for those who are not 'successful' in the normal domains, and of supplying us with the most plastic, malleable objects of desire. Pornographic images are unreal in the sense that they are filtered technically and structurally to remove the wrinkles. But they change to keep slightly ahead of the current mode of objectification. In *Penthouse*, for example, it is no longer enough that women are portrayed as inviting men to devour and demolish their bodies, but narratives are constructed around individual models to allow a more personalized access to the image. What remains the same is that such images could only be the products of objectification, and cater for a perception in which there is nothing more to women than a physical willingness to be penetrated. The same is to a certain extent true of prostitutes. The difference there is that money and reality intrude and deny the possibility of complete control by men. Out of this, I think, and out of a parallel moral conflict in men engendered by the dual role of women as 'damned whore and god's police', comes the attenuated vulnerability of prostitutes to male violence.

This satisfaction of our ongoing daily needs has, on the whole, given us as men the freedom and opportunity to develop a language which need confront and contain only the truth of our own, self-contained, masculinist world. Our assumptions and perceptions thus become so generalized as to part company with the recurring machinery of daily life. It is frequently pointed out that men are perfectly good at doing things which need some general engineering perceptions, but that the finer details are often missed out. I think that's very true. We need look only as far as the kitchen or child's bedroom to see it in action. I remember being taken aback and mortified when I was looking after children on a daily basis and was pleased with myself for the success I was having in getting them dressed in the morning. The problem was, I kept asking their mother what they should wear, where the socks and knickers and other little things were kept, until she got so pissed off that she pushed me aside and did it herself. It is a question, I think, of men failing to take responsibility for the things we regard as petty but which are primary and essential to life.

The fact that as men we are taught and encouraged to think and feel in generalities means that we demean those areas of production which we see as petty. For the most part, it is women who carry out those functions, and they therefore take on an appropriate status. Those of us who have somehow been forced to recognize the importance of such activities find that the recognition challenges our sense of our own importance so thoroughly that we can frequently become abusive as a result. An example: seeing myself as a writer, often locked myself away from the house I was living in to get on with the job of writing, which I valued very highly and expected everyone else to value as well. This meant that childcare, cooking, and cleaning up became the responsibility of those whose work was less important than mine. This is a familiar scenario. What I think is significant is that when I was challenged about my withdrawal, physically and emotionally, I became frustrated and resentful that she did not understand the importance of what I was doing. I also managed to channel guilt into my response, which ended in clenched fists, verbal abuse, and finally my kicking a hole in the kitchen door. I suspect that in various ways the same kind of violent response has been experienced by most men.

'Nagging'

The most common experience of such a response is to what we have learned to call nagging. Nagging is insistence. Yet as men at work or in education we live daily with many forms of insistence to which our response is different. Why is it, then, that when it is women in the home who insist that we recognize a need or that we do something really useful, we often respond in rage or assault? One reason is that what is being insisted on frequently confronts us with what we want to evade, thus forcing us to consider or act on something which alters our sense of ourselves. Another is because it denies the harmony, agreement and collusion on which our authority and importance are based. What makes it irritating to the point of violence is that this is a truth coming from nowhere, from beneath us. The supposed invisibility of its source has changed, and we are confronted with what we do not wish to accept. Thus, for those of us involved in alienated work situations, the expected language of comfort and ego-building has altered and become a language nearing truths that are threatening in both their sense and their delivery.

Because women are understood in terms of their reproductive function, their domestic position and their physicality, it is in those terms that the phallic power of male sexuality is expressed in penetration. Because they operate for us in the physical domain, it is women's bodies we penetrate. When we can't penetrate women's minds, we deny their importance, evade their questioning, and relegate them to petty categories. For the most part this works, and over the centuries women have been forced to comply by developing languages of their own which we call 'intuition', 'gossip' and so on. It is when that language threatens to move our of our control, or challenges our understanding and authority, that we become violent. Because it is only through abuse, assault and battering, that we can establish and maintain the dominance which supplies us with our sense of ourselves.

Similarly, when women begin to assert their own sexuality, especially if that does not involve a dominant position for the man, the response is frequently automatic violence (though sometimes it is organized as in gang rape). Attacks on lesbian women, on prostitutes and women who appear aggressive in some way (for example, academics) seem to me the result of this kind of reaction. A combination of phallic arrogance and threat is involved. In the more frequent cases of rape within the family, for example, the threat may not be there but the arrogance is, on top of the assumption because a girl or a woman is no more than her body, it doesn't really matter.

Given the reality of violence, it has become the habit to explain it away as a legitimate response to nagging, or an urgency of desire. Were I to explain it that way to a judge and jury at the Old Bailey I would probably, on recent evidence, get away with it. Where the extent of violence becomes intolerable, as in the case of the Yorkshire Ripper murders, we either reduce the question to one of 'individual psychosis' and thus evade our own complicity, or fall back upon our position as 'protectors'. Much of the public urgency surrounding the Ripper investigation was the indignant response to the threat Sutcliffe posed to other men's women. Indirectly, the same response made it possible for prosecuting counsel Sir Michael Havers to make a moral distinction between the prostitutes and the murder of women who were girlfriends or daughters.

Much of what needs to be done is being done now. Women are organizing perhaps more than they have ever done before to resist and combat the proliferation of sexual violence. But rather than retreating into silence, men need to come out now with attempts at getting to the bottom of why we resort to violence, and doing something about it at that level. Pious moralism is more dangerous even than silence. This article, while making no claims to being exhaustive, is an attempt to move the discussion of violence on to our ground, where we can make some sort of contribution to understanding and resistance.

Peter Bradbury
October 1981

Notes

1 Two accounts of this history that I have found useful and absorbing are Ann
  Foreman: *Femininity as Alienation* (London: Pluto, 1977); and Eli Zaret-
  sky: *Capitalism, the Family and Personal Life* (New York, 1976).
2 Susan Brownmiller: *Against Our Will: Men, Women and Rape* (London:
  Secker and Warburg, 1975).
3 Marie-Antonietta Macciochi: 'Female sexuality in fascist ideology.' *Feminist
  Review* 1 (1979).
4 Ibid, p. 69.
5 Ibid, p. 75.
6 See Herbert Marcuse: 'Aggressiveness in advanced industrial society', in
  Negations (London: Allen Lane, 1968); and Jean-Paul Sartre, *Critique of
  Dialectical Reason* (London : New Left Books, 1976).

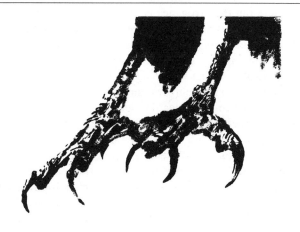

MACHISMO POLITICS: REAGAN AND EL SALVADOR

In his brilliant essay in *The Male Machine*[1] called 'Viet Nam and the
cult of toughness in foreign policy', Marc Fasteau traces through US
Presidents Kennedy, Johnson and Nixon and their policy makers the
tendency to make their foreign policy in accordance with a strong
personal desire or need to be seen as 'tough'. Fasteau details his
amazement at the lack of real evidence, even for the reasons publicly
given, for the early involvement of the US in Vietnam, and claims,
partly by analysing the language and the reported remarks of the
Presidents, that such personal concepts as 'tests of will' played an

enormous part in the decisions that were made: 'The test of will seemed at most an end in itself rather than a means to a political end.'

Of Vietnam, Kennedy said: 'We have a problem trying to make our power credible, and Vietnam looks like the place.' West Berlin he called 'the greatest testing place of Western courage and will', and of the US intervention of Cambodia, Nixon said: 'It is not our power but our will and character that are being tested tonight .... When I have to face an international crisis, I have what it takes.' Fasteau regards Johnson the most overt in his conscious association of aggressive foreign policy with his own sexuality; witness his remark following the bombing of targets inside North Vietnam: 'I didn't just screw Ho Chi Minh, I cut his pecker off.'

Men 'live out their masculinity' the world over. Patriarchy. When one of those men happens to be a ruler/president of the US, the power he wields means that, by some crazy mathematics, the smallest twitch of his insecurity can lead directly to the deaths of thousands of men, women and children. And the expectation of most of his brothers is that he should act precisely like that.

'Power accrued to the "can-do" men, men whose mastery took the form of visible action, not those who expressed doubts.... To answer "Nothing", to the question "What can be done about disagreeable development X?" was passive, the mark of a loser and a weakling.' Towards the end of the essay Fasteau writes:

> We may even avoid ... Vietnams of the future. But the lesson of enduring value – the lesson that our policy is in danger of being pushed in stupid, costly and dangerous directions by the cult of toughness – has not and will not be learned from public debate which does not focus critically on the existence and influence of the biases created by the masculine ideal.

In 1977 I travelled through Central America, staying a week in San Salvador. My knowledge of Latin American politics was scarcely deeper than the stereotypical western view of this collection of crazy little countries always having revolutions and coups in between harvests and hurricanes. I was on my way to Peru to look at ruins and mountains. The week I was in San Salvador General Romero had just faked another election win. Various opposition groups were 'generously allowed' to hold a weekend-long mass meeting in one of the central squares of the city on the condition that they dispersed by midnight on Sunday. I was amazed at strangers coming up to me, an obvious foreigner, saying 'please take our story out of El Salvador, it's impossible to tell the world what's happening here'; and in cafes coming over, telling how desperate people were, no chance of a living wage even if you have got a job; and so much fear. At midnight the meeting was still there. Tanks appeared from the side streets; some 70 people were shot there and then, the entire centre of the city sealed off again, and further hundreds killed over the next few days.

Since then, I have followed, and felt a lot closer to events there, and in Central America generally.

But I felt what I am sure many post-war Europeans have felt at their first experience of the activities of extreme fascist, militaristic regimes, so helpless, and scared, in the face of their violence. And later, safely back in England, comparatively safe at least as a middle-class, straight, white man, sometimes I couldn't help thinking how peripheral, trivial were our concerns, politically and in the men's movement. Hadn't some Latin American women, at the International Conference and in articles in the press recently said that feminism as we know it was a largely irrelevant luxury when you are fighting for your survival?

Apart from a few statements of fact, the press cuttings which follow in rough chronological order contain what people have said, rather than editorial or interpretative material.[2] The parallels between what Fasteau talks about in relation to Vietnam and previous US Presidents, and Reagan, Haig and co. and El Salvador are clear even down to the ludicrous 'evidence' story. Indeed the wide opposition which is now manifest in Congress and in the country to any major military involvement in El Salvador and the growing alarm at the brutality employed by the regime, spectacular even by Latin American standards yet sanctioned by the US government, throws Reagan's investment in El Salvador into awful relief. Despite the great differences between the situation in El Salvador and Vietnam, Reagan's foreign-policy stance underlines Fasteau's thesis in a particularly graphic and alarming way.

16.2.81 Central American Representatives of Joint Commission of FMLF and FDR:[3] 'The trouble with the US decision makers is that they believe the propaganda they themselves have invented, and then design policy on the basis of those myths.'

18.2.81 In a briefing to Congressional leaders in Washington, the Secretary of State, General Haig, said there was 'hard evidence' that left-wing guerrillas in El Salvador were receiving arms from Cuba, Ethiopia and Vietnam.

23.2.81 Mr Haig told Allied ambassadors in Washington that the United States:

> will not remain passive in the face of this Communist challenge ... and it's time that Cuba and the other nations that seek to subvert other counties wake up to the fact that we have a new Administration, a new national resolve, and we will take the steps that are to keep the peace any place in the world – and that includes El Salvador.... We believe in all sincerity we have no alternative but to act to prevent forces hostile to the US and the West from overthrowing a government on our doorstep, particularly when that government offers the best hope of progress towards moderate democracy.

The Americans are leaning on evidence drawn from guerrilla documents captured over the past few weeks. These, they maintain, show plainly the extent of outside countries' involvement in the supply and shipment of arms to the people's revolutionary army.

Ex-El Salvador Army Captain, now joined the FMLN[4] speaking of his experience of the Army: 'beheading and sexual mutilation were standard procedures'.

4.3.81 Mr Haig views the conflict in El Salvador as a test of US will.

6.3.81 In Washington, the row about American policy in El Salvador continued with claims that Cuban and Russian 'interference' there had become a test of President Reagan's resolve.

5.3.81 Lord Carrington: 'I think that President Reagan had no alternative, in the light of what is happening and the subversion by the Soviet Union and Cuba, to support the present Salvadorian Government.'

7.3.81 Reagan:

> The situation here, you might say, is in our front yard.... It isn't just El Salvador. What we are doing is going to the aid of a Government that asked for help against guerrillas and terrorists ... who aren't just aiming at El Salvador but who are aiming at the whole of Central and South America, I'm sure, eventually North America.

By aiding the defence forces, the US was 'Helping forces which are keeping human rights in El Salvador.'

March 81 8000 Salvadoran refugees attempted for two days to cross the River Lempa ... while the Salvadoran Air Force dropped bombs and strafed them, and the Army fired mortar shells and machine guns. FDR/FMLN representatives in France: '... repression without precedent like that of Sumpul near the Honduran border, where pregnant women were mutilated, raped, and their foetuses removed from the wombs with machetes.'

12.3.81 'The US yesterday declined to support the appointment of a special UN investigator into human rights violations in El Salvador, after the UN Human Rights Commission called for an end to the supply of arms to the country ...'

April 1981 Bulletin of El Salvador Solidarity Campaign:[5]

> Over 1500 children, women and old people were fleeing towards the Honduran border to escape from 'cleaning operations' by the Salvadoran army around San Francisco Gotera.... They had taken refuge in caves.... The army received reports of people hiding in caves and without warning filled them with poisonous gas. Those who tried to escape from the cave were killed by artillery fire.... There were no survivors ...

Reagan: 'Those who say we are in a time when there are no heroes, they just don't know where to look.'

27.4.81 Government forces have massacred 13,000 people in one year.

El Salvador Commission on Human Rights:

> We do not know what the chemicals are that do this to the skin, but it strips it all off. There is a body of a young woman, her torso dressed in a bright patch-work T-shirt, the flesh of her face stripped to the skull.... Decapitated bodies, children, students, trucks full, lorry loads, breasts cut off, eye balls shot out, explosive bullets entering through the chest and exiting through the head, and always the tell-tale signs of the security forces, thumbs tied behind the victims' backs with nylon rope. Anything vile you might ever imagine could happen to a human body.

May 81 *Spare Rib*. Miriam Galdemez, FDR representative in Europe:

> Nobody has seen any Russian sub-machine guns or tanks in El Salvador but they have seen plenty of US ones .... Tons of military arms that are being used to kill the people. Green Beret paratroopers who are already inside the country. We are also fighting

US imperialism, which has dominated our country and backed the oligarchy, because the oligarchy does its dirty work. What people don't know is that the US has been intervening in El Salvador for years training officers in techniques of counter insurgency; spying; imposing programmes of population control; sterilising women without their consent; dumping dangerous drugs which kill us. Many things. Had it not been for the US my people would have been at the door of their liberation many years before now.

El Salvador Solidarity Campaign Bulletin: James Cheek, Assistant Secretary of State for InterAmerican Affairs: 'We have never maintained that this government (El Salvador) has broad-based popular support ... it is not looking for popular support.' Salvador Army Officer: 'If it took the slaughter of 32,000 in 1932 to quell the revolt, and if it takes the slaughter of 100,000 today, so be it.'[6]
15.6.81 Noam Chomsky:

> The cold war ... a marvellous device by means of which the domestic population could be mobilised in support of aggressive and interventionist policies under the threat of the superpower enemy.... It is a very unstable system and could blow up at any time. But planners of both sides are willing to accept this risk for the utility of being able, in the case of the US to control its Grand Area, and of the Soviet Union, its minor Grand Area.

9.6.81 The document on which the State Department relied to persuade Allied leaders to back American policy in El Salvador was yesterday described by its principal author as 'misleading' and 'overembellished'.
El Salvador Solidarity Campaign bulletin: a leaked draft document from the CIA's Foreign Assessment Centre concludes 'the evidence (see 18.2, 23.2.81, etc.) is murky at best and at times there is none'. However the CIA's own report may never see the light of day. Defence Secretary Caspar Weinberger and CIA director William Casey are 'asking' the team to change their conclusions. Philip Agee, former CIA agent analysing the reported documents 'captured' from the guerrillas which the US based their international media campaign on foreign involvement in El Salvador (except their own) has stated they are complete fabrications.

To look at the question of the US policy makers' decisions from Fasteau's angle in this way is not of course to present a total picture of the overall process. For one thing it overlooks the extraordinary hypocrisy whereby they seek to divert attention from the massive US military aid to the regime in El Salvador, by affecting horror about, and pouring condemnation on any supposed or actual flow of arms to the guerrillas from elsewhere. (It makes little difference which.) It also concentrates, in the manner of most of the UK press coverage, from which many of the cuttings above are taken, on the rottenness of the Junta and the stance of the US, rather than on the strengths of the FMLN itself, the powerful involvement of women in all aspects of their struggle, the support for its ideas throughout the Salvador society. These last are anyway of little concern to Reagan, who sees them mainly as *representing* this thing out there he feels he has to fight.

Also, as Fasteau describes, it is characteristic that this aggressive posturing shows itself mainly in foreign, rather than domestic policy. Not even a US president could afford electorally to gamble in such a way in the field of home issues. There is perhaps an analogy to be drawn here by taking the 'masculine' imagery further: Reagan needs his support at home at all costs, to stay where he is. Away from home he can be aggressive and disgusting in his affairs on the side with this or that little number. Reagan keep your prick out of El Salvador. And everywhere else!

Nor does this piece intend to claim that US presidents and secretaries of state have a monopoly on such motivations in foreign policy. It does exhibit itself peculiarly blatantly in them because of the premium placed at the heart of American life on tough maleness. The 'winning' of the West. The appalling irony of Reagan's past(?) career, acting cowboys. But the covering of personal insecurities through aggressive political action is worldwide, not least in the arms race and in the whole question of nuclear 'defence'.

To see the process, and to see it reinforced by the expectations of masses of people, is to have no option but to put male sexual politics at its most vital in a place very much more central to world affairs then it has so far occupied. It's precisely because political action is largely defined by, measured by such supposed qualities as decisiveness, courage, will, that so many world leaders, male and quasi-male have wrought such havoc for so long on the poor and oppressed, on women and all of us. If non-sexist men together could grow to exert influence politically (as women, and in some areas gays, have in the US) by supporting feminist politicians, and encouraging any hint in male politicians of a rejection of the traditional ways of operating, misusing trust and power, abusing opponents, macho posturing, then there will be a change.

Tom Weld
September 1981

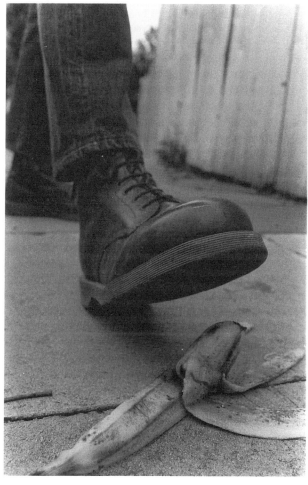

James Swinson

Notes

1 Marc Fasteau, *The Male Machine* (Dell Publishing Co.: New York, 1975).
2 All quotes from the *Guardian* or *Sunday Times* except where otherwise indicated.
3 FMLF and FDR; FMLF: anglicized initials of FMLN, see note 4. FDR: Democratic Revolutionary Front, now part of the FMLN.
4 FMLN: Faribundo Marti Liberation Front, see note 6.
5 El Salvador Solidarity Campaign, 29 Islington Park Street, London, N1.
6 1932 was the year of the peasant rebellion lead by Faribundo Marti. It was suppressed, with 32,000 deaths, by the military government which seized power in 1931 and has remained in one form or another ever since. The FMLN is named in honour of the peasant leader.

Chapter 6

Men's health
Body and mind

SEX WITH CONTRACEPTION

A woman to whom one of us mentioned our intent to write this article said with some bitterness and anger: 'What are men doing writing about contraception?' Many women and men seem to have concluded that if women bear the risk of pregnancy, men ought not to be involved in sharing decisions about contraception. However, as we are opposed to sexism, we have assumed that men should take more interest in and responsibility for contraception. But when, four months ago, we started talking about our experiences, we found that each of us had failed pretty fundamentally to develop a sexual practice which avoided the risk of pregnancy. As we had generally become more 'liberated', more knowledgeable about different devices, more open to our partners and more responsible, so the problems involved in avoiding pregnancy increased.

Our developing awareness, our experience with self-defined feminist women, seem to exist alongside deeply rooted, rather primitive definitions of our sexuality. We started by exploring what was actually happening in sex that made contraception so difficult: problems of communication, lack of clarity about who was responsible for what. In some ways these issues had become more difficult – perhaps because the preconditions for satisfying our needs for emotional and passionate relationships were to discard our intellectual control.

'I can't explain my confusion'

We'd known each other for 12 years and now we were in bed together for the first time. Sitting by the fire, whatever we'd been talking about, my mind had kept coming round to the idea of us sleeping together. It got later and later. Eventually she suggested

it, I wasn't ready, but then, after a few microseconds as nonchalant-
ly as possible I said in a careful sort of way 'Yeah, that would be
okay', acknowledging whatever it was, I wanted it too.

It was nice the two of us in bed, I quite unexpected her desire to
touch me and offer her body's warmth. We started to feel closer
and gradually I realized that the light softness between her legs was
different to anyone else, her hidden beauty. We didn't know each
other and yet we were starting to make love – I wasn't sure this was
right and as we were getting excited and close to fucking I said
questioningly 'What about contraception?' A few seconds later
she said, now firm and mature, 'It doesn't matter.' I waited patiently,
trying to understand and as I waited I sensed a closing up. I asked
again – there was no answer. And now 6 months later after another
night together, I'm still confused. Was she too involved to care? Too
unwilling to talk about herself? Had I created the distance? But I
feel good and we're friends – and maybe one day ... who knows what?

Behind this however, we began to realize we didn't understand why
we were actually having sex. Neither of the two traditional reasons –
procreation and pleasure – fitted. 'Therapeutic' explanations worked
only a little better. Sex has been on occasion a 'beautiful experience',
but this doesn't explain the enormous investment we were making for
this particular 'beautiful experience'. Moreover, we seemed satisfied
when it wasn't beautiful, a satisfaction which wasn't replaceable by
even the most intense physical and emotional release of masturbation. Sex and having a sexual relationship has often been a crutch
with which to face a destructive world.

One of us considered that in sex he had found a missing part of his
masculinity – he felt unable to create that outside of being 'possessed'
by sexual passion with/for some (mainly women) friend.

Needing to have sex in order to express himself. But this lays a
terrible burden on contraception, because heterosexual sex cannot
ultimately be divorced from pregnancy. The risk is always there, to
create a fantasy world in which emotional conflicts can be explored
through the vagina communicating with the penis places acute demands
on our ability to cope physically with contraception.

It is a dangerous game where the object is to keep in control of contraception whilst letting go of everything else. It's a bit like being into rock-
climbing – the better you get the more dangerous the game becomes.

For 18 months now Jane and I have been together, learning about each other, about our bodies, about how to make love together, and about contraception. We use three methods – Durex, the cap and Jane checks on her ovulation by examining her mucous and sometimes using a thermometer. We don't get on too well – we've split up a lot – and sometimes our being together is strangely distant. But we can acknowledge and talk about it. Sex has always been important. We spend a lot of time in bed having a bit of a cuddle, then stopping, penetrating a little, then coming a lot, talking a lot. It's felt like a growing process. Gradually we've made less mistakes. I've come inside her less often when she's unprotected. Eventually we got contraception under control. Then we split up for a bit. Then she found out she was pregnant. I couldn't believe it. After all those mistakes. We're always so careful nowadays – there was only one possible occasion – she used the cap. Jane thinks her body has changed and the cap no longer fits. I feel guilty – I think it's because we fucked a bit and only then put the cap in. Perhaps there was semen in the Cooper's fluid.

Perhaps I came a bit. I feel my whole practice in fucking is wrong. I know now I wanted her pregnant, and that for me procreation is still bound up with sex. The Pope's got it right and procreation still rules.

One central problem is the lack of safe and effective methods. Nearly all medical research in the field goes towards looking for new methods for women and not for men, a classic example of the dominance in conventional western medicine of a male disregard for female anatomy, an attitude which moreover regards 'side-effects' as acceptable, although to the user so-called side-effects are just as much effects as the desired effect, here, of preventing pregnancy. Some researchers[1] wrote:

In recent years the Pill has largely supplanted condom use among sexually active couples (from 32% of couples in 1960 to only 15% of couples in 1972) ... [and] has become increasingly associated with several serious health risks.... The excessive 'high technology' bias of contraception research led to over $63.9 million being spent on hormonal and intrauterine methods in the US during 1976–7, and only $193,000 spent on barrier methods during the same period....
... Male doctors working in the contraceptive field do not regard male hormonal methods as being viable 'until at least the year

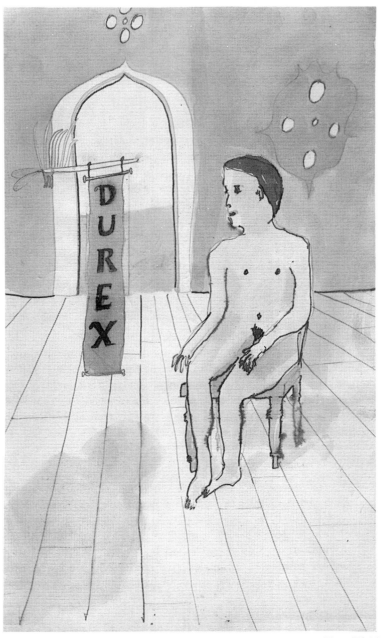

Tom Weld

2000. Ten years or even 30 years of research would probably not be enough to assure their safety.' On the other hand, 'Female hormonal contraception was introduced on the market after only five years of racially prejudiced research that is now considered to be of dubious ethical, methodological and scientific credibility.

The authors go on to argue that contraception techniques are tested under exploitive conditions in the Third World, and the way they are marketed puts profit before people's lives and health.[2]

The suppression in this country of some of the better forms of female contraception (cervical cap,[3] post-coital low-dosage pill[4]) points to a male conspiracy to keep sex and contraception a problem, to maintain men's control over women.

Men want 'their' women to be 'safe', to take care of contraception completely, but not in such a way that it allows the woman the freedom safely to have sex with someone else.

There's a deep-rooted idea that there should *not* be the perfect contraceptive, and that sex between women and men completely freed from any remainder of its reproduction function would somehow corrupt us.

Unlike sex, it is difficult for many men or women to get enthusiastic about contraception; it seems to be negative, about *not* doing, like locking things up, or wearing a crash helmet. There's an irresponsible part of most of us, certainly of me, which recoils at and would like to be free of involving ourselves in such non-productive precautions. There are also times in the lives of many women and men when, sometimes without acknowledging this, they want to know if they are fertile.

So many gaps between what we *know* and what we *do*. Very few people, especially those brought up as Catholics, ever really accept the validity of sex with contraception.

I cannot fail to draw attention to the negative phenomena which are a corruption of the idea and experience of freedom, with subsequent self-centredness in human relations. That means serious misconceptions about the relation between parents and children, the growing number of divorces, the scourge of abortion, and the spread of a contraceptive and anti-life mentality.

(the Pope in England)

What would 'perfect' contraception be like anyway? Is the search or desire for it as fruitless as the desire for the ultimate sexual experience, as marketed in pornography (where no one ever mentions contraception)? The Pill was billed as perfection at first, even as revolutionary perfection. In fact one major effect has been to shift responsibility for contraception firmly onto the woman. Before the Pill, the main method was the sheath, so that the man *had* to take responsibility. This combined with the probably greater fear than now for the women of getting pregnant, and of abortion/illegitimacy.

The Pill[5] meant for the woman – autonomy ... side-effects ... sole responsibility. Although clearly much more attention should be paid to developing more satisfactory mechanical and perhaps chemical contraception for women and especially for men, looking for an ideal method for *one* partner to solve the whole problem of contraception in a relationship is not likely to provide good answers.

It was a disaster if the sales assistant said 'I beg your pardon' so that I had to repeat the word in what seemed like a raucous shout, the other customers looking at me as if I had a large blue penis sticking out of each ear. Twenty-one years old, nearly married, my first sexual relationship with a woman involving intercourse. Buying Durex in a shop felt like – was – announcing to the public: I AM GOING TO FUCK WITH A WOMAN IN THE VERY NEAR FUTURE. That was difficult and intensely embarrassing, both because I still felt a 'romantic' distaste for sex being anything other than spontaneous and unplanned, and because I also at that stage still thought of sex as somehow possibly dirty, and certainly didn't want to be seen by strangers having anything to do with it.

Machines in pub toilets were wonderful but I never quite trusted them, with things like 'Beware – second-hand stock' scratched into the grey paint of the battered dispensers, remarks which seemed all too plausible. And they clank horribly when you turn the handle. As for the 'exotic' selections you can buy from mail order firms, mine arrived in an anonymous brown envelope – good. But 'French' this and 'Turkish' that turn out to look and feel like those moulds for plaster-of-Paris figures – (set of six, The Three Wise Men and their Camels).

Many more men could/should consider, and having vasectomies: 'In Britain about 100,000 female sterilizations are performed each year and the number of vasectomies is not much smaller. Over a quarter of couples, one partner or the other will have been sterilized by the time the wife is 35.'[6]

However, vasectomy confers very unequal benefits as soon as either wishes to sleep with another, as the woman is then unprotected. This is no reason for a man to discount vasectomy, but is something a couple in which the man has had one may need to consider.

Any 'invisible' method, IUD, cap, pill, vasectomy, safe period – can be problematical when there is an issue of trust. One partner may never be sure the other really has taken precautions. It's probably unusual for any one method to remain satisfactory for many years. What all these considerations, and all the stories, point towards is a situation where both partners, in short- or long-term relationships – i.e. everyone, male or female with any possibility of a sexual relationship of any kind – has access to contraception all the time. If he has not had a vasectomy, the man always having and always offering to use condoms is one way the woman can really feel he is sharing responsibility for contraception.

All non-chemical or non-'side-effect' methods, Durex, cap, jelly, can become less of a mystery, more a part of sex if both partners involve themselves putting them on/in.

Acquiescing in the culture which makes sex a fantasy and seeks to ignore contraception leads to situations like:

He: Shall we have sex?
She: Okay.
He: Are you on the pill?
She: No, I use a cap.
He: Are you going to put it in then?
She: No, it's all right, I've got it in already.
He: Oh ... so you planned to have sex with me, did you?
She: Well, yes, I thought we *might*. ...

which in a new relationship *might* lead to positive developments, or might well not. Or, with Durex, the classic problem:

He: I'll just get fixed up ... (turns away, scrabbles under the pillow, on the table, under the bed; sounds of tearing paper ... Minutes later, still turned aside ...) I er ...

(though for one of us an advantage is that the rubber ring at the bottom of the sheath presses enough on the vas deferens sometimes to inhibit orgasm).

Rolling a Durex Featherlite over my erect penis with her help day

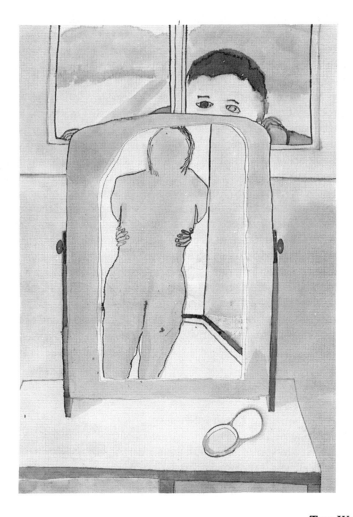

Tom Weld

after day for 10 years isn't going to remain a joyous experience, any more than together coating her cap with cream tasting of petrol, not very conducive to oral sex, and putting it in place. But in using these visible methods, sharing or being prepared to share their use is really important, and can help both partners become aware of the meaning of contraception.

A short walk from the cottage, we start kissing by the stream in the chestnut wood. Gradually we are both naked, and she takes me inside her standing up, last year's twigs and leaves don't look too soft, then she kneels and I'm behind her, and then we collapse on the ground anyway. I have ejaculated in her. She knows – and I know by now – she stopped taking her pills a few weeks before. And we've been through this before, much of our lovemaking similarly outdoors, spontaneous, essentially in circumstances and in a frame of mind where either premeditated or on-the-spot contraception would have seemed (or where each *thought* the other might think it seemed) ludicrous, bathetic, inappropriate.

This time she sits hopefully in the middle of the stream on the stones, I hoping nothing else swims into her and those others swim out.

Our first child was conceived a month or so after this in a similar way. For the next few years our indecision was directly reflected in how we approached contraception. Brief periods of the pill; an IUD, removed one night by pulling the string; the cap, only used once and usually in its box in the bathroom; Durex occasionally, often discarded during lovemaking; the use of the safe period either side of her fortunately clockwork-like ovulation, so finely calculated they almost met in the middle, and often, withdrawal, non-ejaculation, and attempts by her to make me come while inside her.

Finally last year deciding together to be pregnant again, living apart, meant my staying overnight on the right day; and to fuck without any thought of contraception, and to orgasm in order to make a child seemed in a way outlandish and almost anti-climatic after all that; and at the same time, wonderful and what I had always wanted to do.

These contradictions came after, and almost as a result of my awareness of feminism. Because it means women being independent, it can also mean more arguments, less communication and more problems with contraception. Seven years earlier, 'before' feminism:

We met when we were students. We became totally in love with each other. We had neither slept with anyone before; both ignorant about sex and contraception. We were very frightened of getting pregnant. After some early fumblings with condoms, I really expected her to go on the pill. It was down to her to find a doctor who would not tell parents or college and would co-operate.

Her being on the pill meant we could have sex without (my) thinking about contraception. Sex had to be, ought to be, and needed to be beautiful, spontaneous, the/a joyful expression of what was in other ways a lovely relationship. It never was, and *partly* because of contraception. When we wanted each other desperately at the beginning, we were too ignorant to contain, explore, savour our sexuality. By the time we knew a bit more, the pill had quite possibly taken its hormonal toll on her, which together with the psychological effect on her of repeatedly unsatisfying sexual experiences with me, very much reduced her desire for sex.

Later she used a cap because of the health dangers of the pill. I still sometimes shudder at the sight of those oval plastic boxes, from the time when I would look desperately for hers in her drawer, when she first had a sexual relationship with someone else.

For us, there was never a question of whether to use contraception or not. It was on the face of it a simple matter of choice. But I took very little, and then no responsibility. To me at the time all my attitudes about sex and contraception seemed quite natural; until her growing understanding of feminism began to affect this, and every other area of our lives.

For the same man, another side to the 'sexual revolution' resulted in:

We had talked theoretically about sex with other partners, realizing that much had to be lacking in our own sexual relationship. I talked to this woman with long, blonde curls at a party we were both at. I felt a determination to break my sexual monogamy, and somehow I decided she was to be the one I would try to use. I dropped my wife off first after the party – her husband was on nights. I went into her living room with her and in a few minutes I was lying on top of her. I never asked her about contraception. I went into her, came almost immediately. She said: 'You didn't did you? I didn't have anything.' I put my pants and trousers back on and walked out and drove home, feeling disgusted by the entire episode.

She saw me a year later in the street. She called over angrily, sarcastically to me: 'So you don't recognize me without the wig, eh?' I imagine why she was angry; I'd rather not think about it.

How a man and a woman approach fertility depends on some very fundamental aspects of their relationship. When both are confident that neither wants pregnancy, there can be a clarity about the choice and use of contraceptive, which isn't there when one or both feels unsure, when contraception can involve fear and mistrust and finally can become a battleground.

Friday she came home from work and made meat loaf. When they sat down at the table, she couldn't find her pills. She looked all over the table and then under it and then all round the kitchen counter. Finally, afraid already, she asked Jim.
'I poured them down the toilet.' He made a gesture of flushing. 'All down.'
She ran into the bedroom to look in her dresser. He followed.
'I flushed down next month too. No more pills. Now you'll have to shape up and do things the right way.'
'Why are you doing this to me? I don't want a baby! I don't want one right now!'
'Well, you're going to. Because you're my wife and I love you and you're supposed to love me. So you're to have a baby, and from now on we're going to have a real marriage.'[7]

Contraception is so easy. There are several really good devices available. Yet there's something strange about sex that stops our rationality. I can fix a meal or a bike, but we can't seem to put on a Durex at the right time or get out the diaphragm. Is it just the problem of two people having to decide together? Or is it that sexuality is so essentially emotional and irrational that simple, practical decisions become hard?

For some formerly heterosexual people, especially lesbians, one result of becoming gay has been an enormous relief at no longer having to cope with contraception in their lives. For me, a heterosexual man, realizing slowly that sex is not the same as, and need not include my penis in a woman's vagina, elicits fantasies of having no penis (to worry about), or making love with a woman being as a woman myself; and, it brings up 'non-penetration' (or less penetration) and non-ejaculation. Both have been sexually enriching for me, as well as having contraceptive implications.

In our discussions, for him non-penetration meant, in a particular relationship with a feminist, a political decision on her part. Later he said: 'Well, actually, she was afraid of penetration.' Then he said 'But they are the same.' I.e. to refuse to take part in penetrative sex because one fears it, and one fears it because it is so inextricably linked with, or even the hallmark of oppressive maledom.

For me, non-penetration was *incidentally* a form of contraception, in that each of us had decided to draw that particular limit on what we did sexually together. Both these resulted in our broadening our ideas of our own sexuality, bodies becoming so much more intricate and responsive than when penetration had been the, or even a, goal for either partner.

Each relationship needs a fresh approach to contraception. We cannot take all we've learnt directly from one into another. But we can never assume contraception is 'up to her'. And the balance between a kind of irresponsible, reckless, male version of sex and its attendant risks of pregnancy, and on the other hand, an obsessive and joy-killing fear of sex and hatred of our penises as the 'root causes' of unwanted pregnancy, is perhaps best kept by looking hard at why we have sex, and why our penises usually figure so insistently in that.

Tom Weld and Steve Gould

June 1983

Notes

1 *Health Promotion Philosophy*, Ronald N. Labonte and P. Susan Penfold, Ministry of Health, BC, Canada 1981.
2 See also article in *Spare Rib* 90: 6, and on Depo Provera see *Spare Rib* 42, 47 and 69.
3 See article in *Spare Rib* 105: 18.
4 See *Spare Rib* 95: 13.
5 See Shere Hite's short chapter on contraception in *The Hite Report*.
6 *Guardian* Woman's Page, May 1981.
7 From *Small Changes* by Marge Piercy.

DEPRESSION

All the studies on depression show that it's mainly women who get depressed, or, at least, diagnosed as depressed. In Europe and North America, according to Maggie Scarf, for every man being treated for depression, there are from two to five women in treatment. So, naturally enough, what work there's been on the sexual politics of depression has tended to concentrate on women and on important questions like: Are women biologically predisposed to depression? Are women more likely to get depressed because their upbringing encourages suppression of anger and other 'unfeminine' feelings? Or are women diagnosed as depressed because of the desire of the male-dominated medical profession to keep them in their place? In this discussion of the sexual and social politics of depression, I want to give more space to the male experience of depression. Choosing to approach things from this angle isn't arbitrary; understanding and coping with depression has been a vital task for me for the last four years.

It's 'real'

How far it's possible to generalize from one's own experience is an open question. As I'm writing this, I'm in a sitting room in South London with two male friends also diagnosed, at some stage in their lives, as depressed. One is out for the day from the South London mental hospital where he's been for the past 6 months: his wife hit him with a candlestick, but the greater blow was, apparently, the very fact that she would attack him at all. My other friend was in hospital for treatment 10 years ago; during his 2-week stay he had a couple of sessions of electric-shock therapy. Anyway, after 4 months on anti-depressants recently, he's landed a good job, and is now only swallowing the occasional Triptazol.

Tom Weld

The problem is that though each of us is struggling with depression, each of us seems to find it difficult to share his experience, and to generalize from it. But the difficulties men have in sharing and coping with their experience of depression seems to me to make the task of opening a dialogue about this experience all the more urgent. And it *is* a real experience; this is one thing all three of us can agree on. Depression may be a catch-all term, but the suffering it labels is real, not the invention of our psychiatrists.

A permanent lump in the throat

So, assuming the label 'depression' describes a real experience, or, more accurately, a number of real experiences what are they? What does it feel like to be depressed? Well, the word itself says a lot about symptoms. Everything – energy, excitement, feelings, interests in the outer world – is lowered, 'pressed down'. Instead of the normal ups and downs of emotional life, there is a continual feeling of hopelessness, of being unable to act on the world, and a persistent sense of sadness, a permanent lump in the throat. Most distinctive for me is the feeling of sadness and numbness on the surface, while underneath flows an agitated current of anxiety and irritability. This suppressed anxiety accounts for the early unrested waking so characteristic of the depressive life-pattern. Feeding this anxiety is diminished self-esteem. You feel contemptuous of your own inability to concentrate on abstract ideas, and of your inability to experience the pleasure and purpose which people around seem so naturally endowed with. I've made this description impersonal, but these are the symptoms I've experienced; this is the kind of depression I'm talking about.

Some unravelling

I think the causes of depression will always remain a little mysterious. After all, what we're looking at is the loss of a commitment to life, a faith in life, as Alexander Lowen puts it. And if what creates this faith is a mystery (which people like D.H. Lawrence and Wilhelm Reich spent years trying to unravel) so what causes us to lose it, even temporarily, must stay something of a mystery too. But some unravelling seems possible and helpful.

A common assumption is that female depression is caused by the loss of a dominant other, and male depression by the loss of a

Tom Weld

dominant goal. (The terms are Silvano Arieti's.) To take the first case first, studies show that women's depression most often comes from the relationship with a parent, or with someone who has become a symbolic parent. In the normal course of life, loss leads to grief, and grief releases the hurt from the system. George W. Brown and Tirril Harris say that what makes the difference between grief and depression are the 'vulnerability factors' in the situation of the women experiencing the loss. Most important factors are: the state of self-esteem and the availability of intimate relationships.

The point is that a women is likely to lack self-esteem at the time of a loss of an important relationship, precisely because her upbringing has probably encouraged her to identify her value with the way she is valued by others, to establish her identity by dependency and passivity rather than by assertion. So when she loses a dominant other, she is also losing a source of self-esteem, often *the* source of self-esteem, and she has few alternative sources of self-valuation to fall back on. The result is that grief locks itself into depression.

Male upbringing, on the other hand, typically encourages emotional investment in achievements, dominant goals, and male depression comes from disappointment in these goals. The interesting thing is that the disappointment is often not so much at the *loss* of the goal, but at its *achievement*. What disappoints is that the achievement fails to fulfil the emotional needs invested in it. My depression, for example, followed the completion of a PhD. A matter for rejoicing, you'd think. But I had, in fact, subconsciously got the degree for my mother, whose unstated ambition it was for me to restore the family to middle-class status. Since she was dead (and probably wouldn't have been satisfied if she had been alive), getting the degree didn't give me the emotional security I'd always expected it would, but rather left me desperately wondering what to do next.

My own case shows that there's some point in linking kinds of depression with kinds of upbringing. To put this point in general terms: the difference between male and female depression corresponds to the difference in male and female socialization, and this in turn originates in the sexual division of labour in our society. The belief in emotional fulfilment by dependence justifies female domestic labour, while an orientation to achievement, competition and emotional isolation is the condition for performance of labour outside the home.

Root causes

Having said that, I have to add that I think that the differences between so-called male and female depression are, when you get to the bottom of things, illusory. I say this not just because one can see examples of men primarily orientated to relationships and women primarily orientated to goals. More important is the fact that commitment to a dominant goal is only a disguise for commitment to a dominant other. It is this domination by the other, this need to run one's life in a way that will please some dominant figure, that is the root cause of depression.

To see what I mean about dominant goals, consider the typical steps in evolving such goals. At some early stage in his development, the child does not receive the 'unsolicited positive regard' (Carl Rogers) which confirms his right to exist as he is. Protest fails, or is too dangerous. Instead the child's natural anger at this state of affairs is directed in on the self. ('I'm not good enough.' 'I must try harder.' 'I'm not trying hard enough.') To exist without love is not conceivable; the child seeks for an achievement that will win back the love he lacks. This is Alexander Lowen's account of the origins of achievement-orientated behaviour, and I think it's a most insightful one, provided we add that what makes such behaviour so available an option is that it slots in so exactly with the kinds of rewards our society is prepared to offer.

If there's no root difference between depression in men and women, why you might ask, is there such a disproportion in numbers treated? If part of the answer is that women do get the rougher end of the stick in our society, part is also surely that men's upbringing is a bar to acknowledging bodily and mental signals of disturbance. My own reaction to my crisis was that if getting the degree hadn't made me happy, it must be because everyone at my stage of my career was getting a book published. Through one long, hot summer, I struggled to rewrite my thesis into a book, managing a page a day if I was lucky, sleeping terribly at night. Only when I started getting dizzy spells and falling over was I forced to give what was going on inside me some attention.

Male ignorance isn't enough to explain such stupidity. There are also the factors of male emotional isolation, and the secret terror of not knowing what else to do. For me, ill as I felt, everything that wasn't academic writing seemed like a waste of time. I wasn't able to find any pleasure in the activities I'd dropped along the road to the degree. And, to make matters worse, I hadn't the skills to be able to share my predicament with anyone, even the person I was living with. In all this, I suspect I'm pretty typical of men with depression: we're very slow in acknowledging what's going on, and slower still in dealing with it.

Not that dealing with depression is easy. It isn't. For, as I understand it, depression marks the crisis of a way of life built up over a good many years, and reconstructing your way of life takes time. I certainly don't have a sure-fire formula for getting out of depression. But I would like to share with other men what I've thought and what I've learnt about the alternatives to depression.

Alternatives

Personal or group therapy, if it's available and affordable, is one valid way to tackle depression. If it's to get at the root of the problem, the therapy must help you to find pleasure in the expression of your own needs and feelings, rather than in the fulfilment of someone else's real or imagined needs. In my experience, this means being able to express anger as well as love, to establish distance as well as permit closeness. For, to win approval, depressed people often pretend to be loving when their real feelings are anger and resentment; they believe that expressing their anger means the immediate loss of loving contact.

Of the therapies I've tried, the one that has helped me most is bioenergetics, a therapy developed by Alexander Lowen from the work of Wilhelm Reich. According to Reich, repressed feelings are structured into the body by muscular 'armoring'. For example, when a child is continually forced to repress tears, she/he may develop muscles in the neck and jaw that will inhibit crying throughout her/his life. Bioenergetics uses a combination of analysis, stress exercises, expressive exercises (like pounding a mattress, twisting a towel) and often, group work, gradually to unlock this 'armoring'. It also has techniques to work on the various neurotic defences people use to fend off others and their own deepest feelings.

However, though I'm personally committed to bioenergetics, it isn't the only therapeutic solution to depression. Any therapy that recognizes the role of the body in depression, and that discourages the male tendency to take refuge in talk, would probably work just as well. What won't do, as far as I'm concerned, is purely chemical or electrical treatment. I can see the point of such treatment as a stop-gap measure, or when there's a very clear brain dysfunction involved, but not otherwise. Certainly my own 6 months on anti-depressant drugs didn't do me the slightest bit of good. I was as depressed and anxious when I stopped as when I started. I've known them work better for other people, but only when other factors (like a new job) were involved.

How far any therapy is the complete answer to depression is, though, something I question. Time and time again what you achieve in therapy is undone by how you have to live in the outside world. And, in any case, I don't think you can work on depression in a vacuum, because you need to move from a submissive, self-destructive relationship to persons and institutions to an assertive, critical and creative one. Recognizing all this makes me feel the need for a politics, a way of acting that can use the experience of depression as a springboard to changing the things that cause and reinforce that experience, and helping other people in the process. It's easier to define than to find such a politics, however. Since many of the causes of depression come from our present society, the depressed person should be able to look to the left for her/his politics. The problem is that the usual style and content of left politics reinforces rather than helps the depressed state.

The left and self

To my mind, the best analysis of what's wrong with conventional left politics is still Wilhelm Reich's *The Mass Psychology of Fascism*. Most relevant to depression of the negative features of left politics Reich identifies are: the denial of pleasure, the development of submissive personality, the separation of intellectual and emotional life.

Typical left activities like leafletting, postering, picketing, marching through hostile crowds or empty streets, writing campaign material in a committee may be useful. But they're not usually much fun. Some groups do hold activities like discos, socials and fairs, but their prime purpose is to slip in propaganda, not to give pleasure to people. And if the left discusses culture, it's never to recognize its 'play' element but always to debate the 'correctness' of the book, play or whatever under the microscope. So while depressed people can

Tom Weld

slot very nicely into left activities, it's only at the risk of intensifying their inability to reach out for pleasure.

Self-sacrifice in a political movement as a temporary, self-generated choice is often necessary; co-ordination of political work would be impossible without it. But if the group or party comes to symbolize the dominant other for the depressed person, then she or he simply sinks deeper in the swamp of self-destructiveness.

The root of the problems of left politics for the depressed person is the left's habitual separation of intellectual from emotional and bodily life. Granted socialist analysis has to be abstract in some ways. It tries to show that causes of events are not what they appear on the surface, it proposes a state of affairs that doesn't exist, and so on. But what goes on in left practice is often abstract in a much more negative sense. I can't count the times I've struggled, with a sinking heart, to argue about subjects where I've no personal experience to guide me. (Did the Trotskyists betray the revolution in Ceylon/Sri Lanka?) Or suppressed a true feeling because it hasn't been politically correct? (How can I talk about my fear of emotional closeness with men in a meeting on gay repression?) Or forced myself to act like a cardboard militant, never sad, always combative, and always submissive to the general good. This kind of stuff encourages public acquiescence and private despair. For a depressed person, it's poison.

Can a politics helpful to the depressed person emerge from left politics? There are signs that it could. For one thing, the women's movement has evolved very practical ways of arguing from feeling and experience as well as ideas (see Gracie Lyons, *Constructive Criticism* for some of the techniques). And the development of men against sexism and men's consciousness-raising groups offers people like myself a chance to break out of our intense emotional isolation. Also, radical therapy is developing in a few centres. On the other hand, the drive towards abstraction is very powerful. For just one example, current Marxist psychology is saying that self-construction comes from language, not from the body, and that the self is illusory anyway. Even in myself I find this drive; evolving a theory of depression helps ward off the living experience of it.

'Unconclusion'

If this all sounds rather inconclusive, well, that's the note I feel it's right to end on. Five minutes ago, someone rang, cancelling a meeting I was looking forward to. The familiar sinking feeling in my stomach (What shall I do this weekend? Why can't I make more friends?) reminded me that depression hasn't vanished from my life. Nor is the question of the politics of depression resolved for me. But I'm working on the issue, for myself and for others, and I'd like to hear from anyone else who's doing the same. So I'll conclude this unconclusion with a series of questions: Are other people's attacks of depression like mine? What do they do about them? Does depression lead one to politics? If so, which politics?

Chris Bullock
January 1980

References

Arieti, Silvano, *Severe and Mild Depression* (New York: Basic Books, 1978).
Brown, George W. and Tirril Harris: *The Social Origins of Depression* (London: Tavistock, 1978).
Lowen, Alexander: *Depression and the Body* (New York: Penguin, 1973).
Lyons, Gracie: *Constructive Criticism* (Berkeley: IRT).
Reich, Wilhelm: *The Mass Psychology of Fascism* (London: Souvenir Press, 1972).
Riesman, David: *The Lonely Crowd* (New Haven: Yale University Press, 1950).
Scarf, Maggie: 'The More Sorrowful Sex.' *Psychology Today*, April 1979, pp. 44–52, 89–90.
Slater, Philip: *The Pursuit of Loneliness*, Rev. edn (Boston: Beacon, 1976).

NSU

The first time I had no symptoms. But somebody else had it which made it likely that I did. For some reason, I went to Westminster Hospital that time. Friends had gone so I did. There it's called 'Clinical Measurement'. And it's not in the basement but the floor below that. Well out of the way of the respectable linoleum bustle of the wards above. It was hidden.

What I most dreaded was pain. I knew they'd put something down it. To have my urethra scraped from inside: that made me shake. I did not feel humiliation. Nor at that stage guilt. But I was frightened it would hurt.

For years – maybe since I was 10 – I have felt that my penis is too small. Knowledge that millions of other men do has only slowly eroded that shame. Knowledge that my feeling that it was too small has made no difference to my fucking has also been slow in getting rid of my inhibition. Besides, its not really women's response to my penis that I fear, but men's.

So an added fear as I sat in the waiting room was the knowledge that another man would take my penis in his hand. What would be his thoughts? And what if he was gay?

Fear and apprehension make me want to shit. About three in all which completely emptied me. It also makes me sweat. So I was sticky.

Signing on was no problem. A fast moving queue, men into one booth, women into another. Behind the counter a huge filing system. The venereal histories of thousands of people. Many connections.

NO SMOKING

In the waiting room (men only now) was a nervous silence. And the usual thumbed *Punches* and *Autocars*. No *Weekends* or *Titbits* though. All kinds of men were there of different colours and classes. That was reassuring: everyone gets it.

In front of me a young man collapsed. No more than 19 the fear and shame were too much for him. He cried out and fell as they were testing him. The lab workers, who make the tests, were kind to him.

The doctor was jolly. A retired naval officer? The file on me opened. Who had I fucked with recently? No one else? Ah! Piss into this jar will you old chap. Oh ... you have already ... well just do what

you can. So I pissed an inch or two into the wine glass. He held it up to the light. Nothing there. Just go for a test though.

Now they were going to hurt me. A wire with a small loop on the end. An eighth of an inch in diameter. Quickly in. But only an inch down. He moved it around inside. My urethra was very very sensitive to internal touch. But my idea of the pain made it worse. Not so much hurt as much discomfort. Out it came and was rubbed on a microscope glass. Not enough so in again. Oh no. But it was done quickly. On to the glass again. Please not again. He doesn't do it again. I pulled up my trousers and went to the waiting room again. So the worst is over. Now only the verdict and my sentence.

You've got NSU. (I couldn't have. I don't feel anything. Why me. Shit.) The information he gave me was all about what isn't known about it. Hence its non-specificity. No word about complications. A simple diatribe on un-science. And the sentence:

> No alcohol and no intercourse for a month. Alcohol irritates the urethra. Intercourse is a bit like playing football on a sprained ankle. What. (Haw! haw!) Don't want to bounce around on the old thing too much ay? (Haw! Haw!) Come back in 3 weeks. Goodbye.

Prescription: 3 weeks' tetracycline. That is four yellow Smarties a day each beautifully inscribed with Roche.

Our child was born on 9 November. I had NSU. S had it. So the child's mother must have carried it. (Women can carry NSU I think but are not infected.) She was carrying it all the birth. Though we didn't know it.

The birth was all that they're made out to be. I was high for a fortnight. J went into the Prem Unit. She was two ounces below the mark at 5 lb 4 oz. But she was alright and fed from M's breast from the third day. There were two tiny creatures in incubators there. One of 2½ lb and another 1½ lb. Nixon was bombing Hanoi with laser guidance that month. The newspapers were death, napalm and bomb damage through all those days. The bleeps and screens and dials and knobs allowed the 2½ pounder life. The other died in spite of science. It was simply too small.

J's eyes were sticky. Somedays she couldn't open one of them because it had dried shut. In fact they seemed to spend a lot of time close together and gungy round the lids. It was my only worry. We were told: 'There's a channel from the eye to the mouth. If it blocks the child will get sticky eyes. That's what's happened. Take this cream.' With no effect. They just got worse.

Still 3 weeks old and her eyes were sticky and much closed. Another examination: 'Well ... I don't know. A TRIC is highly unlikely. But I suppose I'd better test.' A test. But no results for a few days.

Still sticky. Worse if anything.

In a bookshop I looked up TRIC. In Medical Science I found a huge tome. 'Triple Inclusive Conjunctivitis ... could be caused by NSU at birth ... the most common cause of blindness in the world ...' Then I panicked. She might go blind. What if ... what if ... what if. Huge moral questions reared themselves up. Our lifestyle had caused her blindness. Guilt began to set in fast. And resentment. I began blaming others. How could it be me? I didn't even feel I had it. And besides, I'd caught it from them, not them from me. He shouldn't have fucked with her with NSU when she was pregnant. He must have known. The bastard. So what I thought I'd avoided – the sexual guilt that surrounds NSU, VD etc. – set in fast in a way that I least expected. And what was worst was the way I was projecting my guilt onto S and making him, in my mind, the scapegoat for it all. What jealousies surfaced here? In the event J did have a TRIC. And it was transmitted from the vagina to her eyes at birth. And it is the most common cause of blindness in the world – if left for months and months with no antibiotic. J immediately responded to antibiotic and her eyes cleared in days. In Britain it was not serious.

Meanwhile, I was on my diet of tetracycline. And it was horrible. In days it had reduced me to a state of prickly lethargy and depression.

Felt permanently post-flu. The side-effects of that stuff are big: it racks my body. And what primitive medicine: 'We know nothing about NSU, except that it's a viral infection anyway and is unlikely to respond to antibiotics, but we'll give you a sledgehammer dose of TC to see what we can hit.' It's like Hiroshima in your body. Nothing lives through it. Barely you.

Eventually I was cleared. I pissed in another wine glass. Nothing there. That was 20 December 1972. At least I drank at Christmas. Well actually I had one or two booze-ups before the green light with no bad effects. Just got pissed quicker on antibiotics. Joints are OK I think, though I didn't ask him. That time I'd felt nothing physically. NSU hadn't existed for me. Only the diagnosis that I had it and all that followed.

Three years later I got a real itch. Which in two days became sore. The discomfort was in my urethra, right at the end. For a few days I said to myself: 'It can't be it. No. It's just sore. Some mild thing that'll go away.' Pissing began to hurt. Hot, searing as the salty uriny piss first touched my raw, infected urethra. It was still only at the end. And I still didn't want to believe it.

My main fear at this stage was not going to the clinic and what would happen there. I'd been through all that and it was bearable. No. It was the thought of more strong antibiotics and the way they would make me feel. Bad.

I'd put off pissing into a glass first thing to check my piss. Then I did it. And there were the tell-tale threads of pus. So off to the clinic. This time Paddington.

I hoped it would be gonorrhoea because I knew that could be cured in days. It's that specific. Again the tests.

Paddington clinic is purpose built. It stands on I-beams above a small car park. I can't remember its title but it's certainly not as elusive as 'Clinical Measurement'. At Westminster the 'test' cubicles feel isolated. They take the sample away to some back-room lab. At Paddington there is a row of cubicles off a door in a corridor. They have lights outside: red and green for stop and enter. There is a green curtain opposite the door wall. By the curtain, I think, a chair and perhaps a bed. The technician comes through the curtain to do the test. The curtain, which might be open after your test while you wait, opens on to a long laboratory, which all the cubicles open on to. In the lab are rows of microscopes, lab taps and sinks, shelves of reference books, bottles of this and that. There's a bustle of white-coated technicians in there. Some examining smears through microscopes, others consulting each other on their findings. Two discussed my smear and reached a verdict. Or at least a non-specific verdict. What was reassuring about seeing into the lab was its demystification. They were examining life through microscopes. The life happened to be from the end of my prick. Never mind that. I felt part of the enquiry. Later I was summoned back to the doctor. NSU. Not even so much patter as the last time. Simply a prescription on the basis of 'We'll try this this time.' A week only this time. The pill looked different and it was one a day. That mildly reassured me.

I collected the pills from another basement. This time in St Mary's, Paddington, main hospital – of which the VD Clinic was a separate part. I followed white road sign lettering on a blue background with a white border and little arrow. Dispensary. Down into a Victorian central-heating system. Huge iron pipes. Along corridors that bent and twisted this way and that up and down. Past rooms full of piled-up hospital beds. Consignments of NHS bulk orders: stacks of drips, hypodermics, medicines, etc. Hot and stuffy. Recently painted to alleviate the Transylvanian heaviness of the place. To a little door with a counter in it. Inside a mass of medicines. I handed in my prescription defiantly. I'd got over buying Durex years ago. At least I could do this boldly. Not guilty!

But it didn't get better. In fact much worse. We were in final stages of rehearsing a show at that time. The most totally exhausting time. And there was no way I could rest. Pissing became agony. And the more I dreaded that first pain the more I wanted the piss to be over so the more I brought it forward and pissed when I could have waited a bit. Consequently, I was pissing more than I needed have been. Sometimes in the morning there'd be caked discharge on the end. The first piss had to reopen the channel. That hurt.

Now it hurt all the time. And even more when pissing. Fucking was not only *verboten*. It was out of the question. An erection was very tender and oversensitive to any touch. Coming particularly hurt, through the pleasure. (It wasn't totally out of the question because I did try a couple of times.) Coming hurt when the sperm rushed through my urethra, like pissing. It also began to hurt further back.

For a few days I didn't want to be believe it was getting worse. The thought that the pills weren't working was not on. But in fact the soreness was creeping back up my urethra. It began to hurt while pissing more and more along the external (to my body) length of my penis. Still from the inside only. In a few days I had a bad itch in or around my anus. I couldn't precisely locate it.

I knew about prostate glands. But not much. There was something that ejaculated sperm. And it was back there somewhere. The pain when coming, and the arse-itch, were making me suspect that the NSU had got to the prostate gland. But that was even harder to want to believe. From being uncomfortable, sometimes in pain, washed out and depressed, I now got worried. What if it did permanent damage?

I went back to the clinic. He hummed and harred. Hmmm. 'We'll try a jab and a Kelfizine in a single tablet ... you take it diluted in water ... and it acts in your body for a week ... it's a sledgehammer.' So down came my trousers again. In went a needle. Off to the dispensary. Another pill. It was strong, too. At about 5 p.m. in the afternoon its side-effects (which hadn't been too bad on the first batch of the pills) hit me. Sudden exhaustion. Weak brain and jelly limbs.

I looked in a Penguin book. There turned out to be many complications of NSU of which prostitis was one ... infection of the prostate gland. Hence my itchy bum. The doctor wasn't any help. He was in too much of a hurry. Simply acknowledged that such complications can develop and prescribed the above. No clue as to its seriousness or not. Whether I should take time off work (which I couldn't have done anyway). Let alone the psychological effects of the worry and lack of knowledge.

Meanwhile unanticipated tangles developed on the fucking (or more specifically, lack of fucking) front. It was a down time emotionally anyway. Relationships underattended. Problems. This compounded into my inability to get erection and fuck being interpreted at times as sexual rejection. This in itself was I think worked through easily. But it had effects inside me: what if the effects of NSU were permanent anyway; what if my fucking capacity was permanently damaged. My penis had been becoming progressively less sensitive in its most sexually sensitive places. The jab and the new pill seemed to have cured the infection. But it left me with a wartorn genital area. First terrible itching all over the outside of my penis and all over my my scrotum. Pissing not entirely back to normal. Erection still very tender. Prostate gland not hurting but still very tender. Then came a generalized skin irritation – a kind of acute prickly itch around my abdomen and all down my thighs which needed constant scratching to tolerate at all. This latter stage lasted about a month. And at the end of that: no sign of NSU but considerable after-effects on my sexuality. I was feeling generally less randy, sexual appetite low, as if there were fewer hormones around. And my penis was still very insensitive. Foreplay wasn't what it was. Coming felt as if I had two Durex on – distant and removed. No respite even in masturbation. I began to reconcile myself to being older and that maybe it happened to everyone (I was 30 then). I thought maybe fucking will never be what it was. I worried about its effect on my relationships: if I appear to want to fuck less maybe I'd become unfuckable with (extreme thought). This period – the early months of 1976 – coincided with a prolonged absence from M. I wasn't fucking hardly at all anyway. Gradually into the spring, life seemed to creep back into my penis. It became slowly more sensitive. What I'd thought was turning to leather was rebecoming sensitive flesh. Masturbation helped this rediscovery, which coincided with a *conscious* recognition of how sensitive and erogenous my prostate area is. Maybe having prostate infection put the focus on the sexuality of that area in a way which might have happened more slowly otherwise.

My first thoughts that time on getting it were: I've caught it from someone else. And the link only led one way. So I began stoking up resentment in the old way. I thought it was somebody else's carelessness. Hopeless (of me). I then discovered that NSU can be contracted without sexual contact. And that in fact I had developed it from within myself, or at least certainly not caught it from someone else. Instead given it to someone else and sent a half a dozen people to the clinic. My low physical state had given me a cold in the prick instead of the nose or throat. And the fact that I didn't and couldn't rest complicated it. So, NSU needs rest like flu or anything else.

It also has a lot more complications than prostate infection and needs care. There is also very little information on it: I think 'they' (certainly not we) know what it can complicate into, but not how, or what it is. It would be interesting to know how much the NHS/state allocates for research into what effects so many men in quite a big way. Very few people seem to understand that the non-specific in NSU is a pompous way of saying we know nothing about it. Yet it's as common genitally (relatively) as the common cold. It would be useful to men to popularize what is known about it and to share some experience of it in print. NSU – especially when it repeats and resurfaces (which it does unpredictably) – can be a lonely and worrying experience.

I think we should make a point of pressing doctors for information at the clinic. There's usually such a queue – which is no fault of the doctors – that they really want to rush you through. I tried to ask on my third visit (second bout) about my prostate gland. There was no way of persuading the doctor to linger and discuss it short of a shouting match. I was hustled out, having been given the all clear, when my prostate still hurt and I was not convinced myself that I was cured.

It would be also useful to share (among men) ways of curing other than antibiotics, which are so disastrous in their side-effects (on me). We might include in what was produced some information on what antibiotics do and don't do to you. My local GP dishes them out like sweets. What about herbal and/or homoeopathic alternatives to the antibiotics rack?

Chris Rawlins
July 1978

Antecedents: a poem

My grandfathers had a men's group too
There's a picture that I keep above my desk,
Sepia-tinted,
Of the four of them together:
Berezny, Mirsky, Moskovitch
And Plotkin.
Two of them sitting – Plotkin and Moskovitch

With their hands folded on their knees,
Berezny standing straight,
And Mirsky standing with one foot
Planted on the bench
And an arm around Plotkin's shoulder.

They all wear high starched collars
And double breasted suits
With waistcoats
And look proud and serious
To be photographed together.

I don't know how much they consciously
          communicated about their inner lives.
I imagine they talked about themselves
In metaphors
About Art and Politics
They were immigrants.
They went to the anarchist club
And read in the library,
Listened to the speeches
And ate sausages.
It was warm there.

Maybe I romanticize:
I am looking for precedents
For my own deep need for men's love.
Yet I know they were very close.
On the night that Berezny died Mirsky, 3,000 miles away,
Had a black dream about him.
Berezny's soul was calling out to him,
He said.

I believe it.
He wasn't a religious man or superstitious.

Berezny and Moskovitch became my grandfathers.
Mirsky became my great-uncle.
Plotkin became a family myth
Because he was always on the scrounge.

                              Paul Morrison

Chapter 7

Men and therapy

SEXUALITY AND SELF-DENIAL

In this article I want to look at what is happening around the area of male and femaleness, particularly in relation to people's felt identity. The individual subjective experience of what is male and what is female is much more important to me as a therapist than to involve myself in abstract debate about what is the nature of maleness and femaleness.

Relationships go through fashions; they have always done and whether we like it or not we are all to some extent victims of current trends in thinking and deeply influenced by the times in which we live. What wasn't acceptable behaviour 10 or 20 years ago becomes part of everyday life now: being nude, women living alone and people getting divorced are just some.

We constantly come under pressure to accept new models of health, sexual lifestyle and living in general. In a society that is moving so fast we are vulnerable. Vulnerable in the sense that we don't give ourselves time to consider in any depth or gather information about what choices we are making, only conceptualizing conditioning as an historical event and not a part of what is happening now. We are half asleep in the process of our changing.

Our sense of ourselves as men and women is to a large extent the result of these pressures. Time and time again in groups I hear men complaining of not having a sense of themselves as men, of not feeling their maleness and of women saying their sexuality is too much for the men they are involved with, that they scare away men by the strength of their feeling and need.

It is interesting to stop and ask why this situation has occurred of men not feeling enough and of women feeling too much.

On the one hand, these men are undercharged, weak and depressed which influences them in such a way that they lack clarity and become indecisive.

The women become overcharged, have strong feelings of personal power to the point of frustration, become strong in the knowledge of what they want and hungry for change. This particular syndrome interests me as I think we are beginning to see a role reversal between men and women which is a result of the way some men and women have attempted to achieve sexual equality through the process of over-identifying with one another. In other words men using images of women or real women as models for how to be more soft, nurturing, receptive and giving and women using men as models for how to be powerful, achieving and more sexually satisfied.

Anyone who has worked with people knows that immediately someone realizes something about themselves which they feel is negative or out of balance the first impulse is to take the opposite position. In other words, to give up the position they are in.

One of the ways I have seen men attempt to achieve some of the qualities I mentioned is through suppressing that which feels or is recognized as being male. It's got to a point that any wilful feelings such as anger, aggression or assertiveness are judged as negative and counterproductive to the vision of sexual equality. Another way I have seen men attempt to achieve these qualities is by indiscriminate outpourings of emotion in the hope that this emotional flooding of the character will dissolve indirectly any aspects of themselves they find dissatisfying or at the very least will meet deep neglected needs for contact.

This is not what I see happening at all. I see these men becoming ineffectual, confused and dependent and that's a high price to pay for closeness and emotional relief from the realities of being male.

There is a difference between emotional relief and emotional expression. One is getting rid of emotion and the other is learning to direct it in such a way as to deepen your relationship with yourself and others. The first is giving up and in a sense excluding, where as the latter has a more inclusive and self-gathering feeling about it and also assumes a certain amount of responsibility and self-discipline.

I have outlined two basic ways people attempt to deal with their experience and feelings of excitation. One is to suppress it, deny it and pretend to themselves that they are not what they are. We could call this person the actor-inner, and the other person, the actor-outer, attempts to get rid of his experience by sharing everything (Mr Honesty). Though in appearance they seem opposites they do in fact have one thing in common and that is an inability to contain and stay with their experience in such a way as to be able to use it wisely.

Both of these characteristics weaken people and make them feel incomplete. They breed feelings of inadequacy and make the person negatively dependent on others.

One of the ways to deal with self-denial is through self-recognition. We all have ritualized patterns of holding and letting go, contact and withdrawal. My personal view is that if we can find out what the nature of these rituals are for each of us, in other words the how of letting go and the *how* of holding on, then we have an opportunity to engage ourselves in a process of self-regulation which is what choice is. As we begin to feel we can disorganize and maintain our rituals of being in the world, we can begin to have a vision of creating our own world. A moving world as opposed to a static world of conditioned responses.

What I am proposing is that self-denial, however expressed or however reasonable, is responsible for people feeling incomplete, that our sense of maleness and our sense of completeness are one and the same and are inseparable, that we tend to separate in our minds our feelings of gender from our feelings of maturing and of moving towards wholeness, and that the feeling of wholeness for a man is the feeling of maleness as is the feeling of wholeness for a woman the feeling of femaleness.

Though I recognize that we are in an age of change, moving out towards new limits and new definitions we also need to learn how to participate in these changes without losing our sense of self.

Terry Cooper
June 1983

A SEXIST STORY

I like sex. And so, it seems, do lots of people. Because so much store is put by it, we have expectations beyond our capacity to fulfil them. I judge myself by my performance. I know this is stupid and counterproductive, but still my guts tell me that I am a man only to the extent of this narrow assessment. My guts are still very sexist and I catch them at it when I least expect it. It all goes back a long way.

As a teenager I climbed our neighbour's bathroom window to have a peep over the top of their curtains, the only way I could see what a female body looked like. The rarity value of this hidden mystery was confirmed when I at long last managed to file myself a key that fitted my father's locked drawer underneath his bookshelves, to discover it filled with pictures of nude women in various states of display. Even today, so many years later, and so many bodies shared, I still have this hunger to discover the most secret place that most people want to hide from each other. Sex to me is like food to the aborigines, it has its rarity value. Sometimes it seems even better because of all the taboos and rituals around it.

So I can see that I am a damaged person and when I am asked to write about sex I may well show my unconscious slips here and there. No amount of censoring and monitoring myself will save me from making a fool of myself occasionally. Nor do I really want to avoid it completely. I may well learn a little more about the hidden corners of my unexplored furniture, and get my antique gut feelings more in line with what I want them to be in my head.

Workshops

At our man–woman workshops we do a number of exercises which have a bearing on our sexual roles and attitudes towards each other.

For instance, there is a three-way fantasy. First we go and look for the same-sex symbol as ourselves. If I am male I shall look for something to show me my own male role, something which symbolizes masculinity for me. The first time I ever did this, I found a toy bison, a woolly, fluffy, cuddly soft toy. It was quite angry, pawing the ground even though it seemed to me sweetly ineffective. The second part of this fantasy trip is to look for the opposite sex symbol, for the male to find his female bit.

What I found as my female symbol I rejected out of hand. A pink powder puff? I didn't want to know. But go as I might all over the landscape to try and find something more in line with what I thought it should be, she would come back and would not leave me, so I accepted her in the end, reluctantly and unhappily. The last part of this triple exercise was to bring the two of them together and see if they would talk to each other. My powderpuff kept dancing around my toy buffalo powdering his nose, much to his (and my) disgust. At a later workshop the buffalo had turned into the real thing and the female part had become a heavy wooden gate that would not open for him. And so on. Most frightening of all was when my male bit was a straw core of an onion string suspended from a hook in the ceiling, and the female bit was a tuning fork sending out vibrations to the straw, which swished about unwilling to listen, and I was cowering under a heavy wooden table barely daring to look over its rim to see how they were getting on. It held a lot of menacing messages for me.

Another exercise which taught me a lot was to make lists of what I wanted from women. We all make lists of what we would like from each other. When we came to read out these lists I was amazed to find that both men and women had very similar lists. Was it that we were similar sorts of people, quite possibly, or was it more general than that? The only main difference I found over the years is that men seem to live more in their fantasies altogether, and are easily disappointed when the reality is not quite so rewarding; while women seem much more willing to work on and accept reality even if it is disappointing at times.

What puzzles me most of all is that all but four of the several hundred women who had taken part in these groups envied men. And all the men without exception, envied women. If that envy runs right through all our relationships with each other, what must be the size of that hidden agenda?

Women envy men for being in charge. Men seem to be in charge in our world. They feel free to make advances towards women, while women sit and wait for a man to come along. Even women who now-adays 'pull blokes' when it suits them, and feel free to go to pubs on their own and start conversations with men, still feel out on a limb, feel they are taking risks, they expose themselves to being rejected. When pressed, they do recognize that men take such risks and take it for granted that taking these risks is part of their natural existence. But they make this admission in their heads, not in their guts. Their guts still feel very much at a disadvantage, and when they have taken such risks and succeeded, they talk about it and boast about it, just as men do.

Men envy women for being able to sit back and wait for someone to come to them. They can sit and choose, it seems, whom to allow to come to them. Men think that a woman only has to smile at a man or otherwise indicate her interest and any man will fall into her arms. Men feel very much at a disadvantage, it is hard work for them to constantly have to take the lead, or believing they are expected to, in all sorts of decision-making situations including lovemaking. Men are frightened of women who have learned to reverse their traditional roles and make advances, or worse, press men as men have tradition-ally pressed women. And there are many men who won't play that game and then feel even more at a disadvantage because many women expect them to be strong and masterful and able to take responsibilities, and are bitterly disappointed when clay feet get trampled on and the tears are only just under the surface.

What I am mostly concerned with in this motley scenario is what it must do to our expectations of each other, how this undercurrent must affect our day-to-day relationships with each other, the sub-merged anger, disappointment, frustrations. All I can do is to say as much of it as I am aware at the time I may notice it in myself or in my partner, to be free to talk about these hurts. But it is a risky business, and we say to each other – 'I have something to say to you but it feels very risky saying it.' It gets better in time and feels less risky as I learn that we are all in the same boat and in taking these risks we learn to trust each other. There are still innumerable tripwires strung across my path attached to land mines, and I can only see some of them.

Yet what I have found in my long years of running these groups is that people, men and women are respected and admired for taking risks, being open, less pleasing. The more I stand up for myself the more I am liked. So where does all this having to please come from? We all know the answer, and it's a messy situation. Relationships are formed

Poems

A simple shift

The blood forms colour in the light
neck, clothed in red wool
turns maroon in despair
as the knife cleaves
jaggedly through skin, bone and life.
The pleasure of watching the shimmering arc
catch and glance in the light
becomes pained distress as steel slices.
I bleed
images of running out
pouring streams haunting dreams
kaleidoscopes of colour
returning always returning
to the scarlet becoming maroon
in a change of light
A simple shift.

Martin Humphries

Scary man

Deeper than the heart of this blue night,
my dear,
I thrust and plunge,
velvet bruises cupped in my hands, torn
roses at my feet,
I penetrate
and swim about,
arrow in your veins,
peaked mountain under the breast.
Bitter with your stillness
I plough your nature for my seed
searching for new angles.
I am the transgressor,
riding the waves.
To be the other
that is my power,
and my prison;
but it has its satisfactions
and momentary escapes.

Andy Metcalf

Movement

Ever darkening the landscape of our thought
Are the realities of our everyday lives
The tightening of pressure
The awareness of how little we have done
The politics of those in power
Breaking through our imagined movements.

Andy Metcalf

to you

i tried to say what i felt
clumsily it lies on the page
small, stark, unreal
conveying – i hope –
what i feel

writing is so hard
lightly the meanings change
from head to hand

how much more
could i show you
but no it's not to be
this letter must convey it all
i hope it does.

Martin Humphries

Being in a crowded room

The walls of this place
weep with tears
voices never ceasing
sounds which carry and splinter
whilst those unperturbed
in fragile tranquillity
continue never ceasing
for fear of the silence.

Martin Humphries

very early. The script we have brought in with us is not easily changed.
Yet unless we do change it, the same old oppressive play goes on.

Hans Lobstein
June 1983

Note

Hans Lobstein first started leading groups in the 1960s, and has
consistently made a practice of running groups for men and women
concerned with questions of sex and relationships.

LOVE, ANGER AND VIOLENCE: FRAGMENTS OF AN AUTOBIOGRAPHY

*Writing this felt like diving into a pool full of deep, dark and light places
right down. When I was out of breath I burst to the surface gasping and
after a rest dived down into it all again. This pool was sometimes a
simple image of my work. Other times it felt bloody, flesh-torn and raw.
I needed a place where I could see; I felt so exposed that I could only be
a while in there.*

An introduction

I wrote out a sequence of small histories about me and love and anger
and violence, and I felt swamped by the volume of memories and
confused in attempts to analyse and conclude. I resisted writing. The
resistance I felt consisted of, on the one hand, a judgement which said
all violence against women is bad, is wrong, is awful – big heavy
judgement. On the other hand, another judgement surfaced which
said – I should understand my process completely before I write
about it, before I do anything about it at all, I should have a total
understanding of what it is about, where I have learned to be this way
in my life, how to change and what to do about it in the world. I was
bound up between these opposing judgements.

   In the middle was I; I feel anger towards women, I've had a lot of
anger that I have projected out onto women in general and
specifically. Part of the way that anger has manifested itself has been
in violent, in murderous rage. Sometimes some of this has crept into
my relations with women – most of the time, its totality has surfaced
only during my work in gestalt therapy.[1]

I don't have answers which solve this issue for you or for the world: all I can say is that I can make a choice about what I do with my violence. I can choose whether or not to project it and inflict it on women. I can choose to recognize when I am angry and to identify what it is I am really angry about.

So, for me it's OK to feel anger and it's OK to feel violent – it's what I do with those feelings that matters.

Tom Weld

As I wrote this I began to go tense in my abdomen, just below my diaphragm – I was a little frightened to write that last statement. So, message to myself, it's OK to be me. I can't be anybody else now. I can just look at my process, work on it,[2] and understand how I am and allow myself to change. I can't do anything else.

I can start by saying I feel confused and sometimes paralysed – from this, by listening to myself, I can realize that I confuse myself, that I get swamped by memories, thoughts and judgements. I realize that if I focus on what I feel now, I need not be confused; I can recognize that I feel all the things I have begun talking about, I can throw out the judgements and get on with the changing.

A thought about public action against violence against women: it feels dodgy mentioning it because it is so easy to take a position, to be coming from the 'all violence against women is bad' judgement and therefore I must 'make a stand' against it. I could do this and feel 'I'm against violence against women', but the question of my own potential for violence remains.

Some of my process

I talked with my lover, Peggy, at a moment when I felt totally stuck and unable to write any more. I realized that in writing about past relationships I was stirring stuff in me that wasn't yet finished. I had reached another point of change and was resisting.

My strongest feeling – once I let go of the need to write – was that I'd been tricked. That I haven't ever had enough love – not only was I short-changed but the bank was robbed. Somewhere I didn't get love – I felt hard and angry about this. In gestalt therapy I relived my birth:

I was late being born. Labour was very hard work for my mother who had been unwell. I felt stuck in the birth canal for a while as my mother stopped pushing – I twisted and turned, feeling the struggle and nobody there to help me. I was stuck. Threatened forceps delivery, Mum made a last effort and I was born. She was too exhausted to hold me for long and I was placed away from her in a cot by a radiator.

As I spoke about this, I realized the rage I feel. Peggy asked me, had I looked at what my mother's life experience was? I hadn't. I felt this as a further pressure; not from Peggy but from in me. I stayed with the consciousness of my rage before looking out of myself.

I feel tricked. The rape fantasy (see below) and the information around my birth are parts of my truth. I am also carrying a lot more that pushes up hard to the surface and meets my resistance. It sits there. As part of working through that resistance I wrote this, in fantasy, to my mother:

Dear Mum,

Rage sits in me saying, 'fuck you, fuck you, fuck you' and then into 'I want to fuck you' – over and over again. This goes first to individual women I've known and then to you. It just sits there and I have judged it as bad, nasty stuff and locked it away. Then comes in my sneaking 5-year-old voice – 'If I can put that stuff away underneath the me that I show to the world, I'll get love and caring from you, from any woman I am with – you, or she, won't know what I really feel.' A big sneer, nasty and exaggerated, has come across my face. I'm not going to give away my last power to you. I'm going to hold onto it, it feels like all I have left. You suck me dry, like there's an umbilical cord in reverse – you have somehow got me to look after you and by not showing me your anger, made it unsafe for me to show mine.

But it will out. I snipe at you. I criticize you for not taking care of yourself, for your naive politics, for not being aware of stress in your body, for not expressing yourself; then, when you do, you're wrong.

Actually, as I relate out to you now, I know you, too, are loaded with anger from your life that you decided not to show. It seeps out of you too. You judged your anger as bad – you experienced unresolved anger and bitterness in your family and were determined not to give your children the same environment. So I never learned about anger.

You carried your anger about being left at home with us, about Dad being out at work or meetings – union and CP. You had all sorts of earlier stuff – girl/woman in a sexist Jewish family: were you loved by your father? Some poverty, anti-semitism, Nazism, relations in the camps.

I know this a bit now and I still feel you trapped me – you got me and you're still getting at me. Still telling me you love me and I'm not sure what it is you do feel. I listen to you and I don't know. As much as you hid your anger, so I picked it up from you, I felt it anyway. I haven't trusted your love for me. Now, as I grew up with anger around me unspoken and unnamed, I often imagine people are angry with me when they are not. When I do get angry with you or with other women, I punish myself because of course 'you are so vulnerable and need so much protection'.

Mum, I can write now because I have discovered a lot of what is in me. Now I feel more for you and see a few of my games but it's still hard, and all the above still has a hold on me and I'm still not ready yet to forgive you.

How have I reached some of this knowledge?

In talking to my mother (in fantasy) in gestalt therapy, I have moved between 'I hate you' and 'hold me' and 'I'll do whatever you want' and 'Poor, poor me'.

In one session, my anger at a lover turned into an acted-out rape of her. I was 'fucking' and beating this large cushion.

The anger went away from her to being against all women and then onto my mother. I finally went through all the rage and became very small and wanting to be held. ('I want to fuck you/I want you to fuck me/I want you to love me'.) In my imagination, I became 5 years old.

When I was 10 I was left out of trips to the woods near my school with a girl who showed her knickers to groups of boys. I was asked once and refused. I was interested but scared.

Between the ages of 11 and 12, I had a sexual relationship with a boy of the same age as me. We masturbated each other in a tent in his garden, in woods, but never in my house. He asked me to go and see some girls with him and his friends and talked about kissing with them. I didn't want to. I wasn't interested in 'that'. I was afraid. It wasn't long after this that I moved from Ilford to Stevenage with my family. He came once to see me – sex was the same, in some woods and fields in the sun.

It was during his visit that we played in a park with swings and slides and a girl stuck two fingers up at us, and poked a finger in and out between them. We talked from a distance. This was exciting. When we returned home and my mother asked what we had been doing, I said 'Throwing mud up the slide'. I had felt guilty, lied and got told off for what I said I'd done!

When I was 13, in the third year at my secondary school, I talked with a friend in the classroom about 'chucking' girlfriends. I said I would never do that. The statement underneath that for me is I would never let go voluntarily, I wouldn't say goodbye.

Between the ages of 13 and 14, I began to have more contact with girls. I went to a Church of England youth club – kissing would be in a dark side passage. I was clumsy and nervous and instantly dependent and wary of rejection. I was already on the road to 'falling in love'. Told off and banned by an angry father for 'getting his daughter home late', I wrote an obsequious, apologetic letter. I was shirked for this and still not allowed to see her again.

At 15, I had intercourse for the first time. In a darkened room, I orgasmed almost on coming into Jane. She said I may as well be hung for a sheep as a lamb so we made love again – I was no 'better' that time and didn't orgasm. Jane pursued me at school. This was my first love affair – before, I'd just had fantasies fenced by fear and gaucheness.

I am 17. I went for a walk with Jane. She was in my class art school. I had fallen in love with her. I felt high and often full of wonder with her and then pain and incompleteness when away from her. I planned, purchased (bottom-drawer) and fantasized my way into a married future – children, security, for ever, etc.

I remember the excitement of seeing her half-naked for the first time – we were in a wood together. I felt admiration and amazement. I had no doubts about having what 'we' wanted. I don't remember feeling that she and I were separate and distinct. 'We' were the one feeling that I felt and she reinforced that for me. I didn't think or question what happened very much, if at all.

We would fuck in the hallway of her parents' council house whilst they watched TV 6 feet away. I would come very quickly – 'was it nice?'. I didn't know anything about a woman's sexuality then. The being in her was enough. Now I know – then there was nothing else, no information for her or for me. She seemed excited by our discovery and adventure. We would fuck in an armchair in the kitchen after Sunday tea – the danger of her parents breaking from *Sunday Night at the London Palladium* made it all the more urgent and fun.

I went to Scotland for 3 weeks and she wrote to me at every youth hostel – I wrote back. Long, long love letters. That's how it was, or so I thought.

One day, we were walking along a main road through the centre of our town; woods on either side. We were by a stile that had to be crossed en route to her house. In some way she'd told me that she wanted to end our relationship. I remember feeling numb, feeling a heavy shock like a blow to my head and abdomen. I turned towards her, she was on my left, and began strangling her. I remember the power of my hands around her throat, my total rage at her rejection of me. She went backwards – she was hurt. I stopped. As she got over the fear and choking, I apologized again and again, saying I was just frightened and I couldn't stand it if she left. I was desperate.

What her process was after that I don't really know. We stayed together. I don't remember talking about it with her.

A friend, Martin Humphries, read this and was horrified by the time we stayed together after that – it was about $1\frac{1}{2}$ years. At the time I had little self-knowledge; I blocked my attack on Jane right out as something unpleasant. I suppose I didn't question because at the time I secretly enjoyed the violence for the power I had to get what I wanted, and be in control of the woman I was getting it from. I won that time.

An end

At the point where this writing began to flow together, I had a sense of victory and a sexual urge. I masturbated using pornography to turn on. The pictures that worked for me were those where the man was being fucked by the woman – yet behind my flicking for these pages, was a search for those photos in which women were being 'taken' by the man and being passive, being fucked.

I came safely with no retaliation from the objects 'who' excited me – I was still translating my feeling of power in my work into a way of scoring over women, of beating them; the undercurrent of violence was still there. This is all a very deep game and it caught me again.

The end

All this leads me back to the beginning of this article and how, for me, it is not enough to take a simplistic, rigid position against violence against women – our own violence as men will out so long as we repress and seek to forget 'it' and the pasts from which we come.

It is also not enough for me to stay constantly in trauma – that also leads to dysfunction; I would remain locked in an inner, exhaustive and confusing turmoil. For me 'An End' expressed a point of transition. Here I am aware of how I function at the moment in relationship with the world, and particularly with women. With that awareness I can choose to change, and in changing, act on the world.

Chris Nickolay
October 1981

Notes

1 Explanatory note on gestalt therapy:

Gestalt is an experimental and therapeutic learning framework developed by Fritz Peris. It is concerned with enlivening the whole person, encouraging integration of body, feelings, intellect and intuition.

The focus of attention in this work is on the minute-to-minute process of the individual and the purpose of the techniques used is to heighten awareness of that process, so that the person 'working' comes to recognize and take responsibility for how she or he is living.

Dreams, body posture, breathing, guided fantasy, talking, in fantasy, to a person and then switching to discover how you imagine 'they' feel towards you – all these are used to increase self-awareness.

Internal conflicts, including those left over from the past, are made explicit, thus releasing locked-in energy and allowing personal choice rather than conditioned, patterned response.

Gestalt centres upon taking responsibility. The form for this can either be one to one with a facilitator or by oneself.

2 'Work on it' – see above.

A WAY OF WORKING ON ONESELF

I would like to share some of my own experience of sexuality and also say a little about my work in running men's sexuality groups.

I started working on myself in groups of different kinds in 1970. Like a lot of people at that time I never got into anything specific about my sexuality and looking back on that time now it seems incredible that it was not really an issue for me then. I had a big resistance to sharing this area of myself that I felt vulnerable and unhappy about. I saw a few other people, people close to me, begin to work on their own sexuality, and I realized that it was something I was going to have to do for myself.

The first sexuality group I attended was a mixed one. The specific focus was sexuality, but it seemed really difficult to be able to focus just on sexuality; there were so many dynamics, so much fear of rejection, of competition with the other men in the group. It was a very confusing time for me and although it was a good weekend and I learnt a lot from it, it did not help me as far as looking at my sexuality was concerned.

Some time later I attended my first men's basic sexuality group. The group was run by Terry Cooper. Once again I approached with fear and trepidation this dreadful area of myself that I felt no one else shared. I had never heard anybody else talking about feeling

inadequate with women or about feeling insecure about their sexuality around other men; about feeling like they were in competition for women's affection. If anyone had in fact been saying any of those things to me I certainly had not been listening.

This group was different, that was clear from the very beginning. There was a structure and there were just men around, mostly men who seemed to be feeling quite a lot like me. I found that I was not the only one who confused, upset or angry as far as my sexuality was concerned. I was not the only one who was fearful. It seemed possible to share these feelings a lot more in an atmosphere which was structured, somewhere where people had obviously put some thought into other people's sexuality.

The strongest thing that struck me was this sense of structure, this sense that other men had been here before, it helped in a very powerful way to make it safe to share.

My experience of structure up to now had been largely counterproductive. School had not been a good experience for me. I resented having people I would not respect telling me how I should feel and how I should be. The structure in the group was different, it was like a scaffold, something to build from, rather than something to have to memorize, or learn internally or shape myself to. It encouraged me for the first time to look at my own sexuality, separate from others, different from others, as unique and personal as my face or any other part of my body. It was a validating and self-confronting experience.

The group carried on for eight Monday evenings plus a Saturday at the beginning of the group. By the end of that time I had a sense of my own individual sexuality in a way that I had never had before. I was very impressed.

When Terry asked me if I wanted to be supervised in running men's sexuality groups I accepted the offer gratefully. I completed three other men's basic groups as part of my supervision, each time learning something more and something new about my sexuality. I have since participated in the entire spectrum programme of sexuality groups, through the intermediate and advanced group and I am now running the men's basic sexuality groups in London and Portsmouth.

Each group is different and reflects the different men, their feelings and their individual sexuality. However, there are some important common themes which run through all of the groups and it is particularly important to look at some of these patterns, to question the expectations, possible disappointments and resentments that we bring into our sexual and social interactions with others. It is easy to say that the best way of being is being yourself, it is somewhat more difficult to find out what yourself is when you are shaped by parental pressure, advertising, sexist attitudes in society, other people's ideas and prejudices of what is right and wrong. It becomes difficult to tell the wood from the trees. One way of approaching this problem is with the physical exercises which are a component of the group.

A lot of people who do the basic sexuality group are surprised by how little they know about their own bodies; what they like having done to them; what they don't like having done to them; how they allow themselves pleasure and how they limit their experience of pleasure. Recognizing that you are actually stopping yourself from getting what you want and that you can do something about it can be a very joyful thing.

The homework component of the group is to set aside an hour a day just for focusing on you. First, you spend 20 minutes in a bath, not washing or scrubbing yourself, simply being there in the warm water, letting go of thoughts which keep you away from bodily awareness with your bodily sensations. Then, after the bath, you have a series of breathing and physical exercises to do for a further 20 minutes. These are also to help you raise your consciousness of areas of your body. Through focusing on genitals, stomach, chest, legs and your breathing you can recognize and learn to release tensions and resistances you have in these areas. The last 20 minutes of the hour is spent focusing on a specific subject for that day, for example, influences on your sexuality, such as your parents, or peer-group expectations, looking at your attitude to sexuality generally, perhaps masturbation or homosexuality. Obviously you need time to cover issues which are important to you, all the homeworks are followed up in the group so there is a lot of opportunity to share feedback with other men on these issues. It is a good way of questioning your sexual patterns.

The outcome for me of exploring my sexuality in these ways was a terrific change in my relationship with my partner. I found that by understanding myself more I could be much easier around my sexuality, this in turn allowed Pat to relax and share more. Instead of blaming one another and holding back, being resentful of one another's pleasure we are able to take pleasure in being with each other in a way which had not been possible previously.

It's good to be able to see how I have been stopping myself over the years from having the kind of flowing sexual relationship I have always wanted. I realize now that if I take on the responsibility for my sexuality, I give myself the power to do something about it, rather than blaming others and being like a resentful victim, that's also something I've taken out to other areas of my life with good effect.

I think if we take responsibility for our sexuality, rather than putting it on others we gain a sense of clarity which frees us, and helps us as individuals and in our relationships.

Rex Bradley
June 1983

DANCING EVOLUTION

For many years I was terrified of dance. Nowadays dance is at the centre of my life. I want to describe my evolution. My hope is that some people will respond, whether through dance or through writing. I (an able-bodied, white, Jewish, middle-class man, a co-founder of London Crèches Against Sexism, of the London Men's Centre and of the Anti-sexist Men's Newsletter) feel very isolated and want to make contact with like-minded people. My fantasy is of a loose network of children and adults who go together to non-sexist bops and participate in creating at such events – and elsewhere too – an environment which will nurture both creative expression and non-oppressive, non-alienated forms of relating.

Prague, around 1963 – I was 13 or 14. Our mixed-sex school class was taken for one dancing lesson. I remember being bought some clothes for the occasion. I found the event very scary.

My next memory of dance is London, 1965. Our parents took us to visit some old friends of theirs. While they were talking, the girls took us to their room and put on some records. They encouraged us to dance. We tried, but were very rigid and didn't enjoy it at all. Then came four years at a boy's school in London, with prefects and jokes about sexuality and the agony of Saturday-night parties. Forcing myself to approach a girl, desperately thinking of something to say, my mind spanning furiously. Asking her to dance ... hating every minute of it. And if she refused to dance with me, then feeling bad in a different way. I felt it very important that I try to behave as I saw others doing.

And then university and more of the same.

But then a surprise. In the hippy community of 1972 Brighton I found people for whom dance was a joy in itself, rather than a painful courtship ritual. People who danced autonomously, rather than in couples. I started going dancing more and more often, usually with John, with whom I worked in a vegetarian cafe. On one of these occasions I had a very memorable experience. I was completely lost in the music and in my dance. Waves of energy flowed up and down my body. I danced on, and the waves grew wavier and stronger and slowly built into an orgasm. That was 7 years ago. It hasn't happened to me since.

John and I travelled around music festivals that summer and danced. We made our living by cooking vegetarian stews for hundreds of hungry people. Then the cafe closed down and I moved to London, started teaching in a tough school, and stopped dancing.

The next time I encountered dance for pleasure was at Lauriston Hall in Scotland, about 4 years ago. I found most of the workshops at that particular event alienating and I gravitated to the crèche room. The atmosphere there was warm and relaxed. The gramophone was often playing and sometimes people danced. In the evenings more people drifted into this room and there was lots of dancing. Some of the dancers were very expressive – they weren't just bopping along to the music, they were creating/improvising. No longer consumers of music, but co-creators of dance-with-music. I was amazed. I found out from someone there about the Natural Dance Association and decided to go there when I got back to London.

It actually took me 9 months to find the courage to go to a day of dance at the NDA – I still felt that people who did things like that were in some mysterious way different from me and that I would be an outsider. But I loved it. And joined a weekly group. And when that one finished, another.

I was intentionally celibate at that time and this made me feel much more open than previously to the possibility of expressive/improvised/creative dance. The decision to be celibate made me much less concerned with what others thought of me and also less concerned with what my internalized self-critical voice thought of me. I hadn't realized till then just how much my behaviour is shaped by my ideas of what would please others. Even writing this piece I find it very difficult to say what I mean to say, without constantly looking over my shoulder in fear at other people's (possibly hostile) responses.

When I haven't danced for a week, my body feels half-dead. When dancing, I feel a freedom greater than any other, a freedom to be anyone at all, a freedom to be all my selves. I explore sensations, moods, ways of being which I feel too scared to explore at other times. Dancing, I don't feel any need to be consistent. Changing from moment to moment, improvising in response to the music. I am ... exploring the air with my fingers, hands, arms ... then crouching down to the ground and slowly growing upwards till I'm on tiptoe with my fingers reaching high up ... then I'm spinning round ... leaping in the air ... and then standing still.

I don't feel this freedom when dancing with another person. Though the sexual relationships I have had have been with women, I feel much more at ease dancing with men than with women. This is so whether the dance involves or does not involve physical contact. My discomfort in dancing with women makes me unhappy and I want to learn more about it and the reasons for it. I think it is because my relationships with men span a smaller spectrum of pain and joy than my relationships with women. As a result I am more scared of the potential consequences of an interaction with a woman than with a man.

I started searching the pages of the alternative press for bops. By now I knew I was looking for a particular atmosphere. One where I wouldn't feel scared of physical or verbal aggression. One where there wouldn't be many smokers, as I can't dance when I'm gasping for air. One where there wouldn't be broken glass on the floor – I like dancing barefoot. One where I could feel good dancing expressively.

So I searched *Peace News*, *Spare Rib*, *Time Out* ... and found next to nothing. A few years have passed and things are now slightly better. This spring I've gone dancing every couple of weeks. Usually I go with Anna, a friend of mine. She's 2 years old and loves dancing. For me, being with her at a dance is a delight. I feel there is a pool of warmth around the two of us. I feel much, much safer in Anna's company than when I go to a bop alone. She is a very alive person and quite evidently feels good about herself. That's probably why people consistently mistake her for a boy.

Very few children come to bops. I think this is because a lot of adults have the idea that music and dance are for adults, which I think is based on the cultural connection between dance and patriarchal sexual rituals. Most dance takes place under one of a few very rigid sets of cultural rules.

Dance at parties and bops has the most inflexible rules and typically has a sexual purpose. By 'a sexual purpose' I do not mean the physical and emotional enjoyment of dance. I mean a purpose subservient to a patriarchal, alienated sexuality. A purpose such as communicating to others one of a few boring stereotyped messages, such as: 'Look at me, I'm cool/sexually desirable/feminine/masculine/liberated/sophisticated.'

These messages are the very same messages which leap at us from advertising billboards, newspapers and TV. The product being marketed, in this case, is not a car or a cigarette or underwear – the product is a person. Not surprisingly, the act of projecting such a message produces anxiety and isolation: 'Am I sufficiently convincing?' 'Is someone else's advertisement better than mine?'

Most (though not all) dance today is immersed not only in patriarchal sexual rituals, but also in other, related forms of alienation, such as the performer/consumer duality. I am speaking not only of the dominant culture, but also of movements and subcultures which describe themselves as 'radical'. Most (though not all) musicians are projecting images which are not different in kind (though they are much more powerful) from the images I've described above.

Small children love dance – until they're taught, by adults, to be scared and dishonest. Their idea of dance – I'm glad to say – is very different from that of most adults. Anna does not distinguish between dancing/running/jumping/cuddling/shouting/climbing under and over people and objects.

When I go dancing alone, I am usually terrified of other people's responses. Sometimes people laugh or are verbally aggressive when they see me dancing expressively. I very rarely get an encouraging smile or gesture. I very much want some such indications of empathy. Sometimes I dance with my eyes shut – hoping to avoid some of the pain by not seeing the coldness. I also don't start dancing as soon as I feel like it. When I start responding positively to the music, I experience a conflict between the part of me which wants to get up and dance and another part which is crying out 'Danger!'. Eventually my desire to dance overcomes my fear. I sometimes remain tense, though.

Despite my internal conflict due to my fear of other people, I find that dance expresses my emotions (except for anger – I'm still scared to show more than a small bit of my anger in dance) better than any other activity. This is often a healing process. When my sister Dana killed herself in February 1981, dance helped me deal with my enormous grief. I remember, in particular, one dance during a workshop at the NDA in March of that year. About fifteen of us stood in a circle, arms loosely around each other's shoulders, swaying and letting sounds come out freely. We each connected this dance to our own life. I re-experienced standing in the wintery sunlight by Dana's grave as her coffin was lowered, then the lumps of damp earth falling with a thump, and my feeling of utter desolation.

I am sad about not seeing people in their sixties and seventies at dances. I'm also sad to see so few people with (visible) physical disabilities. I'm not surprised, though. Patriarchal sexuality worships youth and able bodies. Almost all of today's dance events do the same. I very much hope that when I am old I will still be physically able to dance. I'm sure I'll still be burning with the desire to do so. If I can and do dance, I hope others won't subject me to ridicule.

Recently, at the end of a large meeting advertised as being for men who want to take positive steps against male violence against women, I announced that I want to contact others who enjoy dance. I heard ugly laughter and turned to find a few men sneering and saying contemptuously to one another: 'Dance?!'. I understood them to mean 'Dance?! While we have a revolution to make?!' That is not the kind of revolution I am or want to be involved in.

The revolution I see myself as part of is concerned with slowly, honestly and painfully building a world in which all people, black and white, women and men, young and old, with physical disabilities and able-bodied, can freely and publicly enjoy being creative. This involves working on many levels and in many places.

In most human societies, past and present, dance is an essential part of the fabric of the community. It is only in the highly-industrialized societies that dance has lost this meaning and has become a marginal, unimportant activity. I want to work – with others – to bring dance back into the centre of our lives.

Dancing as a grass seedling growing into a blade of grass, as a sapling slowly growing into a mature tree, touching the sky, blown about by the winds is – I feel – an expression of life within us which challenges the patriarchy, the death machines, rape, exploitation and murder.

Misha Wolf
July 1983

Poems

Most happiness is an illusion
the product of myopic vision
and a convenient memory
but that's not to say
there is no true happiness

Most love is confusion
created by blind desire
and obsession
but that's not to say
there is no true love

All good children go to heaven
Some do. No they don't.
They're already there.

I love you madly
You are mad
I hate you

I think about you all the time
All the time i think
About you hardly ever

There is only one thing i care about
I don't care about just one thing
Just one thing. I don't care

You are everything to me
What are you to me?
Am i to you? Nothing.

I wish i was dead
Glad to be alive
What's the difference?

If my mind goes blank
What does it do – go blank?

Who are you?

---

i wrote my poison pen letter
pretending to make it all better
but now i know
i would rather have you

i used to talk of pain and strife
but now i want to live my life
now i know
i would rather have you

i tried hard to understand
to find the promised land
now i know
i would rather have you

i used to have ideas about you
used you as my muse
made you a sparrin partner
to try out all my views
and i always blamed you
when i had the blues
and everything you did
seemed like a woman's ruse
and everything you said
always seemed to be bad news

always something i was tryin to get
now i want to forgive and forget
now i know   now i know
i would rather have you

Keith Horne, from *Public & Private Parts*

Postscript
Men, therapy and politics

EMOTIONAL WORK

What is the relationship between personal and political change? Feminism and gay liberation helped to challenge the idea that society has to be changed before individuals can change themselves. These movements helped to strengthen the idea that individuals have to change themselves as part of a process of changing society. They also questioned the idea that the liberation of women and gay liberation would have to wait for the socialist revolution. They refused to subordinate their struggles to the overthrow of capitalism, recognizing clearly that sexual relationships had to be transformed as part of the transformation of a capitalist patriarchal society. Change could not wait but it had to be initiated *now* and it had to take place in individual lives. Since individuals needed the support and solidarity of others, their attempts to change their lives could not be separated from attempts to create alternative forms of community.

But if consciousness-raising helped us to recognize how individuals changing themselves was inseparable from the process of transforming social relationships, this was often conceived in moralistic terms. People generally assumed that they could change themselves through acts of will and determination. If there were feelings such as jealousy and possessiveness that were judged negatively, then we would eradicate these feelings through an act of will. We could learn to relate differently towards each other, through gradually weakening the hold of these feelings on us. But at some level this sustained notions of self-rejection as we refused to accept parts of ourselves that did not fit in with these new conceptions of our identities. For heterosexual men this went further, as it was often assumed that it was only with a rejection of masculinity itself that they could refuse positions of power in relationship to women, gay men and lesbians.

Often it was felt that if we changed our relationships, moving towards more collective forms of living, then we would change ourselves. But people were often forced to recognize that they did not change and that some of our patterns of relating were more deeply embedded in our childhood experiences. This initiated a rethinking about the relationship of psychoanalysis to politics and different attempts were made to re-evaluate the significance of Freud's work, which initially had been regarded as patriarchal in its formulations. There was also a growing interest in alternative forms of therapy and the ways in which they broke with the assumptions of traditional analysis.

As certain insights from therapy were combined with consciousness-raising, it helped to reformulate our conceptions of personal and political change. People were encouraged to take greater responsibility for their emotional lives. Women refused to do the emotional work for men but insisted that men learn *how* to draw support from each other. Men were to explore their sexualities and to recognize how the rationalist structures of modernity had worked to estrange men from their emotional lives. As heterosexual men, we were struck by how dependent we were on women to interpret our emotional lives for us, and how blind we had been to this dependency. Since it compromised our vision of ourselves as being independent and self-sufficient, able to live our lives on our own, we resisted understanding the nature of our dependency. Often we acted defensively and withdrew when we were challenged. Often this meant that men felt even more isolated and alone.

Men were frequently drawn towards alternative forms of therapy because they recognized the ways that they were trapped by their own language. Consciousness-raising had often proved a frustrating activity because men knew how to intellectualize their experience rather than to share. Our relationship to language seemed to stand in the way of developing more contact with our emotional lives. It was partly because we were only used to allowing ourselves to have the feelings that we could rationally justify in advance, that we were so controlled. But this control could also be threatening because, beneath the surface, we often felt quite different. There was a *tension* between the ways that we presented ourselves to others and the ways that we felt inside. We had learned to sustain a certain image of ourselves as capable and independent within the public world of work where our identities as men were established, but often we felt quite inadequate inside.

Alternative forms of therapy which were more expressively based could help suspend the judgements that we so readily made of ourselves. They could help us to express our feelings, whether or not they were 'rational'. This was particularly significant for men who felt that they had adapted to the images and demands of feminism while at another level they carried a lot of suppressed anger and rage. These feelings were not allowed expression because they were deemed to be 'unacceptable', but often they were held as tension within men's bodies. It was a strength of more bodily orientated therapies which had developed out of Reich's work, to recognize that emotions could not be simply conceived in mental terms but were held in the organization of the body. Frequently, it was this tension that was most difficult to deal with, because as men we were so used to living with it that we did not acknowledge its existence. We would often react defensively when our partners pointed it out to us.

Alternative forms of therapy had their own forms of blindness and often they treated reality as something that was within an individual's control, as if we always make our reality. But for a time this bias could at least encourage men to recognize the complicity involved in their own relationships and the ways that we unwittingly made certain choices for ourselves. As men we often denied that we have *choices*, thinking ourselves into a situation where we simply had to do what was expected of us. Often we blind ourselves to the choices that are available, as a way of denying the responsibility that we have in our relationships. Within sexual politics there was relatively little discussion of relationships, either because women felt guilty about being involved in heterosexual relationships with men or else simply because we were bereft of a language in which to illuminate them. There was a clearer focus upon issues of autonomy and independence and an understanding of the importance of challenging sub-ordination and dependency, but there was less sense of the *complexity* of relationships. Only later was this silence broken as people began to take seriously the complexities of an emotional relationship.

Since men with different class, racial and ethnic backgrounds were so used to drawing their identities from the public world of work, they unwittingly treated relationships as a background that could be largely taken for granted. Only when problems occurred in relationships did men feel that they needed to give them time and attention. As men we were so used to women doing this emotional work for us, that often we were used to putting up with whatever was going on in the relationship. It is much rarer for men to complain that they are not getting enough from their partners than it is for women to feel this way. This reflects the way that male identities and masculinities are structured within the public world of work. At some level this has left many men feeling that they are barely capable of having a relationship. There has been so little in our background that has educated us into knowing how to care for ourselves, let alone care for others.

In the 1970s people were much more hopeful about the possibilities of change. Men were challenged by feminism to take responsibility for their emotional lives. As men, we sometimes accepted this as a task that with the help of therapy we could work on with great determination. This was part of the attraction of bioenergetics and other forms of alternative therapy that seemed to foster the idea that if we really *worked hard* on ourselves emotionally, then not only would we change but also the world around us. Even though Reich was much more sceptical about undoing our bodily armour, recognizing that the patterns we had established served some purpose in our lives, the ways his work was interpreted were within the spirit of the time. If only we could undo our repressive sexuality, then our relationships would change. While we might have momentarily felt different about ourselves, old patterns soon seemed to re-establish themselves and we seemed to be back on the old treadmill. As men it seemed much harder to slow down and learn how to identify and communicate our needs within our relationships. We hoped for much more profound changes through non-verbal forms of therapy and often learned to discount our understandings as we identified with our 'gut feelings'.

An interest in psychoanalysis gradually developed as people became more sceptical about the possibilities of change and recognized that they had to deal with much more deep-seated patterns in a slower and more patient way. With analysis, the source of change became appropriately offered insights. These were to be grasped not only intellectually but also emotionally. But often the source of these insights remained with the analyst who was the source of wisdom and understanding. This was reinforced within the transference situation. With certain forms of Kleinian analysis which focused upon early infant experiences it was easy to say that if people did not feel better, this was because the analysis had not gone deep enough. Implicitly, this was to blame the patient. The analyst remained invulnerable within a position of power, even if he/she learned to deal with his/her own countertransference.

As Foucault has it in his later writings, we are exploring different technologies of the self, different ways in which people can challenge the objectification of their experience as part of a process of becoming subjects themselves. As alternative forms of therapy learned from their own experience, they learned to value both expression and containment. As men, if we are constantly active as a way of assuaging an unacknowledged feeling of inadequacy or low self-esteem, then we never learn *how* to nourish or really give to ourselves. There is also an appreciation within therapy that often we carry unexpressed resentments from the past and that unless we have a way of actively expressing them, we remain locked into these patterns even when we have gained insight into their workings. No doubt many people work through these feelings in analysis, but it can take years and often there is very little change to show for it.

The point is that men change, not only through exploring childhood experience, but also in learning to relate differently in the present. As we learn to reach out to other men, learning how to draw support from them, so we feel less isolated and alone, so in the context of a men's therapy group we can explore a whole range of feelings within a relatively safe environment. This is part of taking responsibility for our emotional lives, so taking the stress off our sexual relationships. In part, this also involves *accepting* certain things about ourselves rather than always judging ourselves according to some externalized standard so that we gradually define ourselves more clearly.

This is part of a process of developing an emotional language that is able to illuminate the contradictions of our experience as men. It involves acknowledging the power that we have in relationships both with women and other men of a different class or ethnic position to put down and diminish the experience of others. But as we learn to undo this power, we learn to appreciate the different *qualities* we can bring into a relationship. At the same time it is important to recognize that women have their own sources of power within relationship, so that they are not simply treated as passive victims. Both partners, whatever the differences of power which separate them, are often involved in sustaining existing patterns of relationships and both have to learn to take responsibility for their part.

Since male identities are structured within the public realm, it will involve a constant struggle to give time and attention to our personal relationships. As it is hard often for men to give time to ourselves, so often it is difficult to give time to our relationships. Often it is through developing particular practices, like putting aside a particular time every day to share what is going on, that we gradually develop habits of communication. It is only when we embody our intentions within particular frameworks that we begin to transform our relationships. If this is not to be a complaining session, it can be important to begin with appreciations for our partners, recognizing how rarely we take time to appreciate what they do. Similarly, it can be significant to share our hopes and dreams for the relationship, even at a mundane level of hoping to make time to go to the cinema. This is part of a process of learning *how* to nourish our relationships and to give them the space that they need.

As men we often pay lip service to the idea that relationships are important, but we have never learned how to make this an actuality. This can help sharpen our awareness of the ways that a capitalist society is organized around consumer goods and constantly takes people and their relationships for granted. As men, we often satisfy our children with new toys because we do not know how to be with them ourselves; but what they often want is time and attention. This is what we cannot give. As therapy helps us to listen to our own *inner child* and to recognize how we often felt abandoned and alone in our own childhood, so we gradually learn to develop a different relationship with our own children. It might mean that for a while at least we put less emphasis on our careers and work towards a different kind of balance between the different parts of our lives. This involves investigating our inherited forms of masculinity and gradually learning to change ourselves.

Often we learn that it is only through our activities that we can take our unhappiness away. Within a utilitarian culture we learn to eradicate our negative feelings, as if to give them any recognition is to give them greater weight. As rational agents we learn to control our emotions, not allowing them to get any grip on our lives. As we fail to listen to ourselves, so we rarely learn how to listen to others. This is reflected in men's instrumental relationship to language, as I have explored in *Rediscovering Masculinity*, where we use language as a way of sustaining particular images of ourselves, or else as a means to solve problems we face. If our partners are feeling sad or unhappy, we automatically think our task is to 'find solutions', for it is hard to realize that what our partners often want is to be given attention and to feel listened to. Often we do not have to solve anything nor do they expect us to take their unhappiness away. But as men it can be easy to blame ourselves or think that somehow it's our fault and that we are being asked to 'solve' their situation. Otherwise we assume that they would not have shared themselves with us. Since we learn to withhold our emotions, we expect others to do the same.

Therapy has helped to break the intellectualization of men's experience, which had often made consciousness-raising a frustrating and difficult experience for men. Often we found it easier to talk about our experience than to share it with others who we felt could easily put us down. As we recognized ourselves in the experience of other men, so we also had to face *difficulties* in our expression of emotions and feelings. It could help to recognize that this does not reflect a feared personal flaw or inadequacy but was often shared by other men, growing out of the way that we learnt our masculinities.

As men we were used to talking, not to listening. Our relationship to language, especially as middle-class men, was constructed around self-protection and self-assertion. We focused upon our agreements or disagreements with others, being so used to finding weaknesses in what others say. It was hard to hear and respond to the emotional content of what was being said. Often we felt embarrassed and uneasy when other men were emotional. We often felt easier with providing 'solutions' for the problems they were sharing. It took time to learn *how* to resonate emotionally with what was being said, learning to connect it to our own experience. Often we did not want to connect to our own pain because this reflected badly on ourselves and tempted us to feel that others would simply think worse of us.

Since our male identities are largely established within the public realm, it becomes easy to forsake our emotional lives and relationships. They are a background against which we venture into the public realm. Somehow this reflects in the impersonalization of our experience and the sense we often inherit, of living at one remove from our experience. This is perpetuated within theories of discourse that are largely set within rationalist terms. If they help us grasp how we use language to achieve or sustain a particular vision of male identity, they too often forsake what is not said as having no reality.

We learn to conceive of reality in linguistic terms and to treat experience as if it were constituted through language. This renders invisible the tension between language and experience and so the difficulties that men can have in expressing themselves emotionally.

This was a theme we were constantly struggling with within *Achilles Heel*. A social theory which limits itself to analysing how language works to achieve particular identities unwittingly gives weight to those who have the power to speak. Truth is supposedly an *effect* of discourse, so that different discourses sustain their own vision of truth. Relativism becomes difficult to avoid. There are supposedly no neutral vantage points from which these different discourses can be evaluated.

Feminism can help us to challenge the rationalist terms of discourse theory in recognizing the power that men have traditionally had to diminish and silence women. With therapy it also questions the way that language is placed *at one remove* from our experience. It helps to bring into view the emotional intensity with which men feel they have to prove themselves to be right. It also recognizes the importance of what is not said, as part of an ongoing relationship. Traditionally, discourse theory has conceived of context in linguistic terms, so that we lose a textured sense of how what is said is embedded within particular relationships of power and subordination.

Gramsci understands the importance of coming to know ourselves in ways which link our thoughts and feelings with the larger social and political relationships. He challenges the reductionism of orthodox Marxism which would treat individuality as a bourgeois myth which blocks our grasp of the ways in which identities are socially and historically constructed. In this crucial respect Gramsci helps challenge a structuralist tradition, which would treat identity as an effect of the dominant discourses within society. Supposedly the only way of avoiding essentialist conceptions of human nature is to acknowledge that our identities are socially and historically constructed. This unwittingly takes on an externalized view of the self.

We lose touch with Gramsci's insight that in coming to understand our own gender, class or ethnic experience, we are not becoming less individual but rather are strengthening and defining our sense of individuality. It is in helping us to *rethink* the dialectic between 'individual' and 'social' that sexual politics can be so significant. Not only does it help us question the distinction between public and private, but it helps us rethink the relationship between 'inner' and 'outer'. It can help us to learn to take greater responsibility for our emotional lives as we refuse the traditional escape from the self which is perpetuated in the idea that we can now blame 'society'. It was an important insight of libertarian left politics that we could not wait for society to change but we had to learn how to change ourselves. Slowly we also had to acknowledge that this meant taking responsibility for our emotional lives as much as for our ideas.

EXPRESSION AND CONTAINMENT

As men living within the terms of an enlightened modernity, we have often learned to deny our emotional needs and deny our emotional expression. Often we learn to withhold ourselves emotionally because we do not want to burden others and we do not want to show our weakness. We learn to acknowledge only those emotions that rationally we can justify in advance. This is the way we contain our emotions, only allowing ourselves to express what we know we can defend rationally. So it is that we are constantly adapting to images of ourselves, feeling what we are supposed to feel, not allowing ourselves to express emotions which somehow challenge the visions that we have of ourselves.

Our inherited traditions of politics and social theory seemed limited in their visions of how people can change. Largely, we are left bereft of an emotional language and of any sustained understanding of the connections between our thoughts, emotions and behaviour. Traditionally, we had learned to curb our emotions and feelings as interferences with our rational action. But as men became aware of the disjunction between what we were feeling and how we were supposed to feel, we looked towards therapy as a place where these tensions could be explored. Often in response to the challenges of feminism we could not acknowledge our anger, jealousy and resentment within the context of our heterosexual relationships so we needed a different kind of space in which we could explore these aspects of ourselves. As we allowed ourselves to express these feelings, sometimes tracking them back to their source in our early family relationships, we would often find that these feelings would change. They were part of a process of exploration in which we learned to accept the integrity of our emotions and feelings. It also meant acknowledging how emotions and feelings are part of our reality, rather than something that was deemed 'merely subjective' and so sustaining no claims to knowledge.

Group therapy provided an important context in which men could resonate with the experience of other men, so breaking the isolation and loneliness which is often a part of men's emotional lives. Men learned to reach out to others in distress and so learned both to give and to receive critical support of other men. This took the strain off heterosexual relationships as men learned to explore their pain and resentments stirred with women's withdrawal and so to give and receive support from each other. As men learned to acknowledge the differences of class, race and ethnicity, they could also recognize aspects of a shared humanity. We learned that we could cry together. Learning to express ourselves emotionally was part of a process of re-education as we surrendered powers we had so long taken for granted. We learned to identify that we have emotional needs and that it was not shameful to express them. We learned to acknowledge our vulnerability and our need and to appreciate that it was all right for men to have needs too. With feminism it has been easy for men to learn that having power in relation to women somehow meant men had no right to their own pain. This could be scary to acknowledge, as we had for so long learned that as men we should curtail our needs so as to conceal our vulnerability. Beginning to acknowledge our needs did not mean that they would be met, so this often involves confronting our fears of rejection.

The move that some men made from consciousness-raising towards therapy was partly an acknowledgement of the need to explore our emotional lives in greater depth and intensity. It was here that the tension between therapy and politics began to surface, as often we can seem to focus upon the emotional sources of our 'problems' rather than to locate our experience within the structures of power and sub-ordination. But often this is a false polarity, for the structural and the personal are often so deeply entwined that it is important to investigate the emotional sources of our experience. For men it was important to question the rejection of masculinity which had been part of an early response to feminism, so learning to explore our resent-ment, even rage, at the loss of our own power and the envy we felt at the strength that women seemed to find for themselves. The fact that we feel ashamed of these feelings and think that they are irrational does not mean that we should not explore them, coming to understand some of their sources within our own personal and collective histories.

SELF-ESTEEM AND ENTITLEMENT

Within a protestant moral culture we often feel that it is through activity and proving ourselves as men that we can assuage a feeling of inadequacy and worthlessness. At some level we do not like ourselves and can feel that we are not entitled to our own happiness. We have to *prove* ourselves as men and constantly show that we can endure whatever the world has to present us with. Often the left has reproduced these protestant assumptions, making both men and women in different ways feel that they are not entitled to pleasure, nourishment or fulfilment. It is this politics of self-denial, as I have attempted to explore it in *Recreating Sexual Politics*, that has been so often reproduced within the left.

As men we often grow up fearing that we are not lovable. We can also feel that we are not capable of loving others. We do our best to hide these truths about ourselves, hoping that we will not be found out. Often feminism has helped to perpetuate some of these feelings in its vision of men and masculinity. As men have internalized these images, often it has been felt by men that it is only in the rejection of their masculinity that they could somehow be redeemed. Therapy can help challenge this negative pattern as it gives men a way of exploring the full range of our emotions and feelings. It also helps to question how men use their power in relationship to women, gay men and lesbians and the ways in which we take out our feelings on others. In helping men to take greater responsibility for our emotional lives, we become more aware of the ways we dump our feelings on others.

As middle-class men we often learn to sustain our self-esteem through our activities within the public realm but often this is quite at odds with the ways we feel about ourselves. Plagued by feelings of failure, we can often feel that we are not entitled to joy or happiness. It is as if we have to be proving ourselves constantly. This creates enormous pressure, which makes it harder for men to hear with good heart the challenges that are made within our personal and sexual relationships. Secure in the demands that we have to meet within the public world of work, men often feel that they are drifting in their personal relationships, being prepared to put up with whatever is offered. Often we will fit in with the plans of others, somehow expecting our partners within heterosexual relationships to take the initiative within the personal realm. In making few demands ourselves we can feel invulnerable to the criticisms of our partners. It can be a way of protecting ourselves.

As men we are constantly proving ourselves by testing ourselves against our own limits. This works in diverse ways, depending on our class, race and ethnicity. We learn to do whatever is required of us and often we do not even sense when our body is tired. This helps to organize our different bodies. Often it is only when we are ill and have been forced to take to our beds, that we allow ourselves to have a break. In this way we affirm our particular masculinities. This is sometimes the only way that we can feel entitled to the love and support of others and so assuage our feelings of inadequacy and low self-esteem.

Humanistic forms of therapy potentially open up a whole range of unexpected political questions. Since they can help to validate a sense that we can both give and receive love, we do not have to look for others to support and nourish us because we can learn to do this for ourselves. We learn that unless we learn to treat ourselves well, we cannot learn to love others. So it is that our self-respect is at some level the basis of our respect for others. Unless we learn to accept our own feelings and desires it is hard to acknowledge the claims that others can make on us. So it is that therapy, far from being dismissed as individualistic, can help us transform our sense of politics through teaching us to care and take responsibility for ourselves as well as for others.

Psychoanalysis can also help us recognize and develop a relationship with our inner lives and in this sense it can help to change us. But often it refuses to deal with conflicts in the present, seeing them as distractions, insisting on seeing their sources in early childhood relationships. It is only when we have 'worked through' this material that supposedly we can hope to find more freedom in the present. Too often for psychoanalysis, humanistic forms of therapy are offering false consolation. Accordingly, unless we are prepared to undergo a full analysis then we are not dealing with the causes of our emotional distress. But in this way psychoanalysis can lock us into the past and also, somewhat paradoxically, into a somewhat removed relationship with ourselves. We can find ourselves too often being trapped as 'observers' of our own experience.

Of course it is dangerous to generalize, and certain forms of analysis are extremely useful in the ways that they help to contain particular individuals. But the method does not suit everybody and it is important to open up the issues which separate psychoanalysis from different forms of psychotherapy, especially since they are implicitly working with different conceptions of identity, experience and gender relations. Often men have found expressive forms of therapy useful, as a way of linking them more directly to their emotional selves. This is not simply a matter of an 'acting out' as traditional therapy might see it. It can also be a way of connecting us more fully to our embodied experience.

The 1980s saw a move away from humanistic forms of therapy towards more traditional analysis and many men were drawn into an analysis as a way of dealing with their emotional issues. Sometimes this was a tempting way of treating issues of masculinity and gender power as if they were in reality issues of childhood and the failure to 'grow up'. Often learning to 'face reality' can mean coming to accept prevailing institutions and relationships and somehow moving them beyond criticism. A sense of alternative, more equal and freer ways of relating becomes weakened as we learn to see our political questioning and rebellion as a sign of immaturity. Without denying the importance of projection, it is important to be much more analytically specific so that we do not treat our attempts to change our relationships merely as projections of inner conflicts which remain unresolved.

Psychoanalysis which is tied to a vision of transference and countertransference tends to be very wary of any emotional expression or physical contact, which it takes automatically to be an interference in this process. There is no doubt that transference, as Freud discovered it, is a powerful method which helps to elicit childhood dependent and regressive aggressive feelings, but often it creates forms of dependency which people never grow out of, even though the method gives some theoretical space for this to happen. This is partly because the analyst often acts as a mirror, reflecting back comments that are made, rather than a person with his/her own emotional difficulties and problems. Often it is the analyst's task to provide interpretations of experience, even though this can often be sensitively handled. But it means in traditional rationalist terms that the analyst 'knows best'.

The Hungarian analyst Sandor Ferenczi, who was one of Freud's closest pupils, and who began to doubt the effectiveness of traditional transference, was soon blocked in his attempt to transform the analytical relationship. He came into direct conflict with Freud when he suggested that some of his female patients had been sexually abused, rather than creating the abuse as fiction of their own imagination. For Freud this was critically a fantasy produced through unconscious desire.

While recognizing the significance of fantasy within psychoanalysis, it is crucial, as feminists and others have insisted, for this abuse to be validated when it happens, as unacceptable behaviour. Traditional forms of psychoanalytic theory, including Freud's, have tempted analysts to feel that they can take no position on it and that in any case, whether it happened or did not 'in reality' has no consequence for the ongoing therapy, since 'reality' is whatever is presented. This is the only reality that the analysts can work with. Humanistic forms of therapy take a firm position on this, recognizing this behaviour is never justified in relationships between adults and children. It breaks with a tradition of moral relativism that has been implicitly present within much analysis. It also insists that there is a profound difference, however we come to grasp theoretically, between whether an event is imagined and whether it has happened in reality. Feminist theory has constantly returned to Freud's case of Dora because it is the touchstone for the difficult relationship between feminism and psychoanalysis.

VALIDATION AND EXPERIENCE

To validate a person's experience is not to agree with them necessarily. It does not mean offering false consolation, but it does mean listening to what they have to say and accepting the terms in which they offer their experience. This is something that can then be explored together, as for instance the different aspects of a dream can be acted out using methods of gestalt which suggests that the different figures in the dream represent different unresolved parts of the self. In acting out these different aspects, a dialogue is set up between different aspects of the self and communication is opened up. This sets quite different terms from the traditional discussion, between fantasy and reality. Emphasis is placed on exploration and communication. This is not to deny the importance of the experience of the therapist, but they enter the process in a different way.

If someone has been abused, it is often crucial for them to feel that they are being heard and listened to. If the question of truth is placed on one side because the analyst cannot know whether it has happened or not, this affects whether a person's experience can be validated or not. This is equally so when it is said that as long as it is 'real' to the patient, then this is all that matters, since analysis can only be concerned with the processes of an inner psychic life. It has been a strength of humanistic forms of therapy to be able to validate a person's abuse and to recognize that, however painful it was, you have survived to tell the tale. This experience resonates in the present and can be worked on in terms of the difficulties that it presents within present relationships as much as it can be worked on in the past. As a person's self-esteem is enhanced and they feel better about themselves, so often they can also feel more capable of dealing with the pain they have carried from the past.

For men it can be particularly important for our emotional experience to be validated, for often we have learned to minimize what has happened to us emotionally and to discount it. Part of learning to put up with things is to minimize the hurt and pain that we have carried from the past. We do not want to make a fuss about it and in any case we have survived it, so it could not have been so bad. Often we need help in acknowledging how bad it really was, say, for example, in being sent away to boarding school when we were 8. The fact that others seem to have coped with it means that as men we feel that we should be able to cope with it ourselves. It is a sign of weakness or inadequacy if we 'winge' about it.

Unless we can appreciate what we have been made to suffer, it is difficult for us to recognize what others are going through. This makes an enormous difference in our understanding of the impact of institutions upon those who are relatively powerless. We begin to think of the education of our emotional lives in quite different ways. We learn to acknowledge our own emotional illiteracy as men and begin to feel angry at the way our emotions have been appropriated from us. Possibly learning *not* to feel is part of assuming a position of power within the larger society. The high price that we pay in our emotional lives and relationships often goes unacknowledged.

Therapy can help us change in the present and can help us recognize that we cannot simply wait in the hope that others will change but we have to change ourselves. Often we are locked in emotional relationships with our parents, constantly going back in the hope that we will gain the recognition and love from them that we might never have received. But this can be a hook that ties us into a relationship that is not going to change. As we learn to change ourselves, so our relationships begin to take on a different shape. We learn to identify where we are being fulfilled and satisfied, recognizing that some of our relationships are no longer working for us.

Learning about the ways in which our feelings are connected with our behaviour, so that when we take risks and change the ways we behave towards others, we also begin to feel differently about ourselves, can help us begin to forge connections between the 'inner' and the 'outer'. Our inner lives are not autonomous in the different ways they are often seen to be by Jung, Klein and Lacan. Similarly, the ways that we act and behave also help to shape our fantasies and dreams, so that we begin to challenge the dualism between 'inner' and 'outer' as we learn *how* to express our inner lives in the ways that we relate to others. We gradually build bridges as we unlock our isolation and learn to share more of ourselves with others. As we recognize that our emotional needs can be fulfilled, so we are less likely to displace our needs onto others. Sexual politics becomes less a matter of self-sacrifice and more an issue of communicating our needs with others.

This makes us more aware about the extent to which institutions are capable of validating people's experience. Liberal educational institutions talk about encouraging individuals to develop their potential but in reality they often leave people with an abiding sense of failure and inadequacy. Our emotional lives are given little recognition and they are hardly appreciated as an *aspect* of our development. Rather, we grow up expecting very little emotionally from others, learning as men to dispense with the support others might readily give us. Often in relationships we leave our partners feeling that we are self-sufficient and can largely do without them.

As men we rarely learn to care for ourselves so we often find it hard to care for others. Identified with work, our best energies go to those to whom we relate at work and often we arrive home drained with very little left of ourselves. Our identity is established within the public realm. Unwittingly, this tempts us to subordinate other areas of our lives so that it is very hard to discover a balance between, say, our work, our friendships, our sexual relationships and time for ourselves. Our commitment to our sexual partners becomes almost rhetorical as we find that our best energies have been expended at work. We slip into taking ourselves for granted in a way which is similar to how we take our partners for granted. Often only when the relationship hits a crisis do we recognize how distant we have become. Often it is too late to do anything about it at this stage.

Ferenczi in his diaries was beginning to recognize the need for analysts to be able to validate their clients through sharing their own experience with their clients. He questioned the notion that the analyst always 'knows best', recognizing that often people together can draw lessons from their own experience. Sometimes it is important to learn that others do *not* have the answers and that we have to struggle for insights ourselves. Too often analysis has served to institutionalize traditional hierarchical relationships in which we look to those in authority as the source of all knowledge and wisdom.

Of course, it is said that the relationships of dependency fostered through analysis are only temporary and they provide the means through which people can acquire a more genuine autonomy and independence. This is supposedly a freedom which grows out of a stronger inner sense of self. But often this process is not completed as endings are too often unsatisfactory and the dependency survives long after. This can also happen with alternative forms of therapy, but there is also a recognition of empowerment and the importance of individuals growing in their own authority as they learn to define themselves more clearly. It is this emphasis which is shared with feminism and sexual politics more generally, where it is more openly held that people have to take power in their own lives, often making their *own* mistakes because others cannot do this for us. We have to learn from our own experience and there is nothing to say that we will learn the lessons that are available to us. Unless we are *ready* to learn, we will often not hear the advice that others have to offer us.

At least within the context of consciousness-raising we meet others as equals and we learn from our experience together. Similarly, within the context of gay liberation, gay men have 'come out' to themselves and the world. It has been crucially important for them to break their invisibility and to make public their sexual identities. Through this process gay men have felt that they are being true with themselves and with others, often for the first time. A structuralist tradition too often diminishes this experience by holding that it depends upon a unified and essentialist conception of human nature, as if people are discovering what they always were. But again, it is because a post-structuralist theory often has limited visions of change that it is too often left with empty categorical oppositions.

It fails to engage with the experience of people themselves and the process through which they are going. Often it talks about making allowances between different movements, but it does this from an externalized position of authority. In treating experience as itself constituted through language, it takes an externalized view and is often trapped by its own formalism. The categories come to exist in a space of their own, as if they organize our experience externally. Failing to validate people's experience and the struggles people have in finding a voice in which to express themselves, this tradition, for all its insights, becomes part of the problem rather than the solution.

SYMBOLS OF TRANSFORMATION

Both sexual politics and therapy acknowledge the importance of contexts outside the spheres of work and home in which we can explore our emotional lives. Not only does it help to break our isolation to recognize that other men, despite significant differences of class, race and ethnicity, feel in similar ways, but we grasp how our emotions and feelings have grown out of the particular ways we have been treated since childhood. We learn to identify some of the different sources which have encouraged us either to withdraw into a sullen silence or to act out in violent and aggressive ways. Often these ways of responding have become so habitual that we hardly recognize what they are and we certainly do not recognize alternative ways of behaving.

Since we are often ashamed of these ways of behaving, we are wary of sharing them with others, especially if we think they will put us down or think badly about us. There is a sharp division between the ways we often behave in our personal and sexual relationships as men and the ways that we present ourselves to others. Working with other men in the context of a consciousness-raising group or therapy group can help to break the isolation which is often so endemic in heterosexual long-term relationships. Rather than adapting to externally accepted ways of behaving, we begin to give space to our inner lives and to acknowledge the resentments and frustrations we are often living with. Rather than blaming our partners we find ways of taking responsibility for these feelings, recognizing them as aspects of ourselves. Often it is only when we have expressed some of the rage and disgust, say, that we feel at women or at sexuality, that the space is created for exploring other ways of being. Because we are scared of these feelings ourselves and so used to locking them away, we are often fearful of the intensity of their expression.

Unless we are ready to express these feelings in a safe and supportive environment, we will be locked into patterns that will remain largely hidden and unacknowledged. Often it is scary to explore these areas of ourselves with others because we are so used to distrusting the responses of other men. We are only used to showing parts of ourselves within our most intimate personal and sexual relationships and even here we often withhold. Since we often inherit a weak and attenuated conception of self, we often invoke cynicism or parody to sustain some distance from our emotional lives. Only with time can we begin to trust other men and so enlarge the circle of those with whom we feel ready to share ourselves.

We might despise the ways we feel, thinking that it is 'irrational' to feel this way, but our feelings are often not rational in this sense but have a logic of their own. This is particularly scary for men because we cannot control the process in advance or say exactly what it is that we are learning. Partly, it is a matter of being open to a process of exploration in which we will discover what it is we are feeling. As we build more relationship to our inner lives, so we will more easily explore the different aspects of our dreams and fantasies. Rather than dismissing these aspects of our experience as 'irrational' we will learn to listen to them and so to use methods which help to unlock their meaning.

Freud long ago recognized that, in interpreting symbols of a dream, what mattered sometimes was not the correctness of the interpretation but the ways it helped people to a deeper connection with themselves. A focus on issues of meaning and interpretation often suggests that this is part of an infinite process and so loses grasp of the 'reality' of our experience. The extent to which Freud sustains this conviction in his later writings is open to contention. He was wary of Jung for giving up the focus upon sexuality because Freud recognized this as a central way of grounding psychoanalysis. He thought that people constantly escaped from sexual aspects of their lives into different fantasies. The importance of grounding our experience in our bodies was Reich's central insight and has remained a firm focus of bodily orientated psychotherapies. A refusal to separate body from mind has characterized Reich's challenge to a Cartesian tradition which has largely shaped modernity. This is particularly significant for men, who have learned to live in their heads. The identification of masculinity with reason affirms this conception of male identity.

Jung has been particularly helpful in breaking with an enlightened rationalism and with the identification of spirituality with orthodox religion. He has helped acknowledge that if we are sexual and emotional beings, we also have spiritual needs. With the advent of AIDS affecting so many lives and bringing issues of mortality so much closer it has become important to learn how to care and support others in the different dimensions of their being. An understanding of mortality was absent within the politics of the 1960s and 1970s, which were often informed by a vision of agelessness. We were the generation who were supposed to be 'forever young'. But as friends have died young we have been forced to develop rituals which can celebrate and remember their lives.

As men we often grow up learning to deny our own needs so that we rarely learn *how* to nourish ourselves. Locked into a life of endless activity and assured that through activities we can assuage a haunting sense of inadequacy, we rarely learn to give time to ourselves. Within a protestant culture we dismiss this as a form of self-indulgence. Often there is a fear of spending time with ourselves because we are wary of what we might discover or else we are plagued by a feeling that without others we do not really exist ourselves. But at another level it is hard to be with others in a deeper way unless we have learned how to be with ourselves.

As men with different backgrounds and histories we often grow up feeling uncomfortable with ourselves. It can be that we only exist through our activities. When we feel sad or unhappy it is easy to feel that we can banish these feelings through doing things. Often these are ways of escaping from the self. Sometimes men use alcohol or drugs for a similar purpose. Since we are doing what we 'ought' to do, we easily convince ourselves that we are in control of our lives, since we are governing them through reason alone. It is scary, especially for middle-class men, to recognize that life cannot be controlled in this way and that often we are closing off to life in order to control it. A structuralist tradition serves to sustain such a rationalist vision of control. It relies upon a distinction between reason and nature and assumes that our sexualities are socially and historically constructed.

In treating nature as given, it fails to grasp how it is historically reformulated. In only recognizing emotion and feeling as part of a given nature, they are excluded from our grasp of individual change and transformation. Identities are treated as a feature of culture, an effect of language or discourse. If it allows us to think about subjectivities, it does this as rational selves within the realm of culture alone. So it is that it builds the control and domination of nature, including our inner nature, into its deep structure. Only being able to acknowledge a reality which is linguistically constituted, it works to marginalize, if not to discount, other aspects of our experience.

Feminism and sexual politics can help to question this tradition if they are not presented in structuralist terms. The tension between who we are struggling to be and the dominant relationships of society is lost within a structuralist framework which fails to recognize that we are *both* natural beings and cultural beings. The fact that we as men learn to discount our inner lives, identifying with how we are expected to be within the larger society, is something which has its consequences for our sense of self. Identities are not simply articulated in linguistic terms because we are not simply externally defined.

Feminist theory grasped the oppression of women as involving the denial of women's autonomy and independence as women were constrained to conceive their lives in masculine terms. Women demanded to have their own time and space to *discover* their own values and meanings. In part this involves a process of emotional exploration in which women discover what brings them fulfilment and satisfaction. In part it involves learning, for both women and men, how to live in relationship to our own individual natures. Understood in more ecological terms, it involves discovering a more appropriate relationship to our emotional lives. We are too often trapped by a false distinction between a nature which is supposedly given and determining and the freedom to make our own lives within the context of culture.

This unwittingly sustains a Kantian distinction which treats our natures as a source of unfreedom and which treats reason alone as the source of our freedom and autonomy. Because nature is supposedly given and shared, it is only through culture that we can individuate ourselves. This helps sustain a partial vision of freedom which simply involves an absence of constraint. As Simone Weil understood, freedom often involves also coming to terms with necessity, including the necessities of nature.

Ecology can help us appreciate how our natures can also be individuated so that we can come to appreciate that we need quite different things from others. No longer is it simply a matter of invoking reason to work out what the most rational course of action would be, but of appreciating more of what I need for myself. It might seem quite rational for me to accept a promotion that is offered at work but it might not be what I want or need for myself. This helps question an Enlightenment tradition of modernity within which we are all rational selves determining our lives by reason alone. This helps sustain a notion of differences as necessarily being somehow superficial.

Within modernity this has meant, for instance, within the context of medicine, that symptoms are treated as universal, having a similar meaning wherever they show themselves. Alternative visions of health challenge this picture in the recognition that a symptom can have quite a different significance for different persons. It is only in the context of a person's life that we can appreciate the significance of a particular symptom. In this sense individuals are quite different from each other. Getting to know the person becomes relevant in a new way, because it is only in the context of this knowledge that we can begin to appreciate the meaning of the symptoms.

Similarly, symbols have to be interpreted within the context of individual lives. Often we have to discover the meaning of these symbols for ourselves and, in terms of gestalt, it is only when we act them out that we can begin to grasp what they involve. This is an exploration that we have to take responsibility for ourselves and cannot simply rely upon others for. They can help us on the way, particularly through sharing their own experience, but in the end we have to appreciate their meaning within the context of our own development.

A rationalist tradition too often serves to disempower people because it assumes a position of superiority from which it can interpret the meaning of these symbols universally. All too often a post-structuralist tradition has sustained this rationalism in its recognition, for instance, that in 'coming out' gay men and lesbians are falsely assigning an essentialist conception of their own natures, as if they are discovering what they 'always were'. This is taken as a sign of their naïvety. Again, people are locked into their own given experience while the theorist is free to interpret its meaning.

CONTROL AND RESPONSIBILITY

As men we often find it hard to give up control. This is a generalization that needs to be carefully explored within the diversities of class, race and ethnicity. We sustain control in our relationships in all kinds of subtle ways. The fact that we often deny this only makes it harder to identify. Often we are prepared to negotiate but at some level we want things to work out our way. We can act defensively when we feel threatened, since somehow our very sense of male identity seems to be at issue. Often we feel so pressured in our work lives that it is hard to work things out within relationships. Since we give so little time to ourselves it is hard to recognize that relationships need to be nourished and that they take time. We easily feel that we only need to give time when a problem arises, as if relationships can be conceived of in mechanical terms. We only need to fix them when they are going wrong. Also, within a protestant culture, we inherit an inadequate sense of limits so we think that we *should* be able to cope with everything. As men we learn to 'take it' so that often there is very little sense of balance between our different activities, and we end up, for instance, blaming our partners for our own tiredness.

When our partners complain that we are not sharing ourselves with them, it can be hard to understand what they mean. It does not help to set yet another task for ourselves, as if life can be divided into a series of tasks. Often it is a matter of withholding less and learning how to communicate more meaningfully in a relationship. Communication has to do with contact and often it is difficult to acknowledge that, though we might talk a lot, little contact is made. Often we can feel frustrated because we have learned to do without this contact ourselves, so we tacitly expect our partners to do the same. At an unspoken level, we often fail to appreciate our own needs for contact, being too busy with the next task at hand to recognize how little contact we make with ourselves in our everyday lives, let alone with our partners.

As men we can hear a desire for contact as yet another demand which only proves our own inadequacy or hopelessness. Rather than touch these feelings we often react defensively or angrily. We do not want to hear, let alone take in, what is being said, partly because it can remind us of our own unrecognized needs. As men, especially middle-class men, we learn to pride ourselves on being able to do without. We can experience this as an issue of how we can be both ourselves and be in a relationship. Sometimes we feel as if we only exist when we are on our own or doing things at work. We are happy to have a relationship but at some level we often remain unsure about *how* to be ourselves within it.

Women often complain of feeling frustrated or disappointed that they do not get more from their partners. When men have problems they often withdraw into themselves and find it hard to reach out for support. Sometimes we push away support that is offered, thinking that we have to handle things on our own. Often we learn that it is no use dwelling upon our problems and that this can only make things worse. Therapy can help us learn *how* to express our feelings and so to begin to identify what we need. Gradually we might recognize that there is nothing shameful in having needs or in reaching out to others.

Often as men we learn to ignore our negative feelings, learning to go on despite them. We do not let them 'interfere' with what we have set ourselves to do, so that frequently we are surprised when our partners ask us whether we are feeling down or depressed. If we have not registered these feelings ourselves, we can feel invaded or found out, and we can react defensively. We can feel shocked that others seem to know us better than we know ourselves. We take for granted the idea that being in control as men means being in control of our emotional lives, and we rarely recognize how this estranges us from ourselves. As men's language takes on an instrumental form, it becomes difficult to express ourselves emotionally.

Psychoanalysis can help us to relate to our inner lives but sometimes as a discrete and separate realm. It can help to contain our emotions within a privatized relationship between 'client' and 'analyst'. Often it works to locate the sources of our misery or depression within the history of our family relationships. Working with an idea that once we have worked through 'transference' we will feel better because we will have removed not only the symptoms but also the unconscious causes. It fosters the idea that the problems we have in relating to both women and men have their source in our failure to deal with certain conflicts in our early childhood relationships.

Consciousness-raising serves to question this focus, recognizing that the ways we are brought up to be as men and the kind of relationships men have with each other can also have an important influence. So it helps to create a bridge between therapy and politics. In doing so it brings into focus not only the larger structures of power and subordination within which we live our lives, but also the quality of our relationships. It faces us with the difficulties we have in communicating with others and the ways that we often fail to make any real contact with them. It reminds us of parts of ourselves that we have lost or forsaken as we have learned to define our masculinity in rationalist terms.

Having said this, psychoanalysis has often proved indispensable for many people in providing them with an opportunity to deal in great detail with their childhood experiences. This is particularly helpful for people who require containment, but it can be limiting for men who have grown up with so little emotional recognition and expres- sion. Also, its refusal, as I have argued, to deal directly with issues in the present as they emerge can weaken its usefulness for change. Again, there is no correct method that can be found equally useful for everybody, as people often need quite different inputs at different points in their lives.

Often what matters are the qualities of the people we are working with and the experience they have had in working on themselves. It is a strength of alternative forms of therapy to recognize that therapy is not a once and for all process but that both therapists and clients will have to commit themselves to working continually on themselves. There are no easy paths, as often it is not a matter of what we have learned but of whether we can put into practice what we have learned in our relationships and in our everyday lives.

CARE AND RESPONSIBILITY

In the 1970s there was a tendency to see parenting as a series of discrete tasks that could be shared between men and women. With time we have begun to think more clearly about the specific qualities and demands of fathering and mothering. It is important to challenge the traditional picture institutionalized within psychoanalysis, that fathers remain separate as sources of authority who intervene at a critical stage to help the separation between mother and child. This fails to validate men's relationships with children as it fails to recognize the importance of an everyday involvement with children if a meaningful relationship is to be sustained.

How, as men, can we remain identified with our work and develop close relationships with our children? This presents a profound challenge to the ways institutions are organized within industrialized societies. Only as men learn to recognize how much they are losing when they are forced to abandon an everyday contact with their children, will the demands for change develop. With the increasing intensity of work in the 1980s this became an excruciating choice for many men.

Often it is the mental space of women that is taken up with children and housework. It is not that men do not do things, but it is women who are often left with the responsibility, and women often feel that they do things better so that it is often easier for them to do things themselves than to rely on their partners. Little prepares men for the loss of freedom and independence that comes with a first child and the emotional and physical demands of the first couple of years. If adults have not learned to communicate their emotional needs with each other, often conflicts in relationships are taken out on children. Difficulties soon emerge if men have not learnt to give time to their relationships.

Often men behave as if they are yet another child in the

relationship because this seems to be the only way they can be looked after. Since there is so much to be done with a new child this can create enormous tension within the relationship. In any case men often suffer from feeling dispensable as the attention of their partners is focused upon the young baby. We can withdraw into a sullen silence, envious of the love that is no longer going in our direction. If we have little experience in meeting our own needs or in reaching out to others, we often look towards other women because this is the only way we know that we can be cared for. Often this sows the seeds of destruction in the relationship.

As men learn to relate to babies and young children, they often find new qualities in themselves, and discover themselves relating in quite different ways. This can be quite liberating, if also painful when it reminds us of how little contact we often had with our own fathers. I know for myself how important it was to give love and care to my children as a way of also nourishing myself. It was a way of assuaging an inner emptiness that I had hardly allowed myself to recognize. This also involves developing new skills of communication as we have to learn non-verbal forms of contact and expression. It can make us aware of how we feel fearful of touch and bodily contact, being used to placing our experience at one remove and so finding it hard to communicate more directly.

As men learn to form their own relationships with their children, so we can also learn to negotiate a division of labour with our partners. Again it is often a matter of learning to be honest and direct in expressing our needs, knowing that we will also have to learn to contain our needs for the time being, since often, a baby's needs are imperative. If men are to do more than help out, but are willing to develop their own relationship with infants then we have to learn how to take particular responsibility for aspects of everyday care. If we are in at the beginning, then we will not need to have things explained to us separately, nor will we feel that our partners can do it more easily.

Traditionally, fathers have existed in families as the source of authority and men have expected their word to be listened to. As men have questioned this traditional conception of fatherhood, so they have often found it hard to exert their authority in the family, giving children the kind of boundaries they have often needed. It is as if they did not want to spoil their relationship with their children through exerting their authority. But this is a trap because children are often looking for boundaries and feel much more secure if they know where they are with their parents. If there are no clear rules then children are constantly dependent on working out how their parents are feeling today, in working out what they can get away with. This creates much insecurity in the relationship and children are left without a clear sense of the boundaries of their relationships.

But is is also true that children learn through example, so that often it does not matter what their parents say, but how their parents are with them. If as parents we have not learned to respect our own emotional needs, how can we expect our children to learn to respect theirs? Of course this reflects upon how partners are negotiating differences between them and whether they are able to develop consistent policies in relationship to their children. Again, there are no simple answers because, as children grow and change, so what they need changes and our relationship takes on a different form with them.

The point is that we have few models for parenting as we have few models of how to develop an equal relationship, especially where both partners need to work. If equality is not to be reduced to sameness then we have to recognize differences in a new way. We have to recognize that mothers and fathers might bring distinct qualities into their relationships with their children, while recognizing the importance of sharing tasks more equally. Both women and men have to learn *how* to be with their children for there is nothing natural in this process. Often it reminds us of our own childhood experience and can bring up quite difficult feelings to deal with. I had greater difficulty as my son, Daniel, turned 5, because this was the age at which I had lost my own father and I seemed to have little inner experience to draw on. If we are determined to do things differently in our relationships with our children, but have not resolved tensions in our own relationships with our parents, we will often reproduce these cycles unwittingly. It is only as we have worked on ourselves that we can begin to change these patterns.

As we learn to take more responsibility for our emotional lives, so we grow in our own authority. Rather than relying upon our partners to interpret our experience for us, we can take more responsibility both in relationship to our partners and also with our children. It is not what I say that turns out to be significant but what I *do*. We begin to recognize that what we are learning here is *how* to have a relationship. This is equally valuable in both heterosexual and homosexual relationships, for it is a matter of learning how to be more honest and direct in our communication. It recognizes and brings to the surface the emotional aspects of our relationship and so teaches us that communication is not simply a rational process. Rather, its rationality is compromised if we think that in being 'rational' we have to turn aside from our emotional needs and desires.

As we learn to respect our emotional needs, so we will begin to respect others'. This is part of learning how to care for the self. It questions a tradition of modernity which treats individuals simply as rational selves and which discounts our emotional lives. If as men we are to take responsibility, not only for ourselves but also for our relationships, then we have to learn to give time. It sharpens our sense of the destructive quality of institutionalized relationships and the ways in which both children and adults are often devalued or diminished within these institutions.

So it is that it begins to transform our sense of politics as we recognize that we have to change ourselves as part of a process of transforming institutions. Since the institutions within a patriarchal society are largely set within the images of a traditional masculinity, men have a particular role in challenging and questioning these institutions. In part this is to give up a power which we have traditionally assumed in our relationships, but as we recognize how the quality of our relationships has suffered as a consequence, we begin to recognize an alternative vision which can sustain us through these changes.

As we learn to care for ourselves, so we become more sensitive to the ways others are diminished and invalidated. As we learn to trust ourselves, so we can begin to trust others. Often this is a slow process since as men we have learned both to distrust our natures and also to distrust other men whom we see as competitors who are ready to put us down. As we grow in our individuality, so we are more ready to acknowledge the individuality of others. In the process our politics begins to take on a different shape as it is no longer separated from our everyday lives as a series of discrete principles. As we create different forms of communities, so we strengthen our vision of the ways in which the world can be transformed and people empowered.

Vic Seidler
July 1991

Index